WHERE THE DREAMS CROSS
T.S. Eliot and French Poetry

WHERE THE DREAMS CROSS
T.S. Eliot and French Poetry

CHINMOY GUHA

PRIMUS BOOKS

PRIMUS BOOKS
An imprint of Ratna Sagar P. Ltd.
Virat Bhavan
Mukherjee Nagar Commercial Complex
Delhi 110 009

Offices at
CHENNAI LUCKNOW
AGRA AHMEDABAD BANGALURU BHOPAL COIMBATORE DEHRADUN
GUWAHATI HYDERABAD JAIPUR JALANDHAR KANPUR KOCHI KOLKATA
MUMBAI PATNA RANCHI VARANASI

© *Chinmoy Guha 2020*

All rights reserved. No part of this publication may be reproduced, stored in a retrieval system or transmitted, in any form or by any means, without the prior permission in writing of Primus Books, or as expressly permitted by law, by licence, or under terms agreed with the appropriate reproduction rights organization. Enquiries concerning reproduction outside the scope of the above should be sent to Primus Books at the address above.

First published 2000
Reprinted 2020

ISBN: 978-81-947560-0-2 (paperback)
ISBN: 978-81-947869-0-0 (POD)

Published by Primus Books

Laser typeset by Mithu Karmakar
mithu.karma@gmail.com

This book is meant for educational and learning purposes.
The author(s) of the book has/have taken all reasonable care to ensure that the contents of the book do not violate any existing copyright or other intellectual property rights of any person in any manner whatsoever.
In the event the author(s) has/have been unable to track any source and if any copyright has been inadvertently infringed, please notify the publisher in writing for corrective action.

In memory
of
PROFESSOR SISIR KUMAR DAS

Contents

Preface

IT ALL STARTED WHEN I STUMBLED on a line in T.S. Eliot's 1940 essay on W.B. Yeats:

The kind of poetry that I needed to teach me the use of my own voice did not exist in English at all; *it was only to be found in French.* [emphasis mine]

T.S. Eliot, On Poetry and Poets,
London: Faber and Faber, 1969, p. 252

Eliot, I soon found out, said and wrote the same thing many times in many fora, both in English and French. Yet very few critics received the signal and tried to explore this vital connection with French poetry, and no systematic attempt was made to trace the primary texts of the poet's French idols, except for E.J.H. Greene's *T.S. Eliot et la France* (1951), which merely restated stereotyped views. I think that really propelled me into this study.

Access to the original French texts was not easy, especially in India. I am grateful to the Ministry of External Affairs, Government of France, for awarding me fellowships to travel to France and research at the Bibliothèque Nationale de Paris, the Bibliothèque Municipale de Vichy, the libraries of the Sorbonne and the Sorbonne Nouvelle, and the Georges Pompidou Centre, Paris. My visits to the Modern Archives, King's College, Cambridge, and Bodleian Library, University of Oxford, on Charles Wallace India Trust fellowships, enabled me to see the Eliot papers at the John Hayward Bequest, King's College, Cambridge.

After I completed the present research, I found a list of books in Eliot's personal collection in Vivienne Eliot's Diaries, preserved at the New Bodleian Library, Oxford, and was relieved to find those very titles (of Charles Baudelaire, Jules Laforgue, Tristan Corbière, Valery Larbaud, Remy de Gourmont, Julien Benda, and Paul Claudel) which I thought had shaped his destiny.

This book re-examines the creative process of Eliot in the light of his fascination for a poetic tradition, which, as he repeatedly claimed, created him. Some of the documents presented here should hopefully stimulate research and rethinking. This book is by no means the last word on the subject; but it should help to create a little more interpretative space for Eliot studies in the new century.

Some of the essays in this book have already been published in *Essays and Studies*, Jadavpur University, Kolkata; *Jadavpur Journal of Comparative Literature*; *The Journal of the Department of English*, University of Calcutta, and the *Visva-Bharati Quarterly*.

My sincere thanks to Mr John Bodley, Director, Eliot Estate, in the 90s, and one of the directors of Faber and Faber Ltd., for his genuine and spontaneous appreciation of this work, which he thought will 'create a rumpus sooner or later'. 'Perhaps you aren't aware', he wrote to me, 'of how aggressively your polemic appears to come down on Eliot and his earlier critics'. I should also thank the Eliot scholar of Faber and Faber, who found the work 'extremely gifted and powerful' and its author 'a strikingly natural writer of great Ancient-Mariner gifts; he grips one, he convinces'.

I express my gratitude to Professor Arup Rudra, Jadavpur University, and my father, the late Prasanta Kumar Guha, a true friend and guide, for encouraging me. I am obliged to Ms Agnes Maury and Mr Philippe Wiedemann, for sending me books from France that were not available in India; Ms Jacqueline Cox, Modern Archivist, King's College, Cambridge, in 1992; Ms Sibani Raychaudhuri, Ms Urbi Bose, and Ms Philippa Hill for putting me up in London and Cambridge; Ms Marie-Claire Lorrain and Mr Supriyo Mukherjee for their warm support in Paris; Ms Monique Kuntz, Librarian, Bibliothèque Valery Larbaud, Vichy for photocopies of documents on Valery Larbaud; Stephane Carré for sending me photos of the boarding house where Eliot stayed in 1910–11; Professor Dipendu Chakraborty, my teacher, for inviting me to write on Eliot's French poems, and Professor Abhijit Sen for first suggesting a serious work on Baudelaire and Eliot; Professor Syed Manzoorul Islam, Dhaka University, and Professor K. Narayana Chandran, University of Hyderabad, for their kind words about my work.

I treasure the ardent appreciation of Sir Frank Kermode, Professor Ronald Bush, St John's College, Oxford, and Professor Ken Hirschkop, University of Manchester, who invited me to deliver lectures on Eliot two decades ago; the appreciations of Professor Lyndall Gordon, Eliot's biographer, who was present at my Oxford lecture; the late Sisir Kumar Das, former Tagore Professor, Delhi University, Swapan Majumdar, and Amiya Dev, former Professors of Comparative literature, Jadavpur University, the late Professors P. Lal, R.K. Dasgupta and Shanta Mahalanobis; Manasij Majumdar, literary and art critic; Joe Winter, poet and translator; and my old classmate and friend Satyaki Pal, for all kinds of encouragement.

My wife, Anasuya Guha, former Professor of English, Bethune College, Kolkata, gave me her emotional and intellectual companionship, which has been one of the great pleasures of the journey. My daughter Surangama, a bundle of joy, quietly tolerated my engagement with Eliot.

For this edition of the book, I must specially mention Dr Pinaki De, distinguished artist, academician, and graphic novelist, who helped me in every possible way, from preparation of typescript to cover design, and to whom I owe an immeasurable debt of gratitude. I would also like to thank Professor Suranjan Das, Vice Chancellor of Jadavpur University, for his kind advice whenever I needed them; my old friend Jean-Marie Fournier, Professor of English, Université de Paris Denis Diderot, for helping me out with important data; and last but not the least, my kind-hearted students Arindam Ghosh, Suchismito Khatua, Ananya Mukherjee, and Agniva Maity for their generous support and help.

University of Calcutta   CHINMOY GUHA
Kolkata

Introduction

'THE KIND OF POETRY THAT I needed to teach me the use of my own voice', stated T. S. Eliot in his 1940 lecture on Yeats, 'did not exist in English at all, it was only to be found in French'.[1] In 1948, the year he was awarded the Nobel Prize and the Order of Merit, came another crucial confession:

> Without the tradition which starts with Baudelaire and culminates in Valéry, *my own work would hardly be conceivable.*[2]

Despite the continued tepidity of critical response, Eliot himself always remained surprisingly frank about his extensive debt to French poetry of the late nineteenth and the early twentieth century.

The discovery of a different poetic discourse in the revised second edition (1908) of Arthur Symons's *The Symbolist Movement in Literature* (1899) at the Harvard Union Library in 1908,[3] the revealing encounters with the works of the Symbolists ('wholly new feelings . . . a revelation'[4]), and the subsequent pilgrimage to France—a country where, according to his mother Charlotte Eliot, he had distinct family roots[5]—brought about a major transformation in Eliot. And this occurred at a time when there was apparently nothing serious to suggest a new start in English poetry:

> When the loop in time comes—and it does not come for everybody—
> The hidden is revealed, and the spectres show themselves.[6]

It signalled the beginning of a long and intricate relationship with France that helped him, once and for all, to destabilize the prevailing canons of English poetry, give it new life by showing the possibility of constructing a new discourse, significantly different from that of the nineteenth century, and firmly establish himself as a pioneer of the new poetry in his own language.

As the young American groped to find the right verbal equivalent of states of mind, the rich and varied expressiveness of a group of poets writing in a foreign language enabled him to project the inherent paradoxes of human experience in new and unexpected ways. It 'elicited his consciousness' of what he himself wanted to write.[7] It gave him 'that intense excitement and sense of enlargement and liberation which comes from a discovery which is also a discovery of oneself.[8] In other words, his encounter with the French symbolists helped him to make significant readjustments and reorganize himself.

My assumption is that many aspects of Eliot's craft, his variegated themes, the self-destructive, astringent irony, the theory of impersonality, of 'thought-feeling' and 'feeling-thought', the desperate craving for order and belief, and the increasingly persuasive, obsessive force of an orchestrated, incantatory language towards the end—may have been calibrated, sifted, and reconstructed from the French poets he admired. It would be interesting to remember what Eliot said in the third Turnbull Lecture ('Laforgue and Corbière in Our Time') at Johns Hopkins University in 1933:

> Without them (his favourite French poets) the Elizabethan and the Jacobean poets would have been remote and quaint, and Shakespeare and Dante too remote and great to have helped me.[9]

He doubted whether without their help he 'should have been able to write poetry at all'.[10]

> I do think that anyone who would understand contemporary literature should study that generation, not so much in England, as in France . . .[11]

Indeed, at times, T.S. Eliot's poetry may seem to be a chart of the anxiety of influence articulated by reading in which French poetic texts of late nineteenth and early twentieth century played a lead role.

Unfortunately, for various reasons including relative unfamiliarity with the language and literature, impatience with other patterns of culture, and possibly literary politics, this great laboratory experiment with French by Eliot and some of his contemporaries (T.E. Hulme, Ezra Pound, F.S. Flint, and Richard Aldington) has never received the critical attention it richly deserved.

As Herbert Howarth wrote significantly in 1965:

> a whole book should be written on Eliot's debt, which is a debt for all of us . . .[12]

Today, more than half a century after his death, it is high time that such a study was undertaken in order to analyse Eliot's creative responses to his French idols, not merely as the relation of product to source, or effect to cause, but as 'the greater relation of latecomer poet to his precursors'.[13] It may not only illuminate better the method and meaning of his works, but may also help us to determine how, despite his copious borrowings, he cleared imaginative space for himself, while retaining such an irresistibly personal accent and tone. Before I begin, I wish to invoke Eliot himself who has this to say on the methodology and purpose of such studies:

> But there is another aspect of the 'problem' which I can possibly treat more competently, and which is not negligible: what may be called the aspect of comparative literature. I don't mean to say a vain study of origins and influences, but the defining of the type of the poet, established by comparison with other manifestations of the type in other languages and in other epochs.[14]

This is what the present study intends to do.

II

T.S. Eliot's own acknowledgements, spread over almost the whole span of his career, will show that his fascination for certain French poets was far from momentary. If in 1910–11 he believed that France and poetry were synonymous: 'Ce n'est pas un accident qui m'avait conduit à Paris. Depuis plusieurs années, la France représentait pour moi la poésie' ('It was not an accident which took me to Paris. For several years, France, represented for me poetry'),[15] more than forty years later, in 1952, as if in a reappraisal of his career, Eliot once more reminded his readers in an address at the University of Rennes (21 April 1952):

> Quand je suis venu en Europe, tout jeune homme, j'ai eu la prudence et la bonne fortune de passer quelque temps en France pour m'y imprégner de sa culture avant de faire la connaissance de la petite île au nord de la Manche.
>
> (When I came to Europe as a very young man, I had the prudence and the good fortune to spend some time in France in order to impregnate myself with its culture before I was acquainted with the small island situated on the north of English Channel).[16]

The connotations of the statement are significant: the key word is, of course, *culture*, and I would like to draw attention to other important words like *prudence*, *good fortune*, *impregnate*, and *before*.

On another occasion, in an interview with Radio-diffusion française on 19 January 1949, Eliot made a statement which has far-reaching implications:

> J'ai le modeste espoir que mes lecteurs français reconnaîtront en moi un des petits héritiers du legs de Baudelaire, (Laforgue, Corbière, si je n'étais l'artisan modeste que je suis, j'oserais même citer le nom auguste de Racine) ou mouvement symboliste.

(I have the modest hope that my French readers will recognize in me one of the small successors to the legacy of Baudelaire, [Laforgue, Corbière, if I were not the modest artisan that I am, I would have dared to mention the august name of Racine] or the symbolist movement.)[17]

The bracketed part was, on second thought, struck off by Eliot, and he added the adjective 'petits' (small).

In a lecture delivered in French on 'Edgar Allan Poe and France' in Aix-en-Provence in April 1948, Eliot, who had just been awarded the Order of Merit in January and would be given the Nobel Prize for Literature in November, did not conceal his French roots:

Je suis un poète anglais d'origine américaine, et l'influence de Baudelaire et des poètes qui en derivent a été dominate dans ma formation.

(I am an English poet of American origin who learnt his art under the aegis of Baudelaire and the Baudelairian lineage of poets.)[18]

Eliot pinpointed this immediate tradition of his poetry in numerous articles and reviews, very often in suggestive parentheses:

I was passionately fond of certain French poetry long before I could have translated two verses of it correctly.[19]

In poetry (I am only speaking for a certain group) Rimbaud, Corbière, and Laforgue were for us masters of the art, more than any English poet of their time.[20]

I had at that time the idea of giving up English and trying to settle down and scrape along in Paris, and gradually write in French. (*Paris Review* Interview, 1959).[21]

Indeed, during the 'romantic year'[22] he spent in Paris, Eliot had seriously toyed with the idea of actually writing in French, like the two Americans Stuart Merrill and Vielé-Griffin.[23] Later on, he 'burst into scurrilous French'[24] (aided, it seems, by a Frenchman called Edmond Dulac),[25] but apparently the experiment failed because he realized that he could not possibly carry on.

Even as late as in 1948, he still had little doubt that in the final years of the nineteenth century, the greatest contribution to European poetry was certainly made in France.[26] And one of the most remarkable things about his widely known and oft-quoted remark in 1930:

I myself owe Mr. Symons a great debt, but for having read this book [*The Symbolist Movement in Literature*], I should not in the year 1908, have heard of Laforgue or Rimbaud; I should probably not have begun to read Verlaine; and but for reading Verlaine, I should not have heard of Corbière. So the Symons book is one which has affected the course of my life.[27]

is the unrelenting emphasis on the great importance—even indispensability—of these poets to Eliot: as if to take them away would be to take away the soul of his works. In the light of the above remarks, two other observations by him are equally important:

Younger generations can hardly realize the intellectual desert of England and America during the first decade or more of this century.[28]

I look back to the dead year of 1908; and I shall observe with satisfaction that it is now taken for granted that the current of French poetry which sprang from Baudelaire is one which has, in these twenty-one years, affected all English poetry that matters.[29]

Without minimising the importance of Elizabethan and Jacobean literature, Eliot never really paid them the special kind of homage he exclusively reserved for France. And a comparative account of Eliot's tributes to Dante and Laforgue (the former is generally considered to be the most pervasive influence on Eliot and the latter usually dismissed as an early influence in his formative years in Harvard and Paris) would make interesting read:

On Dante in 1950:

I still after forty years regard his poetry as the most persistent and deepest influence upon my own verse.[30]

On Laforgue in 1950:

He was the first to teach me how to speak, to teach me the poetic possibilities of my own medium of speech.[31]

On Dante in 1961:

There is one poet, who impressed me profoundly when I was twenty-two, one poet who remains the comfort and amazement of my age . . . Dante.[32]

On Laforgue in 1961:

. . . Jules Laforgue, to whom I owe more than to *any* poet in *any* language . . .[33]

The emphasis on *any,* four years before his death, shows how crucial and decisive his responses to Laforgue and his brethren were and how grateful he still felt towards them.

Earlier work done on the subject has been perfunctory. Although critics like Howarth, have from time to time underscored the need for a major investigation, few have had the inclination and the occasion to do it. This is made clear by Graham Hough:

. . . the real roots of the novelty in modern literary practice have been very little examined. We shall find the roots of English Imagist poetry in the French Symbolist area. And this is well enough known Mr. Eliot has acknowledged his discipleship to Laforgue and Corbière; both Eliot and Pound in the early days made great play with Remy de Gourmont . . . But these known linkages *seem to have made little impression on the general critical consciousness*.[34]

This remains as true today as it was earlier.

The first critic to give due attention to Eliot's debt to French poetry was Ezra Pound, the co-literary activist and high priest of the dissemination of continental thought. The latter (Eliot called on him in September 1914 at his flat in London) was overcome by the fact that Eliot had actually 'trained himself and modernized himself *on his own*',[35] that he did not have to be told to remember the date on the calendar (1914). In June 1917, 'Drunken Helots and Mr. Eliot' was the first attempt to evaluate Eliot's true heritage, when he attacked Arthur Waugh's ignorance of Laforgue, De Régnier, and Corbière, and pointed out that Eliot had derived from French poetry and achieved a comparable finesse:

Our Helot has a marvellous neatness. There is a comparable finesse in Laforgue's 'votre âme est affaire d'occuliste', but hardly in English verse.[36]

In another important essay in *Poetry* (August 1917), Pound endeavoured to establish Eliot's true position in relation to poetry since Laforgue and Browning, and made clear his debt to the French:

You will hardly find such neatness save in France, such modern neatness, save in France.[37]

In the June 1918 issue of *Future*, he spoke of 'a new, French vitality among our younger writers of today', foremost among whom was Eliot, 'the most finished, the most composed.'[38]

Richard Aldington (who had observed in 1915 in the *Little Review* that 'French poetry is foremost in our age for fertility, originality and general poetic charm')[39] placed Eliot in a tradition of French poetry that included Laforgue and Verlaine, Rimbaud and Corbière going back to Villon and the goliards, but made no mention of Baudelaire.[40]

In 'A Poetry of Ideas' in *New Republic* (30 June 1926), Allen Tate was led to assert that Eliot had all along been under the influence of Laforgue and Corbière, from whom he had borrowed 'not tricks of construction so much as attitudes and particular lines.'[41] Tate was the first to suggest that Eliot's French heritage was more significant than the Elizabethan; according to him, the Elizabethan element was impure.[42] Webster's varied complexity of pattern, its fusion of heterogeneous sensations seems to break down under Eliot's treatment. It seems that Tate[43] was also the first to point out that Eliot's 'Simple and faithless like a shake of the hand'[44] was culled from Laforgue's 'Simple et sans foi comme un bonjour' (a discovery later parroted by other critics, oblivious of many more parallels), but that was all.

Although the comments of Eliot's friends Pound and Aldington have considerable historical importance, they remained skin-deep, making no attempt to support their perception with facts. It was only in the late thirties that a Frenchman, Renè Taupin, came up for the first time with a more tenable thesis on the influence of the French symbolists in the thirty-page chapter VI of his *L'Influence du symbolisme français sur la poésie américaine (de 1910 à 1920)*[45]. Taupin stated that Eliot associated the Metaphysicals with the Elizabethans as well as the symbolists, especially Corbière and Laforgue, a point which he did not elaborate. According to him, Eliot and Laforgue were 'Peintres-penseurs' ('Painter-thinkers').[46] Paris was for Laforgue what Europe was for Eliot.[47] A close reading of Laforgue transformed Eliot, who began to feel in the same way; theirs was the same mode of evasion through 'irony, verbalism and speculation,'[48] though Eliot was 'more elegant, less comic'. Taupin claimed that there was basically no difference between the art of T.S. Eliot and that of Laforgue, from 'the synthetic construction up to the word-play,'[49] that if one called Laforgue a symbolist, there was no reason why one should not call Eliot a symbolist too. Taupin made a historic statement when he remarked: 'Eliot a si bien jouè de ces instruments que la symphonie a paru toute neuve.' ('Eliot played so well these instruments that the symphony appeared all new').[50] He compared the relationship of Laforgue and Eliot with that of Picasso and Cézanne.[51] Unfortunately, René Taupin, too, did not make any textual analysis to substantiate his views. Taupin was of the opinion that Eliot was influenced by the freedom of expression of Corbière's diction, which was 'une presentation d'un objet réel depouillé de toute buée et de toute poussière, d'émotion et de sentimentalisme' ('presentation of real objects devoid of all mud, all dust of emotion and sentimentality'). He also tried to show how, Eliot deliberately imitated the construction of certain poems of Théophile Gautier[52] and named Guillaume Apollinaire and André Salmon as possible sources.[53]

Taupin's book was followed by Edmund Wilson's *Axel's Castle* (1931): the first meaningful attempt to analyse Eliot's symbolist connections by an English-speaking critic, who had a first-hand knowledge of French poetry. Wilson pointed out that Eliot derived from the conversational-ironic, rather than from the serious-aesthetic tradition. 'Corbière and Laforgue are almost everywhere in his early work'.[54] He briefly discussed how Laforgue and Corbière introduced a new variety of vocabulary and a new flexibility in poetry, and how Eliot reproduced Laforgue's irregular metrical scheme and some of the unstressed effect of French verse.[55] He concludes that though Eliot has, in certain respects, applied Laforgue's formula so faithfully, he cannot probably be described as an imitator, because he is, in some ways, a superior artist.[56] Wilson's chapter on T.S. Eliot's French connections remains one of the best because of its rare perceptiveness.

But if Wilson's comments on Eliot in *Axel's Castle* were expected to spread a general critical awareness, this was not so evident in English criticism of the time. G.M. Turnell's pioneering articles on Tristan Corbière and Jules Laforgue in the *Criterion*[57] and the *Scrutiny*[58] written in the thirties, inexplicably ignored their relationship with Eliot. The only exception, to my mind, was Frenchman M.J.J. Laboulle's 'T. S. Eliot and Some French Poets' in *Revue de Littérature Comparée*[59] which made a serious, if somewhat confused, attempt to find out resonances of Laforgue and Corbière, before concluding that 'though not always obvious, the influence of French poets is visible in most of the earlier poems, but decreases gradually as Eliot becomes more mature'.[60] This long-lost article is memorable for at least one observation: 'Mr. Eliot continued where Laforgue left off, strengthening his moral and religious sense . . .',[61] an insight that few other critics have shown.

E.J.H. Greene started his research on *T.S. Eliot et la France*[62] in 1937 and completed it after the war. Like Taupin's book, it has remained by and large inaccessible to readers because of the langauge barrier. It has been, in a sense, an obstacle for critics who regard it as the ultimate book on the subject, without really knowing its merits, thereby impeding further investigations.

Indeed, Greene's book is on the whole disappointing because of the expectations it raises. On one hand, this is the only book till date—albeit written in French—devoted to a serious aspect of the poet, who personally answered many of his queries and has, therefore, great documentary value. On the other hand, it has all the limitations of a non-Frenchman writing a dissertation in French. The language is stiff and uneven, and the painstaking style hinders the arguments. Thematically, it restates the generally accepted views on the subject (like the influence of Laforgue's irony on Eliot, or the 'metaphysical' qualities of his favourite French poets) but, critically, has very little to offer. It merely parrots the general opinion (which is catastrophic in a book of such pretensions) that Eliot had succeeded in eliminating the French resonances by the early twenties: 'peu à peu, elle s'efface' ('little by little the influence disappears').[63]

More interesting is Francis Scarfe's somewhat disparaging article 'Eliot and Nineteenth century French poetry' in Graham Martin's *Eliot in Perspective: A Symposium*,[64] which tends to denigrate his French masters as minor figures but makes a few important points. According to Scarfe, 'Eliot did not seem to be at all interested in the "Baroque" poets, Corneille,

La Fontaine, La Bruyère and other moralists and most of the eighteenth century'.[65] Eliot was on good ground, Scarfe thought, and scholarly, in his remarks on Gamier and Montaigne, Pascal and Racine, the last being one of his main points of reference. Scarfe discussed briefly Eliot's interactions with Laforgue, Corbière and Pierre Janet, rejected the possibility of an influence by Rimbaud because Eliot had told him in 1937 that he was 'not particularly' interested in the latter.[66] Scarfe too toed the conventional line of thinking when he concluded that Eliot's vital relationship with French poetry had withered after a while.[67]

Enid Starkie's *From Gautier to Eliot: The Influence of France, 1851–1939*[68] wished to 'serve as a signpost for those who are not well-tried to chart the large currents to indicate the trends of influences',[69] but in effect merely made a summary of known views. In his six pages on Eliot,[70] Starkie refers to Eliot's appreciation of Baudelaire's 'spiritual aspect'[71] in *The Waste Land* phase, but, as usual, says nothing about the later Eliot. Starkie's scope was limited, and he made no attempt to analyse the influences.

The only prominent Eliot critic (apart from Grover Smith, of course) to deal with the subject is Herbert Howarth. He tried to comprehend with great sensitivity the whole creative process of Eliot, his complex method of assimilating and reorganizing the material. His perceptive analysis stands out among a few disjointed, superficial, and sketchy endeavours since the twenties to assess Eliot's indebtedness to 'French sensibility' of the late nineteenth and early twentieth century. Howarth is one critic who was closely familiar with the works of the Symbolists, and those of even Eliot's Parisian friends Alain-Fournier and Jacques Rivière, and the somewhat lesser-known one-time idol of Eliot, Julien Benda. I acknowledge my debt to Howarth for his instructive comments on Paul Claudel;[72] he corroborates my views on one of the most fertilizing influences in Eliot's career. Unfortunately, Howarth too had to limit himself to only one chapter (significantly entitled 'Some Gifts from France') for he had other considerations. Indeed, Howarth's historic statement: 'A whole book should be written on Eliot's debt which is a debt for all of us',[73] can be said to be the starting point of the present research.

A number of outstanding books were published since Eliot's death (notably by Stephen Spender, Bernard Bergonzi, Peter Ackroyd, A.D. Moody, and Lyndall Gordon) which provided new insights into the poet's works, but continued to ignore what the poet himself considered his real roots as 'un petit héritier du legs de Baudelaire' ('a small successor to the legacy of Baudelaire').[74] This indifference (the only exception being Christopher Ricks's edition of Eliot's *Inventions of a March Hare*, 1996) has not helped in the understanding of Eliot's phenomenal genius in making the glorious discoveries of another tradition his own. And it has helped in denying him some of the seminal aspects of his craft. Consequently, conclusions about his poetry have been, to a certain extent, 'misguided, inconclusive and incomplete'.[75]

Hence the necessity of locating some of the principal elements of the bewildering mosaic, out of which Eliot was able to form an authentic crystal.

III

As a young man, T.S. Eliot had submitted to a derivative Tennysonian-Swinburnian code before he was introduced to the Symbolists by the 1908 edition of Arthur Symons's *The Symbolist Movement in Literature* (1899). It led to 'results of permanent importance'.[76] It was an introduction to 'wholly new feelings', a 'revelation',[77] a 'milestone' that 'affected the course of his life'.[78] Now, what was so revolutionary about this book?

First of all, it instructed him about new text elements very different from the prevailing codes in England and America. For a closer examination of the connotative features of those texts of a different cultural system, he felt the need to have a first-hand acquaintance with some of those, notably those of Jules Laforgue and Baudelaire as well as to go to France to have a first-hand knowledge of the country which produced such palpably different stuff.

He ordered three volumes[79] of Laforgue's *Oeuvres Complètes* presumably of the 1902–3 edition by Camille Mauclair published by Mercure de France, and enrolled in Irving Babbitt's class of modern French Criticism in 1909. Babbitt attacked the cult of personality and urged young writers to cultivate the classical spirit in its purest form, which feels itself consecrated to the service of a 'high, impersonal reason'.[80] Secondly, Babbitt tried to inculcate the theory of the living past, which will help strengthen the writer's grasp of the present. These ideas would correspond with Eliot's responses to Laforgue.[81]

And, no doubt, without Symons, Eliot would not have organized so soon a pilgrimage to France: 'the country of movements'.[82] It was he who introduced him to the French sensibility and the undiscovered, new world of symbols. 'It is in and through symbols that man, consciously or unconsciously, lives, works and has his being,' said Symons, quoting Carlyle.[83] 'What are words themselves but symbols?'[84] he asked. He spoke of a literature in which ''the visible world is no longer a reality and the seen world no longer a dream'.[85] Symons presented it as an endeavour to 'spiritualize literature, to evade the old bondage of rhetoric, the old bondage of exteriority'.[86] Symbolism, thus, was '*a revolt against exteriority,* against rhetoric, against a materialistic tradition'.[87] It was a 'revelation of the Infinite'.[88] Symons's conclusion, I believe, had a far-reaching influence on the young Harvardian's mind:

It is an endeavour to disengage the ultimate essence, the soul, of whatever exists and can be realised by the consciousness . . .[89]

Thus, literature, which bowed down to so many burdens, may at last attain liberty and its authentic speech.[90]

The Pension in Paris where Eliot lived in 1910–11

It is a pity that hardly anyone has quoted a word from this book in eight decades of Eliot criticism. But no doubt, Symons's views on Laforgue (which I shall discuss in the relevant chapter), added to all this, had helped revolutionize modern English poetry. For Eliot and his contemporaries of the new generation (T.E. Hulme, F.S. Flint, Herbert Read, Richard Aldington, Ezra Pound, and the *Nouvelle Revue Française* group in France) were fomenting for change, for 'a new attitude of mind, which should be the twentieth century mind, if the twentieth century is to have a mind of its own'.[91]

It was around 1910 that Virginia Woolf had realized the collapse of the old world and the emergence of the new in arts: for 'human nature had changed in 1910'.[92] In 1908, T.E. Hulme had proposed the first poets' club—a gathering of poets who shared a general dissatisfaction with the present state of mind.[93] There was a 'feeling of discontinuity between the literature of our century and that of any previous one'.[94] The singularity of modern poetry, for instance, is one of the arguments used by C.S. Lewis to support his hypothesis of 'a great rift in our culture'[95] just before the present age. To put it in Graham Hough's words:

It was there (in London in the years just before 1914) that the English cell of an almost world-wide poetic conspiracy was incubated—the first plot against the literary establishment for over a hundred years . . .[96]

In *Make it New,* Pound lashed out at attempts to compartmentalize literature. 'You might as well give courses in "American chemistry" neglecting all foreign discoveries'.[97] He emphasized the role of translations in history.[98] In all this 'blasting and bombardiering' (Wyndham Lewis's phrase)[99] French poetry played almost a pivotal role. In a new volume of her verse *Sword Blades and Poppy Seed* (1914), Amy Lowell admitted her 'immense debt' to French and in her preface to *Six French Poets*, she deplored the ignorance of Englishmen and Americans in the matter of contemporary French poetry, which was 'one of the great poetical epochs of the world', and dedicated her own abilities to its correction.[100]

In Richard Aldington's words, *The Egoist* was 'hammering at people to read French poetry'.[101] 'I salute in the poetry of France,' wrote F.S. Flint, 'an inextinguishable vitality'.[102] Yet the most euphoric (and probably historically incorrect) statement was made by none other than Ezra Pound himself:

For the best part of a thousand years English poets have gone to school to the French . . . or one might say that there never were any English poets until they began to study the French. The history of English poetic glory is a history of successful steals from the French. . . . The great periods of English have been the periods when the English showed the greatest powers of assimilation.[103]

Obviously, this belief was shared by F.S. Flint and Richard Aldington, omnivorous readers of French poetry (Aldington was influenced by the same poets as Eliot), yet none of them (least of all Amy Lowell) succeeded as a poet. But their zeal was no less than that of Eliot.

If the desperate aim of this new poetry was to be more and more introspective in order to catch the exact curve of the thing, Arthur Symons's exposé and his translations of samples of Symbolist poetry provided the glimpse of a world of infinite possibilities offered by the young dead, Jules Laforgue. The 'feeling of profound kinship' changed him, 'metamorphosed' him, almost within 'a few weeks'.[104] This led him to seriously emulate French poetry, particularly that of Laforgue, and despite his mother's admonishment,[105] before long landed him in France, the Holy Land he cherished not only in those years of adolescence, but, as I propose to show in this book, throughout his life.

Paris is 'such a strong stimulus', Eliot would write to his friend Robert McAlmon in 1921.[106] 'I am glad to hear that you like Paris; the right way, of course, is to take it as a place and a tradition'.[107]

This is precisely what he had done in 1910–11, when he decided to go there to study the particular genius of France. His pilgrimage to France was a conscious decision, for he wished to change himself inside out.

According to a cartoon in *Le Figaro* of 30 December 1910, 'it was a miserable year, a year of floods and a long railway strike'.[108] In the new year of 1911, the Seine floods were worse than in the previous years and winter persisted till April. When the great German poet Rainer Maria Rilke arrived in the last week of April, the lilacs were almost over.[109] Yet, in his state of unusual excitement, Eliot was probably not concerned with all that. He promptly looked for a boarding-house in the Latin Quarter, near the Sorbonne and the Seine; this he found in Mme Casaubin's *pension* at 151 bis, rue Saint-Jacques, besides the Panthéon. I found the address in Eliot's letters from Paris.[110] I located the whereabouts of this boarding during my stay in a nearby *pension* in 1992. Eliot's biographer Peter Ackroyd[111] believes that he stayed at 9, rue de l'université, but this does not seem to be true. Even if he did live there for a few days, it is *likely* that he soon moved to rue St. Jacques. It was less than a stone's throw from the Collège de France and the Sorbonne, and just about three minutes' walk to the celebrated Boulevard Saint-Michel and the Luxembourg Gardens, closely surrounded by the new and old bookshops. Three decades later, in an interview with a French paper, he would admit:

Je crois que e'était une bonne fortune exceptionelle, pour un adolescent, de découvrir Paris en l'an 1910. *La Nouvelle Revue Française* était encore vraiment nouvelle; et les *Cahiers de la quinzaine* paraissaient, sous leur austère couverture de papier gris.

(I believe that a young man would be exceptionally fortunate to discover Paris in the year 1910. *La Nouvelle Revue Française* was still new: and the *Cahiers de la quinzaine* appeared in their austere cover of grey paper).[112]

He waited five hours to attend Bergson's lectures every week in the packed classrooms of Collège de France. Walking on the banks of the Seine, he saw Anatole France, and bought the latest Gide or Claudel the same day of the publication.[113]

Tantot Paris était tout le passié; tantot tout l'avenir: et ces deux aspects se combinaient en un présent parfait. Si c'est cela (notamment) que la France représente pour moi, peut-être est-ce grace à un heureux accident du hasard. Mais ce n'est pas un accident qui m'avait conduit à Paris. Depuis plusieurs années, la France représentait à mes yeux la poésie . . .

(Often Paris seemed to be all past; often it was all future. And the two aspects combined to make a perfect present. If this is (specially) what France represented for me, perhaps it is because of a happy accident of chance. It is not an accident which took me to Paris. For several years, France represented for me *poetry* . . .)[114]

Eliot's French, although 'bookish',[115] was 'already good enough' and he 'corrected the French of an American compatriot'.[116] He spoke French rapidly with a singsong accent, bringing down his final syllables and softly rolling his 'r'-s (this piece of information I found in the typescript of an unpublished interview with Françoise de Castro on Monday 23 August 1948, preserved at the Modern Archives of King's College, Cambridge).[117] He took private tuitions from Henri Fournier[118]—a young Frenchman of 'exquisite refinement, quiet humour and great personal charm',[119] who would soon burst into the French literary scene under the pseudonym of Alain-Fournier. Fournier was steeped in Laforgue, like Eliot's fellow-lodger Jean Verdenal, who 'carried copies of Laforgue's poetry and *Moralités Légendaires*'.[120] Eliot and his French tutor, who stayed nearby at 2, rue Cassini, studied Dostoevsky in French as well as André Gide and Paul Claudel, and ripped through the pages of the *Nouvelle Revue Française*. It was amidst this unmistakable atmosphere of Paris that the future of English poetry was incubated.

Though he was washed up to London during the war, he detested London.[121] But Oxford and Merton, 'with its Alexandrine verse, nuts and wine, the professors with pregnant wives and sprawling children, and hideous pictures on the walls, made him long even for London . . .' 'Oxford is pretty', he told his friend Aiken, 'but I don't like to be dead'.[122]

On the contrary, Paris remained the oasis which gave him mental health for many years. Ten years later in 1921, on the verge of a nervous breakdown, Eliot wrote to his mother:

My own health has been much better since my week in Paris before Christmas. It was such a complete change, and I enjoyed myself thoroughly.[123]

Earlier on, he wrote to Sidney Schiff (22 August 1920) from Saumur, 'Pans was a great relief after many months of London'. After a trip to France in August 1919, Eliot wrote a touching letter to his mother on 3 September 1919 and described his excitement. 'It was all so France and so sudden that I was dazed by it. . . . Travelling in a taxi I looked out of the window most of the way, too excited to sleep'.[124]

Eliot wrote to Maxwell Bodenheim (2 January 1921), 'I of course escape to Paris whenever I can get a bit of holiday' because he preferred that to 'the placid smile of imbecility which splits the face of contemporary London', or 'more abstractly, the putrescence of English literature and journalism'.[125] The conclusive statement was made in the *Criterion*: 'The predominance of Paris was incontestable'.[126] It is during his year in France that he took to smoking French cigarettes[127] and fell in love with everything French, including the 'splendour' of French book-binding.[128]

This almost pathological bias for France and Paris has been ignored by his commentators, in the process probably losing the right perspective of Eliot's creativity.

Without those vital months, therefore, there would probably have been no Eliot, or perhaps a different Eliot. I have already referred to his friendship with Alain-Fournier: the latter's correspondence with Jacques Rivière will show what kind of enthusiasm he may have inspired in his American friend.

Fournier had introduced Eliot to Rivière, his brother-in-law,[129] who was soon to become the editor of *La Nouvelle Revue Française*. The priceless correspondence exchanged between them[130] would show the unusual state of creative excitement at that point of time in Paris. Fournier and Rivière endlessly enthused about Jules Laforgue and Paul Claudel: Laforgue and Claudel are mentioned 90 and 258 times respectively. Indeed, Fournier and Rivière's unusual interest in Laforgue and Claudel contained, in a sense, the germ of Eliot's whole creative life.

Fournier's extraordinary thirst for Laforgue strongly anticipates that of Eliot himself. In a letter of 21 March 1906, he wrote:

Tout jeune homme qui se respecte devrait être fou de Laforgue . . .
(Every respectable young man should be crazy for Laforgue . . .)[131]

He had even lambasted a bookseller for not possessing Laforgue's *Moralités Légendaires*—quite an unpardonable sin![132]

Fournier and Rivière were also admirers of Dante and Remy de Gourmont.[133] As for Valery Larbaud, whom I am going to present in this book as an important influence on T.S. Eliot, Rivière exchanged no less than 148 letters with him.[134]

Jean Verdenal, the medical student at Mme Casaubin's *pension*, was by some happy accident an addict of Laforgue[135] and admired Claudel and Charles-Louis Philippe,[136] which too, one would like to believe, helped Eliot to decide on his future course of action.

Equally important were the signals Eliot received from the most significant literary journal of the period, *La Nouvelle Revue Française*, which desperately heralded the new. It had been launched by André Gide in November 1908 and served as a forum for the *avant-garde* in France. It had possibly much to do with Eliot's coming of age. He remained a subscriber even after his return to Harvard[137] and modelled his *Criterion* upon it. I have examined the contents of the *NRF* from its first issue up to 1927, the year of his Conversion, and strongly believe that the review may help in decoding the signals emitted by France, and consciously or unconsciously received by Eliot in the second and third decades of the twentieth century. It is indeed unfortunate that Eliot commentators have never wished to know what he actually read in the *NRF* in those vital formative years.

In all probability, Eliot read the previous numbers of the much-acclaimed *NRF* after he arrived in Paris in December 1910. He would not have missed Jean Schlumberger's 'Considerations':

Quant aux problèmes essentiels, ils ne sont jamais à l'ordre du jour. Chaque artiste les affronte, seul, dans les moments les plus décisifs de sa vie.

(As for the essential problems they are never in the order of the day. Every artist confronts them, alone, in the most decisive moments of his life).[138]

Schlumberger not only spoke of the artist's freedom of choice, but attached equally great importance to his 'dépendance filiale' ('filial dependence') on the past: an approach Eliot himself would adopt very soon. He would have come across a quotation from Baudelaire:

. . . plus l'art se détachera de l'enseignement et plus il montera vers la beauté pure et désintéressée.

(. . . the more detached art is from didacticism, the more it will ascend towards pure and disinterested beauty).[139]

or from Madame de Lafayette's *La Princesse de Clèves*:

Les passions peuvent me conduire, mais elles ne sauraient m'aveugler.

(Passions can drive me, but I shall never be blinded by them).[140]

There were instructive articles on Remy de Gourmont by Gide and on Baudelaire by Jacques Rivière. It is possible that the future style of Eliot as critic and poet has been shaped by such illuminating remarks as:

M. de Gourmont est un critique averti, d'un goût fin, de beaucoup de lecture; il a le mot juste; il sait le juste prix des oeuvres et ne laisse jamais la convention guider son choix ni conseiller ses amours . . . Sa phrase se developpe d'un mouvement tout naturel, sans raidissement, sursaut ni hâte . . . La pensée dans les écrits de M. Gourmont ne se propose pas en object, c'est un instrument assoupli qu'il incline et dirige selon ses fins.

(M. de Gourmont is a careful critic, of fine taste, of wide reading. He has the exact word, he knows the just price of works and never lets his choice or his love to be guided by convention . . . His sentences develop in a very natural way, without stiffening, without jerks or haste . . . The thought in Gourmont's writings does not offer itself as an object, it is a supple instrument which he inclines and directs according to his ends).[141]

There was a debate on *vers libre* by Roger Vildrac and Georges Duhamel[142] (Eliot's essay on the same subject in 1917, 'Reflections on *vers libre*', used a line from this article as epigraph[143]), poems by Paul Claudel (whose indirect influence on Eliot I shall try to establish in the present book), Paul Valéry (whose huge photo hung in Eliot's Faber and Faber office) and Saint-John Perse (whose *Anabase* he would translate into English in 1930), and novels by Gide and Valery Larbaud (the latter's book of poems, *A.O. Barnabooth* [1913], he would later try to emulate in *The Waste Land*. See chapter on Larbaud and Eliot).

Eliot's friend Alain-Fournier wrote 'Notes', which he would not have failed to show his pupil by any chance. For example, Fournier requested Eliot to read his 'Portrait' in his letter of 25 July 1911.[144] His masterpiece *Le Grand Meaulnes* was serialized in the *NRF* from July 1913 to November 1913. And, of course, there were the novels and letters of Charles-Louis Philippe. Grover Smith has shown that Eliot used lines from *Bubu de Montparnasse* and *Marie-Donadieu* in 'Preludes' and 'Rhapsody on a Windy Night'.[145]

By the end of 1911, *NRF*'s list of publications included Claudel's *L'Otage*; and *L'Annonce Faite à Marie* was serialized from the December issue. All this would resurge back in Eliot's memory in two decades.

In 'De la Sincerité envers soi-même', Fournier's brother-in-law Jacques Rivière stated that 'spontaneous poetry is a poetry of lies'.[146] His 'De la Foi' ('Of Faith'), dedicated to Claudel, highlighted the *necessity* of faith, because 'those who doubt stagnate'.[147] All this may have seeped into young Eliot's unconscious and shaped his response as a reader. This is particularly important for his later religiosity and inclination for Claudelian Catholicism.

Non seulement mon esprit, en effet, mais aussi faiblement mon coeur tendent vers la foi.

(Not only my mind, in fact, my heart also feebly moves towards faith).[148]

And the *NRF* published a review of Julien Benda's scathing attack on Bergson[149] by Camille Vettard, which could have exorcised Eliot of his erstwhile Bergsonism.

The present researcher stumbled on the poetry of an insignificant poet whom no Eliot specialist has ever recognized as a predecessor: Tristan Leclerc. His poems in the January issue of 1912 seem amusing to us today because of their 'Eliotic' style:

> Vieux rat, tu peux t'aventurer sur la gouttière
> Sur le beau soir bleu
> Monte une fumée légère de bruyère
> Et le chat joue
> Dans la maison avec sa queue
> Vieux coeur, tu peux t'aventurer chez la bérgère,
> C'est l'heure du loup garou,
> Et le mari dort au coin de son feu;
> La lune rit sans bruit dans ce beau soir bleui.
> Eh! Soyons vite audacieux,
> Vieux coeur: c'est l'heure du loup garou
> Et des amoureux.[150]

(Old rat, you can adventure in the gutter/In the beautiful blue evening/Rises a light smoke of dust/And the cat plays/In the house with its tail./Old heart, you can have a fling with the shepherdess./It is time for the werewolf./And the husband sleeps at the fireside corner;/The Moon laughs silently in the bluish evening./Eh, let us quickly be audacious/Old heart: it is time for the werewolf/And lovers).

> Another poem by Leclerc reads:
> Il a plu. Le matin sourit
> A travers ses pleurs;
> La grenouille saute dans l'étang,
> Et sur un roseau droit du Christ,
> Le beau matin-pêcheur,

En habit beau-clair à la hussarde
Avec son plumet rouge éclatant,
Monte la garde:
Francis Jammes, dormez-vous encore?[151]

(It has rained. The morning smiles/Across its tears;/The frog jumps in the pond/On a reed of Christ,/The beautiful morning-fisherman/In a roughly light blue dress/With its shining red plume/Keeps its guard up:/Francis Jammes, are you still asleep?)

Side by side with this crisp, modernist poetry, there was a distinct bias for spirituality among some of the contributors: a characteristic of modern French poetry since Symbolism.

Along with the intensely powerful Catholic poetry of Claudel, Péguy and Léon-Paul Fargue, *NRF* published articles which had immediate relevance for the intellectual development of Eliot, like Albert Thibaudet's 'L'Esthétique des Trois Traditions' (January–March 1913) (which anticipated Eliot's later view about the flexibility of Classicism and Romanticism in *After Strange Gods*), his review of *Promenades littéraires* by Remy de Gourmont[152] (whom Eliot would compare with Aristotle in *The Sacred Wood*), Valery Larbaud's 'Journal d'un milliardaire' (February–April 1913), Rivière's violently anti-romantic 'Le roman d'aventure' (May–July 1913).

In the last Rivière made a statement which Eliot would wholeheartedly approve:

Le romantisme n'est pas seulement un art démodé. C'est vraiment un art inférieur, une sorte de monstre dans l'histoire de la littérature.

L'oeuvre classique c'est l'oeuvre en acte; c'est celle envers lequelle son auteur est complètement acquitté, celle dont chaque molécule a été lentement amené à sa perfection.

L'oeuvre dont nous avons besoin aujourd'hui avant tout il faudra qui'elle soit parfaite et achevée entre toutes ses parties: c'est en quoi elle sera d'essence classique. Mais tout de suite il faut ici nous garder de prendre cette exigeance de notre goût trop à la lettre, d'intérpreter trop strictement le mot: classique.

(Romanticism is not only an old-fashioned art. It is really an inferior art, a kind of monstrosity in the history of literature.

A classical work is a work in action, it is that which literates an author; of which every molecule has slowly been brought to perfection.

The work we primarily need today is one which is perfect and completed in every part, so that it is essentially classical. But immediately we should be on our guard against taking this exigency of our taste too literally, against interpreting too strictly the word: Classical.)[153]

Eliot, who subscribed to the *NRF*, continued to read all this with the interest of an apprentice and, already before the war, imbibed from it the inherent contradictions of French poetry: its insatiable thirst for *novelty* and its adherence to a rich tradition of *scepticism* and *spirituality.*

The *NRF* was stopped because of the First World War for five years between August 1914 and June 1919. When it was revived again, it contained an important admission:

La guerre est venue, la guerre a passé. Elle a profondément bouleversé toute chose, et en particulier nos esprits. Elle a remis chacun de nous au creuset et a recompensé à plusieurs d'entre nous une âme véritablement nouvelle.

(The war came, the war went. It has deeply upset everything, and in particular, our minds. It has put back each of us into a test and has compensated several of us by giving us a truly new soul).[154]

Amidst this ruin and misery, the *NRF* continued its explorations. Claudel's religious poetry gained in importance. Eliot's friend Rivière paid homage to Claudel's faith which he considered instructive;[155] Proust wrote on Flaubert's style (January 1920); Gide wrote his classic novels *S'il ne grain ne meurt* and *La Symphonie pastorale*; and Paul Valéry became a regular contributor. Valéry's 'Le Cimetière Marin' was published in 1920.[156] And, as if to show respect to the tradition, the *NRF* brought out Jules Laforgue's *Notes d'un Agenda,* the diary of the period when he was Queen Augusta's reader.[157]

All this makes a complex mosaic, which seems to have helped the orientation of Eliot's poetry. And the growing reverence for Claudel in the best minds of France (Gide, Larbaud, Rivière) probably led him to gradually look up to his Biblical, incantatory style as a liberating example to be emulated in the last phase of his poetic career from the twenties onwards.

Thus, there is good reason to believe that both the early and the later works of Eliot, both as poet and critic, received important signals from the *NRF*.

Unfortunately, Eliot's unusual interest in Julien Benda, Charles Maurras, and Jacques Maritain has been little investigated. He mentioned Benda's *Belphégor* (1918), Maurras's *L'Avenir de l'Intelligence* (1905) and Maritain's *Réflexions sur l'Intelligence* (1924) among those books which made a powerful impact on him.[158] All these writers featured in the *NRF*. While Benda's name appeared as early as in 1912 (as already mentioned, in a book review), there was a long article on Maritain, 'L'Intelligence de M. Maritain'[159] by Ramon Fernandez, who would later translate some of Eliot's own articles into French. Benda's *La Trahison des clercs,* which disenchanted Eliot about the anti-romantic polemicist, was also serialized in the journal in 1927.

The *NRF* may have remained for many years a useful reference for Eliot. It is a matter of great regret that no attempt has been made to evaluate its contribution towards the making of Modernism in English poetry. Eliot, fully conscious of his debt to the *NRF*, paid tribute to it by modelling *The Criterion* on it[160] and contributed some significant notes and articles to the French journal in the twenties:

1. 'Lettre d'Angleterre', May 1922, pp. 617–24.
2. 'Lettre d'Angleterre', 'Le style dans la prose anglaise', December 1922, pp. 751–6.
3. 'Lettre d'Angleterre', November 1923, pp. 619–25 (tr. G. d'Hangest).
4. 'Rencontre', April 1925 (Special Number on Jacques Rivière), pp. 657–8.
5. 'Notes sur Mallarmé et Poe', November 1926, pp. 524–6 (tr. Ramon Fernandez).
6. 'Le roman anglais contemporain', May 1927, pp. 669–75.

These pages include confessions such as:

On doit reconnâitre . . . que dans une assez grande mesure l'influence la plus puissante est venue de France.

(One should admit . . . that to quite a large extent the most powerful influence came from France . . .)[161]

He makes a distinction between *maîtres de pensee* ('masters of thought') and *maîtres d'art* ('masters of art'), quickly adding that such a categorization is not always possible. If Remy de Gourmont led him to Flaubert, who was both a master of thought and art, and Maurras and Benda remained for him masters of thought, he recognized:

El en poésie (je ne parle toujours que pour un certain groupe) Rimbaud, Corbière et Laforgue ont été pour nous des maîtres d'art plus qu'aucun poète anglais de notre temps.

(And in poetry [I am always speaking of a certain group] Rimbaud, Corbière and Laforgue have been for us masters of art more than any English poet of our time).[162]

Of course, as I shall try to demonstrate in the relevant chapters, Laforgue and Corbière could inadvertently inject their philosophy through their art into Eliot's psyche. The finest conclusion is drawn[163] by Eliot himself:

(La question) que l'on pourrait bien me poser de savoir s'ils ont assez de points communs, si leur influence, pourtant qu'elle existe, est assez semblable pour me donner raison de parler d'eux ensemble. Je ne suis pas préoccupé de leurs 'idées', mais bien de leur influence sur la sensibilité à travers l'intelligence; el il est moins aisé de dire en quoi cette sensibilité consiste, ce qu'elle n'est point ... La pulsation de son rhythme vibre de toute sa souffrance de la vie de l'esprit.

([The question] one could ask me is whether they have enough common points, if their influence, even if it exists, is quite similar. I am not preoccupied by their 'ideas', but by their influence on the sensibility through intelligence; and it is less easy to say what this sensibility consists of, what it is not . . . The pulsation of its rhythm vibrates through the suffering of the mind's life.)

'The pulsation of the rhythm' of a mosaic of different sources, French and otherwise, vibrated through the suffering of his mind's life for many years. Here it will be my endeavour to try and find out how his French *maîtres d'art* enriched his sensibility *à travers l'intelligence*, a sensibility in the process of formation.

The moment of cross was a bewildering moment of crisis, of surrender, of rebirth. To quote Eliot, it evoked:

. . . a feeling of profound kinship, or rather of a peculiar personal intimacy with another, probably dead author. It may overcome us suddenly, on first, or after long acquaintance. It is certainly a crisis; and when a young writer is seized with his first passion of this sort he may be changed, metamorphosed almost, within a few weeks, from a bundle of second hand sentiments into a person . . . It is a cause of development like personal relations in life, like personal intimacies in life, it may and probably will pass, but it will be ineffaceable . . . We do not imitate, we are changed; and our work is the work of a changed man. We have not borrowed, we have been quickened, and we become bearers of a tradition.[164]

Our understanding of this complex process of quickening, of his becoming a part of a tradition, has remained somewhat theoretical because of our inability to give his French heritage the importance it deserves.

The present endeavour is, therefore, not just yet another source-hunting; it is part of a fresh attempt to rediscover his French roots, his links with a soil which enlivened his mind and which he was never tired of acknowledging throughout his life.

Knowing how conjectural and problematic the question of conceptual influence can be on an innovator like T.S. Eliot, I have limited the scope of my study, and left out the thinkers, Maurras and Maritain, from the purview of the present book. But this is by no means to deny their impact. Eliot wrote in the *NRF*[165] that Charles Maurras's *L'Avenir de l'Intelligence* (1905) exerted a deep influence on his intellectual development. He had purchased his copy of the book while studying in Paris in 1911, his attention being drawn to it by Irving Babbitt in Harvard.[166] One of the central concerns of the conservative, traditionalist, Royalist Maurras, was Man:

Au centre de ce pullulement de nouveautés et d'invidus, cherchez l'homme.

(At the centre of this abundance of novelty and individuality, look for man).[167]

His primary commitment was to 'the immense question of order',[168] symbolized by the altar and the throne. The restoration of order, he thought, would either be wholly Christian or an utter failure. Yet more than for its theological content, Maurras identified the Church as a supremely *cultural* institution, which is reflected in Eliot's own unresolved attempt to harmonize the Catholic and European, the Anglican and English traditions, in *Notes Towards the Definition of Culture*. Maurras seems to have inspired Eliot's description of culture as 'essentially the incarnation, so to speak, of the religion of a people', and religion and culture as synonymous.[169] When in 1928 Eliot described himself with uncharacteristic dogmatism as a Classicist in art, an Anglican in religion, and a Royalist in politics, he was no doubt thinking of Albert Thibaudet's description of Maurras as 'classique, catholique, monarchique' in 1913.[170] Eliot would also use an imaginary conversation from *L'Avenir de l'Intelligence* in 'The Triumphal March':

Et les soldats faisaient la haie?—Ils la faisaient.—En armes?—Vous l'avez dit. Mais que disait le peuple?—Il n'en croyait pas ses cent yeux!

Pareille chose ne se fût jamais une voilà vingl-six ans: des tambours, du canon et le déplacement des autorités pour un simple gratte-papier!

(And the soldiers formed a line?—They did.—Armed?—You've said it.—But what did the people say?—They couldn't believe their eyes!

Such a thing never happened in twenty-six years: drums, canons and displacement of authorities for a simple pen-pusher!)[171]

It is no less important that Eliot shared with Maurras his immense respect for Dante. In Maurras's 1912 essay on Dante, reprinted as *Le Conseil de Dante* (1920), he considered the latter 'le plus intellectuel de tous les poètes' ('the most intellectual of all poets') and 'le plus émouvant' ('the most moving')[172] who was far closer to the 'nature essentielle' ('essential nature') of the twentieth century mind than others on whom the French lost their time and energy.[173] To him: 'C'est le roi des poètes . . . du moins des poètes modernes' ('he is the king of poets . . . at least of the modern poets')[174] whose sensibility held in tension contradictory elements with its ampleness, density and 'un don supérieur d'équilibre' ('a superior gift of balance').[175] This should remind us of Eliot's view that 'Dante's is the most comprehensive, and the most ordered presentation of emotions that has been ever made',[176] that 'Dante's poem is a whole where all fit together according to the logic of sensibility'.[177] Maurras especially highlights Dante's 'rare qualities of suppleness and tautness', his uncanny ability to hit the target: 'comme la flèche au but' ('like an arrow which reaches the target')[178]—a metaphor Eliot would use ('his arrow that goes unerringly to the centre of the target') in 'What Dante Means to Me'.[179] Eliot would also echo Maurras's opinion that one could pick up Italian by studying Dante. Predictably, his booklet on Dante was dedicated to Maurras. The epigraph he chose for his 1929 booklet was also borrowed from Maurras: 'La sensibilité sauvée d'elle-même, et conduite dans l'ordre, est devenue un principe de perfection' ('Sensibility saved from itself and controlled in an orderly way, becomes the principle of perfection').[180] This, as we know, was one of Eliot's chief premises of thought. Eliot remained faithful to Maurras[181] even after the latter was excommunicated by Vatican; but his proposed book on him[182] never materialized.

The other Catholic thinker to deeply impress Eliot from the mid-twenties onwards was Jacques Maritain, whom he came to consider the most remarkable contemporary French philosopher.[183] That Eliot's admiration for Maritain, Sorel, and Maurras was not an accident can be seen from the fact that Maritain himself named all of them, along with Bergson, in the chapter 'Retour au real et absolu' of his major work *Réflexions sur l'Intelligence*.[184] He wanted to revolt against the 'physicisme politique et economique' ('political and economic physicality') which 'poisoned modern culture',[185] and I guess that it was the same with Eliot.

Yet, although Eliot believed that 'poetry can be in some sense philosophic and poetry can be penetrated by a philosophic idea',[186] in the decanonization of the prevalent poetic codes he was primarily aided by poets and not thinkers. More than Donne, he loved to 'pick up like a magpie, various shining fragments of ideas as they struck his eye, and stuck them about here and there in his verse'.[187] He had what he calls the 'fundamental brainwork'[188] to rearrange those fragments in an imaginative order. From the beginning, his world of poetry was truly a laboratory, a workshop (to use his own words) and his use of the vocabulary of chemistry is not to be taken lightly.

The 'fundamental brainwork', which in Eliot's case reshaped the resonances and echoes, invariably reminds one of the French critic he admired the most, Remy de Gourmont, who believed that the style is determined by the physiology of a writer, that it is the product of the brain structure itself: 'On ne se donne pas son style; sa forme est déterminée par la structure du cerveau' ('One's style is not acquired automatically, its form is determined by the structure of the brain').[189] Eliot's brainwork is never in doubt even when he makes a continual surrender of himself, as he is at the moment, to something which is more valuable. This happened in the case of his surrender to Laforgue and Baudelaire. If the mind is a mechanism which devours experience, it also transmutes it.

The whole process of contact is therefore characterised by an unusual self-awareness of the function the poet is called upon to perform. He sees himself quite aptly as a scientist who uses the discoveries of an Einstein in pursuing his own independent investigations.[190] This is precisely what he did during his formative years, even in the twenties, when he dared to remodel his poetic style in the mould of the incantatory texts of Claudel and Saint-John Perse. There was of course the exceptional case of Laforgue who almost completely 'inundated' and 'invaded' the psychic process of the receptor at a tender age. But there too, Eliot recovered from the early imitation in poems like 'Humouresque', 'Nocturne', 'Spleen', and 'Silence' to creative rewriting in the final version of 'Prufrock' and other poems.

But innovation is not enough, significance is also necessary. And unlike the post-structuralists, Eliot was studying not merely the texts but also the authors (Symons, for example, had focused on Laforgue the man). Thus, ironically, despite his seemingly professional approach to the materials of other poets, he inadvertently absorbed some of the basic tenets of thought of his models. After all, the received text is already a received interpretation, already a value interpreted into a poem. I shall show how Laforgue seems to have exerted a life-long subconscious moral-intellectual influence on his psyche, like Dante. In spite of himself, Eliot's masters of art also became his real masters of thought.

Possibly the clearest indication of his affinity of thought with those whom I shall consider as his principal French masters is that they all form a magic circle of mutual admiration:

1. Tristan Corbière and Jules Laforgue shared certain basic qualities. Laforgue's *Mélanges Posthumes* reveals his love-hate relationship with his predecessor. Most of his contemporaries were convinced that he imitated Corbière. (See chapter on Corbière and Eliot.)
2. Valery Larbaud, Paul Claudel, and Saint-John Perse[191] were ardent admirers of Laforgue in their youth and they admired each other. Perse learnt his art from Claudel, and it is Larbaud who had discovered the former. (See chapter on Larbaud.)
3. Laforgue had a keen interest in Elizabethan drama, which is evident from the countless epigraphs in his poems and his obsession with Hamlet. I would like to recall once again Eliot's curious confession

in 1933 that without his favourite French poets, 'the Elizabethan and Jacobean poets would have been remote and quaint'.[192]

4. Larbaud was (along with André Gide) one of the founders of the John Donne Society in 1912 and quoted from Donne in his letters.[193] Eliot's well-known preference for the metaphysical poets was therefore no accident; he was possibly echoing the discovery of other European aesthetes.

5. Strangely, most of them were avowed admirers of Dante, which is very significant from a European point of view. The unusual mental affinity and intertextual closeness of this circle of poets reassured me that I was more or less on the right track.

The most interesting similarity (apart from a 'metaphysical' balance of feeling and thought which primarily attracted Eliot) that I have discovered in Baudelaire, Laforgue, Corbière, Larbaud, and Claudel is that, like Dante, all of them showed a bold amalgamation of the material with the spiritual. All of them seemed to be unconsciously striving for Wisdom, which Eliot himself would later come to regard as 'inseparable' from poetry.[194] This indicates that Eliot's debt to French poetry was far more extensive than is usually believed.

The present book attempts to reconstruct a few bold moments of Eliot's encounters with France and make a reappraisal of his apprenticeship in the school of Baudelaire and the Baudelairian lineage of poets. I believed that despite stray references to Racine and Villon (for example, Eliot compared Villon's directness of speech with Dante's[195]) he never went into any serious interaction with them; despite a few name-droppings, there is no proof of his genuine interest in the French classics. As for Gérard de Nerval, whom Eliot quoted in *The Waste Land*[196] he found him 'baffling' and of 'the day—dream type' about whom he had 'never been able to make up [his] mind';[197] and finally dismissed him as a 'distraction from the main issue'.[198] He told Francis Scarfe in 1937 that he was 'not particularly interested'[199] in Rimbaud and repeated the same thing to E.J.H. Greene.[200] In any case, Rimbaud's 'disorientation of the senses' was very different from the self-conscious discourse of the ironists. As for Eliot's late admiration for Stéphane Mallarmé and Paul Valéry, I have a feeling that he agreed with them more in principle than in practice. By the time he was quoting from Mallarmé in *Four Quartets*,[201] his poetic development had shown a clear slant towards spirituality, and I believe it was no longer possible for him at that age to create a Mallarméan discourse all anew. In his formative years, on the contrary, he displayed some contempt for 'the laboured opacity of Mallarmé which fades colourless and dead'[202] and his 'mossiness'.[203] Sure enough, he lauded Mallarmé's battles to 'transmute lead into gold, ordinary language into poetry'[204] and his insistence on the primitive power of the word,[205] but Eliot's Word was possibly more Claudelian (see chapter on Claudel) than Mallarméan. Indeed, one must realize that Eliot's growing commitment to his ideas, and Mallarmé's adventure *against* a poetry of ideas, do not converge. And if Eliot held Paul Valéry in high esteem for his exemplary classicism and impersonality,[206] he seized every opportunity to criticize him for his unrealistic desire to exorcise poetry of philosophy.[207] Eliot seemed to appreciate Valéry's intelligence and introspection, but finally dismissed him as a 'Narcissus gazing into the pool'[208] and his purist theories as 'eyewash'.[209]

I have consciously excluded Théophile Gautier because I believe that Eliot's debt to him was purely incidental and superficial, like his little encounters with André Salmon, Laurent Tailhade, and Jean de Bosschère. And, in any case, his poetry was definitely not a part of the complex 'metaphysical' Baudelairian legacy. In the *Paris Review* interview[210] given later in his life, Eliot saw the decision to employ Gautieresque rhyme and regular strophes as primarily a disciplinary measure. His quatrain poems were first and foremost a literary exercise, which could not have taken him very far. Critics have not noticed, probably because of their unfamiliarity with Corbière's 'Eliotic' quatrains, the more obvious parallels with the Breton poet, which I wish to highlight in the relevant chapter.

I should like to study the serrated layers of T.S. Eliot's creative responses to the Baudelairian tradition of French poetry. One critic has found in his response 'a close and fruitful tension between Eliot the creative poet and Eliot the translator'.[211] 'In Eliot's early poems', he goes on to write, 'the language is nearer to translated French than to idiomatic English'. This brings into relief the overlappings and interfaces between two value-orientations and two parallel sets of dissident codes. Eliot's reception shows how metatextual relations operate here, bringing about transformation and transfiguration of texts in another language.

'No poet, no artist of any art has his complete meaning along', Eliot reminded us many years before the twentieth century debate about intertextuality. 'His significance, his appreciation is the appreciation of his relation to the dead poets and artists'.[212]

As we step into a new century, this will be a fresh endeavour to understand Eliot's creativity in the light of his love for a poetic tradition of another country, which, as his testimonies seem to indicate, possibly made him what he is. His Laforguian narrative will get more varied and complicated, as he will come to interact with others. In the process, I wish to suggest sources (Valery Larbaud, Paul Claudel) which may provide us with some clues to the vital missing link in Eliot's French connection.

NOTES

1. T.S. Eliot, 'Yeats', *On Poetry and Poets* (hereafter referred to as *OPP*), London: Faber and Faber, 1969, p. 252.
2. T.S. Eliot, 'The Unity of European Culture', *Notes towards the Definition of Culture* (hereafter referred to as *NTDC*), London: Faber and Faber, 1948, p. 112; emphasis mine.
3. Herbert Howarth, *Notes on Some Figures Behind T.S. Eliot*, London: Chatto & Windus, 1965, p. 103.
4. T.S. Eliot, *The Sacred Wood* (hereafter referred to as *SW*), London: Methuen, 1982, p. 5.
5. T.S. Eliot's mother gave this startling piece of information to Bertrand Russell on their French background, in a letter dated 23 May 1916, 'The Tempering of T.S. Eliot, 1888–1915', PhD diss. in the University of Harvard, 1972; quoted in Peter Ackroyd, *T.S. Eliot*, London: Hamish Hamilton, 1984, p. 14.
6. T.S. Eliot, 'The Family Reunion', *The Complete Poems and Plays of T.S. Eliot* (hereafter referred to as *CPP*), London: Faber and Faber, 1990, p. 289.
7. Eliot, 'Yeats', p. 252.
8. T.S. Eliot, *To Criticize the Critic* (hereafter referred to as *TCC*), London: Faber and Faber, 1978, p. 22.
9. T.S. Eliot, *The Varieties of Metaphysical Poetry* (hereafter referred to as *VMP*), ed. Ronald Schuchard, London: Faber and Faber, 1993, p. 287.
10. Ibid.
11. Ibid.
12. Howarth, *Some Figures Behind T.S. Eliot*, p. 158.
13. Harold Bloom, *A Map of Misreading*, New York: Oxford University Press, 1975, p. 71.
14. T.S. Eliot, 'Note sur Mallarmé et Poe', *La Nouvelle Revue Française* (hereafter referred to as *NRF*), November 1926, p. 526; my translation.
15. 'What France Means to You' (Réponse de T.S. Eliot), *La France Libre*, 15 June 1944, p. 94.
16. Typescript marked as H2M in the John Hayward Bequest of *T.S. Eliot* manuscripts, Modern Archives, King's College, Cambridge, p. 4.
17. Typescript marked as H2J in the John Hayward Bequest of *T.S. Eliot* manuscripts, Modern Archives, King's College, Cambridge, p. 1.
18. T.S. Eliot, *Essais Choisis*, tr. Henri Fluchère, Paris: Ed. du Seuil, 1950, p. 391.
19. T.S. Eliot, 'Dante' [1929], in *Selected Prose of T.S. Eliot* (hereafter referred to as *SP*), ed. Frank Kermode, London: Faber and Faber, 1975, p. 205.
20. T.S. Eliot, 'Lettre d'Angleterre', *NRF*, November 1923, p. 620.
21. *Paris Review* interview, 1959, quoted in B.C. Southam, ed., *T.S. Eliot: 'Prufrock', 'Gerontion', 'Ash-Wednesday' and other Shorter Poems*, London: Macmillan, 1993, p. 50. Also see Ackroyd, *T.S. Eliot*, p. 40.
22. Address to the Mary Institute, 1 November 1959, quoted in Ackroyd, *T.S. Eliot*, p. 40.
23. *Paris Review* interview, quoted in Southam, ed., *T.S. Eliot*, p. 50.

24. Ezra Pound's remark in a letter to James Joyce in April 1917, quoted in Peter Ackroyd, *T.S. Eliot*, London: Hamish Hamilton, 1984, p. 81.
25. *Paris Review* interview, quoted in Southam, ed., *T.S. Eliot*, p. 50.
26. T.S. Eliot, *NTDC*, London: Faber and Faber, 1948, p. 115.
27. T.S. Eliot, Review, '*Baudelaire and the Symbolists*, by Peter Quennell', *The Criterion*, January 1930, p. 357.
28. T.S. Eliot, 'A Commentary', *The Criterion*, April 1934, pp. 451–2.
29. Eliot, Review, '*Baudelaire and the Symbolists*, by Peter Quennell', p. 359.
30. T.S. Eliot, 'What Dante Means to Me', *TCC*, London: Faber and Faber, 1978, pp. 125–6.
31. Ibid.
32. Eliot, *TCC*, p. 21.
33. Ibid.; emphasis mine.
34. Graham Hough, *Image and Experience*, London: Gerald Duckworth, 1960, p. 51; emphasis mine.
35. Quoted in the introduction to Michael Grant, ed., *T.S. Eliot: The Critical Heritage*, vol. I, London: Routledge and Kegan Paul, 1982, p. 5.
36. Ibid.
37. Reprinted in Ezra Pound, *Literary Essays*, London: Faber and Faber, 1954, p. 420.
38. Grant, ed., *T.S. Eliot*, p. 14.
39. Quoted in Frederick Hoffmann, *The Twenties: American Writing in the Post-War Decade*, New York: Collier, 1962, p. 201.
40. Grant, ed., *T.S. Eliot*, p. 17.
41. Ibid., p. 244.
42. Ibid., p. 245.
43. Ibid.
44. T.S. Eliot, 'La Figlia Che Piange', *CPP*, London: Faber and Faber, 1990, p. 34.
45. René Taupin, *L'Influence du symbolisme français sur la poésie américaine (de 1910 à 1920)* [1929], Geneva: Slatkine Rpts, 1979, pp. 210–40.
46. Ibid., p. 226.
47. Ibid.
48. Ibid., p. 225.
49. Ibid., p. 232.
50. Ibid.
51. Ibid.
52. Ibid., pp. 236–38.
53. Ibid., p. 220.
54. Edmund Wilson, *Axel's Castle*, London: Fontana Books, 1967, p. 82.
55. Ibid., p. 84.
56. Ibid., p. 85.
57. G.M. Turnell, 'Introduction to the Study of Tristan Corbière', *The Criterion*, April 1936, pp. 393–417.
58. G.M. Turnell, 'The Poetry of Jules Laforgue', *Scrutiny*, September 1936, pp. 129–49.

59. M.J.J. Laboulle, 'T.S. Eliot and Some French Poets', *Revue de Littérature Comparée*, April–June 1936, pp. 389–99.
60. Ibid., p. 390.
61. Ibid., p. 399.
62. E.J.H. Greene, *T.S. Eliot et la France*, Paris: Boivin, 1951.
63. Ibid., p. 7.
64. Graham Martin, ed., *Eliot in Perspective: A Symposium*, London: Macmillan, 1970, pp. 45–62.
65. Ibid., p. 45.
66. Ibid., p. 46.
67. Ibid., p. 60.
68. Enid Starkie, *From Gautier to Eliot: The Influence of France, 1851–1939*, London: Hutchinson, 1960.
69. Ibid., p. 11.
70. Ibid., pp. 162–7.
71. Ibid., p. 167.
72. Howarth, *Some Figures Behind T.S. Eliot*, pp. 162–7.
73. Ibid., p. 158.
74. In the interview with Radio-diffusion française, typescript marked as H2J.
75. Leonard Unger, *Eliot's Compound Ghost: Influences and Confluences*, Pennsylvania: Pennsylvania State University Press, 1981, p. 103.
76. Eliot, *SW*, p. 5.
77. Eliot, *SW*, p. 5.
78. Eliot, Review, '*Baudelaire and the Symbolists*, by Peter Quennell', p. 357.
79. In Eliot, *VMP*, ed. Ronald Schuchard, p. 203, n. 21, it has been wrongly stated that it was a 'two-volume' edition. See also Ackroyd, *T.S. Eliot*, p. 34, and A.D. Moody, *Thomas Stearns Eliot, Poet*, Cambridge: Cambridge University Press, 1979, p. 332.
80. Quoted in Howarth, *Some Figures Behind T.S. Eliot*, p. 130.
81. Ibid., p. 131.
82. Arthur Symons, *The Symbolist Movement in Literature*, London: Archibald Constable, 1908, p. v.
83. Ibid, p. 1.
84. Ibid.
85. Ibid., p. 4.
86. Ibid., p. 8.
87. Ibid.
88. Ibid., p. 3.
89. Ibid., p. 9.
90. Ibid.
91. T.S. Eliot, 'A Commentary', *The Criterion*, April 1924, p. 231.
92. Quoted in Stephen Spender, *Eliot*, Glasgow: Fontana, 1986, p. 41.
93. René Wellek, *A History of Modern Criticism 1750–1950*, vol. V, London: Jonathon Cape, 1986, p. 146.
94. Hough, *Image and Experience*, p. 5.

95. Quoted in ibid.
96. Ibid., p. 4.
97. Pound, *Literary Essays*, p. 218.
98. Wellek, *History of Modern Criticism*, vol. V, p. 154.
99. Quoted in Erik Svarney, *The Men of 1914: T.S. Eliot and Early Modernism*, Philadelphia: Open University Press, Milton Keynes, 1988, p. 13.
100. Glenn Hughes, *Imagism and the Imagists*, London: Bowes & Bowes, 1960, pp. 200, 204.
101. R. Aldington, 'New Poetry', *The Egoist*, June 1915, p. 89. Aldington himself translated a lot of French poetry. See, for example, R. Aldington, 'Some New French Poems', *The Egoist*, June 1914, pp. 221–3.
102. Quoted in Cyrena Pondrom, *The Road from Paris*, Cambridge: Cambridge University Press, 1974, p. 145.
103. Ezra Pound, 'The Approach to Paris, II', *The New Age*, 11 September 1913, pp. 577–9, quoted in Pondrom, *The Road from Paris*, pp. 174–5.
104. T.S. Eliot, 'Reflections on Contemporary Poetry', *The Egoist*, July 1919, p. 39.
105. Ackroyd, *T.S. Eliot*, p. 39.
106. Letter dated 2 May 1921 in T.S. Eliot, *Letters of T.S. Eliot*, ed. Valerie Eliot, vol. I, London: Faber and Faber, 1988, pp. 449–50.
107. Ibid.
108. Howarth, *Some Figures Behind T.S. Eliot*, p. 151.
109. Ibid.
110. Eliot, *Letters of T. S. Eliot*, vol. I, p. 20.
111. Ackroyd, *T.S. Eliot*, p. 40.
112. Eliot, 'What France Means to You', *La France Libre*, p. 94.
113. Ibid.
114. Ibid.
115. Ackroyd, *T.S. Eliot*, p. 40.
116. Eliot, *Letters of T. S. Eliot*, vol. I, p. 18.
117. Typescript marked as M4 in the John Hayward Bequest of *T.S. Eliot* manuscripts, Modern Archives, King's College, Cambridge, p. 2.
118. Ackroyd, *T.S. Eliot*, p. 42.
119. T.S. Eliot, quoted in Robert Gibson, *The Quest of Alain Fournier*, London: Paul Elek, 1953, p. 159.
120. Ackroyd, *T.S. Eliot*, p. 42.
121. Conrad Aiken in Tambimuttu and Richard March, eds., *T. S. Eliot: A Symposium*, London: Frank and Cass, 1965, pp. 20–3.
122. Ibid., pp. 22–3.
123. Eliot, *Letters of T.S. Eliot*, vol. I, p. 433.
124. Ibid., p. 328.
125. Ibid., p. 431.
126. Eliot, 'A Commentary', *The Criterion*, April 1934, p. 451.
127. Artplate, Ackroyd, *T.S. Eliot*, pp. 128–9.
128. Eliot's admiration for anything French is reflected in his speech at the opening of an exhibition of English books at the Bibliothèque Nationale,

Paris, 16 November 1951. He praised the 'splendour' of French illuminated manuscript and bindings: 'Your French bindings from at least the sixteenth century are above comparison, thanks to the great collectors like Grolier, whose pride in their books expressed itself in the beauty and richness with which they clothed them'.

129. Greene, *T.S. Eliot et la France*, p. 10.

130. Alain-Fournier and Jacques Rivière, *Correspondance*, 2 vols., Paris: Gallimard, 1991.

131. Fournier and Rivière, *Correspondance*, vol. I, pp. 334–5.

132. Letter dated 23 July 1903, in Fournier and Rivière, *Correspondance*, vol. I, p. 72.

133. Letter dated 13 September 1905, in Fournier and Rivière, *Correspondance*, vol. I, p. 141.

134. Fournier and Rivière, *Correspondance*, vol. II, p. 615n.

135. Ackroyd, *T.S. Eliot*, p. 42.

136. Eliot, *Letters of T. S. Eliot*, vol. I, pp. 20–1.

137. Ackroyd, *T.S. Eliot*, p. 46.

138. Jean Schlumberger, 'Considerations', *NRF*, February 1909, p. 5.

139. Baudelaire's sentence from *L'Art philosophique* cited in 'Textes', *NRF*, June 1909, p. 457.

140. 'Textes', *NRF*, November 1909, p. 321.

141. André Gide, 'L'Amateur de M. Remy de Gourmont', *NRF*, April 1910, p. 425, 431.

142. Henri Ghéon, 'Une discipline du Vers libre', *NRF*, April 1910, pp. 452–64.

143. Eliot, *TCC*, p. 183.

144. Eliot, *Letters of T. S. Eliot*, vol. I, p. 26.

145. Grover Smith, 'Charles-Louis Philippe and T.S. Eliot', *American Literature*, November 1950, pp. 254–9.

146. Jacques Rivière, 'De la Sincerité envers soi-même', *NRF*, January 1912, p. 5.

147. Jacques Rivière, 'De la Foi', *NRF*, November 1912, p. 782.

148. Ibid., p. 970.

149. Camille Vettard, '*Le Bergsonisme* par Julien Benda', *NRF*, November 1912, p. 941.

150. Tristan Leclere (Kingslor), 'Humoresques IV', *NRF*, January 1912, p. 22.

151. Tristan Leclere (Kingslor), 'Humoresques V', *NRF*, January 1912, p. 23.

152. Albert Thibaudet, 'L'Esthétique des Trois Traditions', *NRF*, January 1913, pp. 157–61.

153. Ibid.

154. Jacques Rivière, 'La Nouvelle Revue Française', *NRF*, nouvelle serie, June 1919, p. 2.

155. Jacques Rivière, '*L'Otage* de Paul Claudel au Théâtre de l'Oeuvre', *NRF*, November 1919, p. 973.

156. Paul Valéry, 'Le Cimetière Marin', *NRF*, June 1920, pp. 781–7.

157. Jules Laforgue, 'Notes d'un Agenda', *NRF*, October 1920, pp. 511–38.

158. T.S. Eliot, 'The Idea of a Literary Review', *The Criterion*, January 1926, pp. 5–6.

159. Ramon Fernandez, 'L'Intelligence de M. Maritain', *NRF*, June 1925, pp. 986–94.
160. Eliot, *NTDC*, p. 115.
161. Eliot, 'Lettre d'Angleterre', p. 619.
162. Ibid.
163. Ibid., pp. 624–5.
164. See n. 104.
165. Eliot, 'Lettre d'Angleterre', p. 619.
166. T.S. Eliot, 'Hommage à Charles Maurras', *Aspects de la France et du Monde*, 25 April 1948, p. 6.
167. Pierre Lasserre, *Charles Maurras et la Renaissance Classique*, Paris: Mercure de France, 1902, p. 17.
168. Albert Thibaudet, *Les idées de Charles Maurras*, Paris: Gallimard, 1919, p. 313.
169. Eliot, *NTDC*, pp. 28–9.
170. In *L'Esthétique des trois traditions* (*NRF*, January–March 1913), Albert Thibaudet interpreted Maurras's traditions as 'classique, catholique, monarchique', which are exactly the adjectives Eliot would use about himself in the preface to *For Lancelot Andrewes* (1928).
171. Charles Maurras, *L'Avenir de l'Intelligence*, Paris: Nouvelle Librairie Nationale, 1925, pp. 8–9.
172. Charles Maurras, *Le Conseil de Dante*, Paris: Nouvelle Librairie Nationale, 1920, p. 50.
173. Ibid., p. 13.
174. Ibid.
175. Ibid., p. 18.
176. Eliot, *SW*, p. 168.
177. T.S. Eliot, 'Dante' [1929], *Selected Essays* (hereafter referred to as *SE*), London: Faber and Faber, 1951, pp. 258–69.
178. Maurras, *Le Conseil de Dante*, p. 24.
179. Eliot, *TCC*, p. 23.
180. Ibid., p. 39.
181. 'Throughout his life, Eliot would continue to support Maurras'—Ackroyd, *T.S. Eliot*, p. 42.
182. Ackroyd, *T.S. Eliot*, p. 76.
183. *The Criterion*, January 1927, p. 3.
184. Jacques Maritain, *Réflexions sur l'Intelligence*, Paris: Nouvelle Librairie Nationale, 1924, p. 316.
185. Jacques Maritain, *Religion et Culture*, Paris: Desclée de Brouwer, 1930, p. 45.
186. Eliot, *SW*, p. 167.
187. Eliot, *SE*, pp. 138–9.
188. T.S. Eliot, 'Preface to Anabasis', in *SP*, ed. Frank Kermode, London: Faber and Faber, 1975, p. 78.
189. Remy de Gourmont, *Le Problème du style*, Paris: Mercure de France, 1902, p. 32.

190. T.S. Eliot, 'Ulysses, Order and Myth', in *SP*, ed. Frank Kermode, London: Faber and Faber, 1975, p. 177.
191. The admiration of Larbaud and Claudel for Laforgue has been highlighted in the relevant chapters. As for Saint-John Perse, Fournier wrote to Rivière on 9 September 1911: '. . . il admire beaucoup Laforgue' ('He much admires Laforgue'). See Fournier and Rivière, *Correspondance*, vol. II, p. 451.
192. Eliot, *VMP*, ed. Ronald Schuchard, p. 287.
193. See chapter on Larbaud and Eliot.
194. 1954 lecture at Hamburg University; see T.S. Eliot 'Goethe as the Sage', *OPP*, London: Faber and Faber, 1969, p. 226.
195. Eliot, *SE*, p. 240.
196. T.S. Eliot, 'The Waste Land', *CPP*, London: Faber and Faber, 1990, p. 75, line 429.
197. T.S. Eliot, 'Clark Lecture V', in *VMP*, ed. Ronald Schuchard, London: Faber and Faber, 1993, p. 153.
198. Eliot, Review, '*Baudelaire and the Symbolists*, by Peter Quennell', p. 358.
199. F. Scarfe, 'Eliot and Nineteenth Century French Poetry', in *Eliot in Perspective: A Symposium*, ed. Graham Martin, London: Macmillan, 1970, p. 46.
200. Greene, *T.S. Eliot et la France*, p. 19.
201. T.S. Eliot 'Burnt Norton', II, lines 1–2, *CPP*, London: Faber and Faber, 1990, p. 172; and T.S. Eliot, 'Little Gidding', line 74, *CPP*, London: Faber and Faber, 1990, p. 194.
202. T.S. Eliot, 'The Borderline of Prose', *New Statesman*, 19 May 1917, p. 158.
203. Eliot, *TCC*, p. 170.
204. T.S. Eliot, 'Prose and Verse', *Chapbook*, no. 22, April 1921, pp. 3–10.
205. Eliot, 'Note sur Mallarmé et Poe', p. 526.
206. See the introduction (by T.S. Eliot) to Paul Valéry, *The Art of Poetry*, New York: Bollingen Foundation, 1958.
207. Eliot, *SW*, p. 159.
208. Eliot, 'Introduction', p. xxiii.
209. Ibid., p. xxii.
210. Quoted in Southam, *T.S. Eliot*, p. 49.
211. V. Cronin, 'T. S. Eliot as a Translator', in *T.S. Eliot: A Symposium for His Seventieth Birthday*, ed. N. Braybrooke, London: Hart-Davis, 1958, pp. 130–1.
212. Eliot, *SW*, p. 49.

1

Jules Laforgue and Eliot
The Return of the Dead

T.S. ELIOT'S ENCOUNTER WITH Jules Laforgue[1] (1860–87) seems like a comparatist's dream come true. It was a mighty impact, both aesthetic and moral, which helped the young American to discover his voice and shape his poetic destiny. In a sense, he *rewrote* Laforgue—a magnificent example of the Return of the Dead in twentieth century poetry.

As Eliot wrestled with his mysterious French 'elder brother'[2] for every poetic trope he chose or refused, his anxiety (which he called a 'crisis')[3] to create an imaginative space became a vital part of his revolt in English poetry. Significantly, Eliot wrote to Mary Hutchinson that for him Laforgue was synonymous with 'poetry' and 'modern culture'.[4] To Eliot, Laforgue's new style, double-edged with its multiple possibilities, was the tool he was looking for at that point of time in history to overhaul the poetic discourse of his language.

PLATE 1.1: Jules Laforgue (1860–1887) who changed Eliot's life

Unfortunately, the biggest obstacle to a reappraisal of the relationship between Laforgue and Eliot is the widespread self-deception that there is

*In the title, I have used Harold Bloom's phrase from *The Anxiety of Influence*, New York: Oxford University Press, 1973, p. 15.

nothing more to be said on the subject. On the contrary, the relationship has remained more of a puzzle that one has evaded for various reasons, not the least among them being a subconscious desire to protect Eliot from further suspicions about his originality. Although Eliot himself has from time to time tried to put back his commentators on the right track by acknowledging his special kind of relationship with Laforgue, they have more or less ignored his suggestion and never really carried their hunt to the last.

It has been the usual pattern of criticism to reiterate a few clichés (like Eliot's early admiration for Laforgue's self-irony) before hastily dismissing the interaction as short-lived. 'The direct influence of Laforgue on Eliot's poetry did not last beyond 1912', writes Bernard Bergonzi.[5] E.J.H. Greene voiced a similar opinion in his French thesis *T.S. Eliot et la France* (1951). Eliot's biographer Peter Ackroyd, too, believes that Laforgue's influence on Eliot was limited to his 'youthful poetry'.[6] No doubt, such generalizations resulted from an inadequate knowledge of Laforgue's poetry and a curious misunderstanding that Laforgue's was merely the *'fin-de-siècle* world of lunar pierrots and hapless dandies'.[7] Even Greene felt that though his technique evolved, his subject-matter did not[8]—which, as we shall see, is far from true.

Towards the end of the nineteenth century, sandwiched between his illustrious contemporaries—Baudelaire, Verlaine, Rimbaud, and Mallarmé—young Laforgue desperately wanted to create a space for himself by doing something different and new: 'Faire de l'original a tout prix' ('to be original at any cost').[9] He wanted, above all, to be *interesting* at any cost. 'En art, il s'agit d'être intéressant' ('In art, one must be interesting').[10] My contention is that since Eliot, too, desperately wished the same, he easily succumbed to the charms of the explosive network of verbal habits and obsessions of Laforgue, his mode of writing, or *écriture*, which took him far.

In the present chapter, I intend to show, for the first time, with the help of Laforgue's four books of poems, his short stories *Moralités Légendaires*, his diaries and reflections on literature *Mélanges Posthumes*, his novelette *Stéphane Vassiliew*, his correspondences, and critical discourse, that the popular view of Eliot's development since *Prufrock and Other Observations* (1917) as one away from Laforgue is merely an *idée reçue*; that, in a sense, Eliot worked out the implications of Laforgue *throughout* his life. In my opinion, self-irony was a part, albeit a very important one, of Eliot's debt, but he was equally receptive to other ingredients of Laforgue's poetic discourse: its fragility, its need for others (the abundance of conversations and quotations), its special kind of lexicon, its craving for order, its dabbling in Buddhism and Hinduism, and its increasingly religious overtones. If, as most critics tend to believe, Eliot 'went beyond' Laforgue by the time he composed *The Waste Land*, in reality he was probably moving in the direction Laforgue himself had threatened to when he died at 27. Remy de Gourmont called Laforgue's works 'the prelude to an oratorio that ended in silence'.[11] I expect to show in this chapter that Eliot was possibly one of the very few to understand this prelude, and in an ironic way, it was he who was destined to complete the oratorio.

No objective assessment of Eliot's poetry is possible without an awareness of his extensive debt to various facets of Laforgue's texts: lexical, aesthetic, and philosophic, operating on multiple levels. Even some of his famous critical postulates seem to have been drawn from his reading of Laforgue.

The historic moment he came across Arthur Symons's *The Symbolist movement in Literature* (1899) (Eliot probably saw the revised second edition of 1908 published by Archibald Constable and Co., London) at the Harvard Union library in 1908, the die was cast (it 'affected the course of [his] life')[12] and his poetic destiny was determined. It was a 'demonic possession' by another poet, which he would later consider an intrinsic part of the poet's development.[13] As he assiduously thumbed the three volumes of Laforgue's *Oeuvres Complètes*, which he had ordered from France at Harvard, he was 'changed, metamorphosed almost, within a few weeks even, from a bundle of second-hand sentiments into a person'.[14] It was like meeting a friend in the flesh through the medium of verse: 'a feeling of profound kinship, or rather a peculiar personal intimacy',[15] which helped him to find his own voice. As his friend Robert Sencourt puts it:

. . . reading the verses of a young man who had died in Paris in the year he himself had been conceived in St. Louis, it almost seemed to Eliot that in his body the flitting soul of Laforgue had sought a reincarnation.[16]

And let us note that simultaneously, Eliot became conscious of a 'tradition':

It is a cause of development, like personal relations in life. Like personal intimacies in life, it may and probably will pass, but it will be ineffaceable . . . We do not imitate, we are changed; and our work is the work of the changed man; we have not borrowed, we have been quickened, and we become bearers of a tradition.[17]

Although the interaction with Laforgue has been viewed as a temporary phase, Eliot himself never failed to emphasize, at every phase of his poetic career, Laforgue's seminal influence on him. In 1919, on the eve of composing *The Waste Land*, when Eliot was supposed to have outgrown the spell of Laforgue, he reasserted that their 'profound kinship' was 'ineffaceable'. He raised the subject once again in 1950, ironically in a lecture on Dante, his other master: 'I abate nothing of the praise I have given them (my tutors)'.[18] He still thought highly of Laforgue, who gave him 'nourishment'[19] in his youth and 'directed [his] first steps'.[20]

Of Jules Laforgue, for instance, I can say that he was the first to teach me how to speak, to teach me the poetic possibilities of my own idiom of speech.[21]

And, finally, as late as in 1961, four years before his death, as if in a reappraisal of his career, Eliot paid his last homage to Laforgue:

I have written about Baudelaire but nothing about Jules Laforgue, to whom I owe more than to any poet in any language.[22]

The poet's own evidence yields new meanings and new questions. The dismissive and stereotyped references to Laforgue in Eliot criticism over the last seven decades have not helped much in probing their relationship.

The question is: why did he not write anything on Laforgue? Eliot, who normally liked to write about those who influenced him (Dante, Baudelaire, the Elizabethans, and the metaphysical poets), furnished a strange excuse for this lacuna: 'The reason, I believe, is that no one commissioned me to do so. For these early essays were all written for money . . .'.[23] He was, I suspect, afraid of writing on Laforgue, of revealing too much, with consequences that could be embarrassing.

I would like to compare the fascinating relationship between Laforgue and Eliot with that of Poe and Baudelaire. In both cases, the successor-poet is a major writer who identifies a recently dead foreigner as a literary Messiah initiating, as Eliot says about Laforgue, a 'system of feeling or morals'.[24] Each one is a very private relationship that others have never been able to comprehend fully. It could be an uncritical fascination with the seductive allure of a foreigner's choice of path.

This enigmatic affinity with another poet may perhaps be best understood in the light of Baudelaire's remarks on Edgar Allan Poe:

Savez-vous pourquoi j'ai si patiemment traduit Poe? *Parce qu'il me ressemblait.*

(Do you know why I have so patiently translated Poe? *Because he resembled me.*)[25]

La première fois que j'ai ouvert un livre de lui, j'ai vu, avec épouvante et ravissement, non seulement des sujets rêvés par moi, mais des phrases, pensées par moi, et écrites par lui, vingt ans auparavant.

(The first time I opened a book by him, I saw with fear and joy, not only the subjects I had dreamt of, but phrases I thought of, written by him twenty years ago).[26]

If the mysterious American, writing in a foreign language, was both an 'initiator' and a 'brother'[27] to Baudelaire, Laforgue too was to Eliot likewise not merely a master in the ordinary sense, but 'an admired elder brother',[28] a 'playmate near [his] size'.[29] Did Baudelaire and Eliot communicate more deeply with Poe and Laforgue than the latter's own countrymen?

It seems that there are at least three historic circumstances which helped Laforgue and Eliot to converge:

1. Arthur Symons's book on Symbolism, which aroused his interest in a different code of poetic discourse.
2. Remy de Gourmont's (whom Eliot compared with Aristotle) enthusiasm for Laforgue, which matches and, at times, surpasses Eliot's own.
3. Eliot's apprenticeship in 1910–11 in the hands of his French tutor Alain-Fournier (1886–1914) and a fellow-lodger in Paris, Jean Verdenal (1890–1915)—both ardent admirers of Laforgue.

Before I analyse Eliot's poetic debt to Laforgue, I would like to examine the factors which may have led to one of the most regenerative literary encounters in poetic history.

Although, as René Wellek asserts,[30] George Moore had earlier written on Laforgue, young Tom Eliot met the Frenchman in the pages of Arthur Symons's book *The Symbolist Movement in Literature* (1899), a revised edition of which he discovered at Harvard in December 1908.

It was a 'transforming discovery',[31] a 'milestone'[32] that once and for all 'affected the course of [his] life', Eliot would reminisce later in 1930, when he had traversed two-thirds of his poetic career. What had he found in Symons's book that was so revolutionary?

Symons's sketch of Laforgue may have instantly appealed to Eliot because it showed traits he himself possessed, or may have been developing (like his outward coldness), not really knowing what to do with them. It may have suggested a resolution of his own crisis. Eliot learnt from Symons that Laforgue was 'scrupulously correct, but with a new manner of correctness,' that his:

Balanced, chill, colloquial style has in the paradox of its intensity, the essential heat of the most obviously emotional prose.[33]

Symons described how the Frenchman made subtle use of colloquialism, slang, neologism, technical terms, for their 'factitious, reflected meanings'.[34] Symons's interpretation of Laforgue has particular relevance for Eliot because of his following observations:

The old cadences, the old eloquence, the ingenious seriousness of poetry are *all banished* . . . Here if ever is modern verse, verse which dispenses with so many of the privileges of poetry, for an ideal quite of its own. It is, after all, a very self-conscious ideal, becoming artificial through its extreme naturalness.[35]

It [Laforgue's poetry] gives expression in its icy ecstasy to a very subtle criticism of the cosmic vision.[36]

It is out of these elements of caprice, fear, contempt, linked together by an embracing laughter, that it makes its existence.[37]

He thinks intensely about life, seeing what is automatic, pathetically ludicrous in it, almost as one might who has no part in the comedy.[38]

Symons's chapter on Laforgue was a revelation to Eliot; it gave him the all-important key to modernism:

. . . the possibilities for art which come from the sickly modern being, with his clothes, his nerves, the mere fact that he flowers from the soil of his epoch.[39]

He learnt from Symons's book that the 'art of the nerves'[40] too can produce memorable poetry.

It is not known when exactly Eliot came across Gourmont's essays on Symbolist poetry, but it seems quite likely that he looked up this 'master of facts'[41] for his opinion on Laforgue. Eliot could not have failed to notice that, of all the French critics, Remy de Gourmont was by far the most zealous admirer of his hero.

To Gourmont, Laforgue's was 'l'âme la plus tendre et . . . l'esprit le plus fin' ('the tenderest soul and . . . the finest mind').[42] He was 'une âme exquise' ('an exquisite soul'), and 'un génie charmant' ('a charming genius')—'we can only love him';[43] '. . . son oeuvre, déjà magnifique, n'est que le prélude d'un oratorio achevé dans le silence' ('his works, already magnificent, is only the prelude to an oratorio completed in silence').[44]

Eliot discovered his own feelings reflected in lines like:

C'est de la littérature renouvelée et inattendue et qui déconcerte et qui donne la sensation curieuse (et surtout rare) qu'on n'a jamais rien lu de pareil . . .

(This is literature which is new and unexpected and disconcerting, which arouses the curious [and especially rare] feeling that one has never read anything like this . . .)[45]

Gourmont's other observations which have far-reaching implications in the context of Eliot's own reception to Laforgue are:

Personne ne représente cette extraordinaire ironie sentimentale dont il est le seul maitre.

(None represents that extraordinary sentimental irony of which he is the sole master).[46]

L'Intelligence était une belle qualité chez Laforgue.

(Intelligence was a beautiful quality in Laforgue).[47]

La sensibilité comprend la raison elle-même qui n'est que de la sensibilité crystallisée.

(The sensibility comprises reason itself, which is nothing but crystallised sensibility).[48]

. . . (A) force de vivre, on acquiert la faculté de dissocier son intelligence de sa sensibilité: cela arrive tôt ou tard, par l'acquisition d'une faculté nouvelle indispensable, quoique dangereuse, le scepticisme. Laforgue est mort avant d'avoir atteint cette étape.

(In the process of living, one acquires the faculty of dissociating intelligence from sensibility. This happens sooner or later by the acquisition of a new faculty of scepticism. Laforgue died before reaching that stage).[49]

Eliot would transfer to literary history what Remy de Gourmont considered an inevitable part of the psychological growth of the individual.

Gourmont's clear bias for Laforgue seems to have proved vital for Eliot: like him, the former regarded him as an admired elder brother ('notre adoré frère aîné'), as an 'incontestable master of youth'.[50]

It is well known that Alain-Fournier (1886–1914) became Eliot's French tutor in Paris, but few have taken note of the French novelist's legendary love for Jules Laforgue. The recently reprinted correspondence of Fournier with his brother-in-law Jacques Rivière,[51] one of the editors of the *Nouvelle Revue Française* (and who was, apart from Fournier, the only other literary activist Eliot knew in France in 1910–11)[52], would reveal the demonic hold of Laforgue on the former. It would be legitimate to speculate that this was unceremoniously passed on to the young American during his regular interactions with Fournier in 1910–11.

In this historic correspondence, Laforgue is referred to at least *ninety* times.[53] 'J'ai des foules de choses à te dire sur Laforgue' ('I have such a lot of things to tell you about Laforgue'),[54] wrote Fournier to Rivière as early as in 1905, and frankly admitted that he was 'vivement et complètement saisi de Laforgue' ('deeply and completely captivated by Laforgue'):[55]

Tout jeune homme qui se respecte devrait être fou de Laforgue pour un certain temps.

(Every respectable young man should be madly in love with Laforgue for some time).[56]

Finally, in a letter of 28 August 1906, Laforgue is called 'notre adoré frère aîné' ('our admired elder brother'),[57] which is exactly the epithet that Eliot would use about Laforgue.[58] Both seem to have a similar approach to Laforgue: in his more dispassionate moments, Eliot could realize that his hero was not 'a great master', but a 'smaller poet', a 'playmate nearer [his] own size';[59] Fournier's letters to Rivière likewise reveal analogous ideas expressed in a disconcertingly identical language: '[Laforgue] n'a été qu'un ami que je plaignais et que j'ai toujours trouvé très petit'. ('Laforgue is but a friend whom I pitied and whom I always found very small').[60] Going by the letters, it seems that Fournier was able to convert Rivière.[61]

The similarity of the sentiments of Fournier and Eliot for a neglected poet proves our point: Fournier, too, was historically an important *agent provocateur* in the Laforgue-Eliot encounter. He could have instigated Eliot to make use of, and even transplant, in English poetry, the special qualities of a dead author which seemed to both of them 'plus vrai que tout, plus profond que tout' ('truer than everything, more profound than everything').[62]

Eliot's first book, *Prufrock and Other Observations* (1917), was dedicated to Jean Verdenal (1890–1915), who died early at Dardanelles during the First World War. The lines in the dedication, quoted from Dante,[63] are a testimony to their friendship.[64]

Everything counts in forging a relationship, even coincidences. When Eliot disembarked in Paris in autumn 1910, he found accommodation at Mme Casaubin's *pension* at 151 bis, rue Saint-Jacques in the Latin Quarter of Paris. There he met Jean Verdenal,[65] a medical student, who carried copies[66] of Laforgue's *Poésies Complètes* and *Moralités Légendaries*. Like Eliot's tutor Alain-Fournier, this fellow-lodger seemed to thoroughly brainwash the American about the contemporaneity of Laforgue. As Eliot trudged back from Fournier's house at 2, rue Cassini in south Paris, through the scintillating Boul' Mich, once haunted by the dead poet, to his boarding house in the Latin Quarter, Jean Verdenal reminded him once more of Laforgue.

Verdenal admitted to Eliot in a letter dated 5 February 1912[67] that even his small ideas turned out to be imitations of Laforgue ('...immediately I realized that the idea was not mine, but I had got it from a letter of Laforgue').

Utterly fascinated, Eliot tried to see the world around him through Laforgue's eyes. As his numerous confessions show, he *became* Laforgue for some time.

Yet another catalyst in the Laforgue-Eliot encounter was the epoch-making *La Nouvelle Revue Française,* which had just been launched on the eve of Eliot's arrival in Paris in 1910. It was to become the platform of the experimental new writers,[68] most of whom (André Gide, Paul Claudel, Paul Valéry, Valery Larbaud, Saint-John Perse) would soon become illustrious names in twentieth century French literature. Fournier himself belonged to the junior group of contributors[69] and his brother-in-law Jacques Rivière (to whom Eliot paid homage in the *NRF* itself in April 1925)[70] was one of its editors. Significantly, all these new literary activists held Laforgue in high esteem. 'Laforgue is my friend', wrote Gide to Valery,[71] while for Larbaud, the tubercular Frenchman was a 'brother', whose works were 'a revelation', 'a consecrated classic'.[72] Laforgue was, to many of them, *le dernier cri.*

Eliot's biographers inform us that on his arrival in Paris, he would soon become a subscriber to this revolutionary journal, which he later identified as a model for *The Criterion.*[73]

Not to see Eliot as a shrewd strategist, who would not hesitate to use others' material, is to miss him entirely. But his relationship with Laforgue was something different.

Herbert Howarth was probably right when he said about Eliot: 'There was an element of Laforgue already in him'.[74] Temperamentally, they were like each other.[75] Both looked very distinguished and correct ('toujours fort correct': 'always very correct', in Laforgue's words[76]), but their outward elegance hid their human warmth.

Stephen Spender[77] has spoken of Eliot's 'marble poise' to Virginia Woolf, Eliot looked 'more like marble than flesh'.[78] On the other hand, Arthur Symons referred to Laforgue's 'formal' demeanour, his tall top hat, his sober necktie, his English jacket, his clerical overcoat and the umbrella under one arm. According to Laforgue's biographer Francois Ruchon:

Laforgue a laissé l'impression d'un homme infiniment distingué, un peu distant, très correct, vêtu toujours de sombre.

(Laforgue gave the impression of a man infinitely distinguished, a trifle distant, very correct, dressed in sombre colours.)[79]

This tallies with the description of Eliot by his contemporaries, like Conrad Aiken.[80]

In his later years, Eliot would often resemble a clergyman.[81] As for Laforgue, says Ruchon in *Jules Laforgue, sa vie, son oeuvre:*

La première fois que M. Lidenbaub le vit, sans le connaître encore, il croit avoir à faire à un ecclésiastique. Laforgue lui-même se reconnaissait plaisamment 'un natif air d'apôtre'.

(The first time Mr Lidenbaub saw him, without yet knowing him, he thought he met an ecclesiast. Laforgue jokingly called himself 'a native with priestly air')[82]

Both Laforgue and Eliot wanted basically to hide their neurosis underneath the marble poise of their exterior. Laforgue's icy nonchalance is matched by Virginia Woolf's description of Eliot: 'His cell is, I'm sure, a very lofty one, but a little chilly'.[83] In Laforgue's 'art of the nerves', there is a painfully self-conscious gaiety of spirit which Eliot may have possessed till *The Waste Land*. Poetry was, as it were, a desperate means of survival for both. If both wanted to be performers, it is because they wanted to conceal a consciousness of exile, the solitude in a crowded desert.

In 1860, at the age of six, Jules Laforgue sailed from his birthplace Montevideo (Uruguay) for France, the country of his forefathers. Eliot, too, would choose to move from America to England, his country of origin. In both cases, it was a symbolic journey, leading to a 'rupture d'équilibre'.

François Ruchon[84] has pointed out how Laforgue was still haunted by nostalgia for America, reflected in some poems of *Des Fleurs de Bonne Volonté*:

On m'a dit que la vie au Far-West et les prairies,
Et mon sang a gémi: 'Que voila ma patrie
Déclassée du vieux monde, être sans foi ni loi

(They told me about life in Far-West and the prairies
And my blood screamed: 'There's my motherland
Displaced from the old world, without belief, without law).[85]

The small town in Hautes-Pyrenées made a deep influence on him. 'A Berlin', Ruchon informs us, 'aux témoignages de ses amis, il parlait souvent de son enfance en Amérique et disait avoir nostalgie de la mer qu'il avait traversée' (In Berlin, according to his friends, he often spoke of his childhood in America and admitted having nostalgia for the sea which he had crossed.'). This feeling of strangeness is possibly one of the reasons for his spleen which never left him.[86] Laforgue himself wrote in a letter to Charles Henry, 'Je m'ennuie prodigieusement. Depuis que j'ai traversé l'Atlantique (6 ans, couchant sur la mer), je n'avais eu d'aussi noires crises de spleen'. ('I am terribly bored. Since I crossed the Atlantic [6 years old, sleeping in the sea] I have never had such dark crises of spleen').[87]

We all know that the American nostalgia stayed on in Eliot in the same way, which is evident in *Four Quartets*, with its memories of the Mississippi. To some extent, Eliot's is a poetry of exile, even of what Marie, in an earlier draft of *The Family Reunion*, called a 'perpetual exile'.[88] According to Frank Kermode,[89] this is most obvious in *Ash-Wednesday*, where exile has to be accepted with patience as the human condition.

Laforgue who was frantically searching for something new[90] noted in his diary:

Il faut être un nouveau . . . En art, il s'agit d'être intéressant.
(One has to be new . . . In art, one must be interesting.)[91]

He provided Eliot with all the ammunition to be 'interesting'. The French poet was an amateur at painting and music, and a voracious reader of books, like Eliot. The astonishing range of his reading can be found in his letters. While in Paris, he spent many hours at the Bibliotheque Nationale, which is obvious from his letters to the Administrator General (dated 6 July 1878, and 21 July 1879), to Gustave Kahn,[92] Charles Henry,[93] and Mme Multzer,[94] and attended lectures at the Ecole des Beaux-Arts, in particular, those of Hypolite Taine.[95] He was a dilettante, possibly more than others in the Baudelairian lineage of poets. In Laforgue's words:

Moi, je mène toujours ma vie de dilettante . . . Maintenant, je suis dilettante en tout, avec parfois de petits accès de nausée universelle. Je regarde passer le carnaval de la vie: sergents de ville, artistes, souverains, ministres, amoureux etc. Je fume de blondes cigarettes, je fais des vers et de la prose, peut-être aussi un peu d'eau forte et j'attends la mort.
(I still lead my life of dilettante . . . Now I am dilettante in everything with occasional small bouts of universal nausea. I watch the passage of the carnival of life: sergeants, artists, kings, ministers, lovers etc. I smoke blond cigarettes, I write verse and prose, perhaps also I do some etching, and await death).[96]

Eliot was possibly quick to realize that this self-conscious dilettantism (not a pejorative word in French) could be used as an effective weapon to destroy 'the institutionalized art of dead cultures'.[97] The abundance of quotations and cross-references to various subjects, the inevitable epigraphs, the polyglot texts, and a dazzling amalgamation of disparate experiences—strewn all over in Laforgue's poetry and prose from *Les Fleurs de Bonne Volonté*, *Les Complaintes* to *Derniers Vers*, and *Moralites Légendaires* are hallmarks of the Laforguian heritage in Eliot's works. It is this characteristic, along with his irony, which often redeems what might otherwise have degenerated into adolescent self-pity.

The French critic Jean-Pierre Richard calls Laforgue's poetry 'quasi-citationnelle'[98] because of the never-ending network of multiple references. Unlike Baudelaire and Rimbaud, Laforgue freely used celebrated texts and names of characters, and epigraphed lines from his favourite works, notably from Elizabethan poetry. The numerous citations from Shakespeare (Hamlet is used at least ten times in *Des Fleurs de Bonne Volonté* and as many times in *Derniers Vers*) show Laforgue's special interest in Elizabethan verse, with which—Francis Scarfe corroborates my belief[99]—

eventually 'cracked' French verification in *Derniers Vers*. It reminds one of Eliot's interest in Elizabethan poetry. (He told E.J.H. Greene that he saw the Elizabethans through Laforgue's eyes.)[100] Eliot's habit of using quotations in foreign languages may have been sparked off by Laforgue's Latin and English quotations in 'Préludes autobiographiques'.[101] Eliot's wide learning is well known, and Laforgue's can be ascertained from his correspondence, especially his reading list to Gustave Kahn on 12/19 December 1880.[102]

It was nothing unusual for poets before Laforgue or Eliot to be voracious readers, but the former showed a tendency (like Corbière and Larbaud) to wear his bibliophilia on his sleeves—a snobbery which perfectly suited Eliot's own elitist taste and temperament. *The Waste Land*—the poem of many voices—remains the best example of this Laforguian fabric of quotations.

This tendency to speak in others' voices was possibly a mask to desperately hide their fear and agony—a mask they could not afford to drop.

'. . . in short, I was afraid', said Eliot.[103] 'J'ai peur de la vie' ('I am afraid of life'), whispered Laforgue.[104] According to Valéry,[105] the nervous system of man is the greatest poet; and Laforgue and Eliot's poetry seems to vindicate that. Eliot's own 'neurasthenic agony'[106] and 'aboulie and emotional derangement'[107] have been much discussed, and we now know of his 'grouse against life'; but it is necessary to understand Laforgue's, which no critic of Eliot has done.

The latter confesses in his diaries that he was always 'sans amour, sans amis' ('without love, without friends').[108] He 'never believed in human happiness—had no roots, no stability, never settled down in life'.[109] In 1881, he wrote a novelette *Stéphane Vassiliew* about a worthless being, a *raté*; this he called an 'autobiographic de mon organisme, de ma pensée' ('autobiography of my organism, my thought').[110] 'Sa vie n'était qu'une suite de chagrins qu'il ne comprenait pas. Nul ne l'aimait au monde' ('His life was nothing but a series of sadnesses which he failed to understand. Nobody loved him in the world').[111] He was, like his Hamlet, 'damné d'avance' ('already damned').[112] It is interesting to know about Laforgue's fragility, nervousness, and his sense of 'incurable ennui':

'l'incurable ennui, l'injustice, le mystère de son existence le prenait à la gorge.

(. . . incurable boredom, injustice, mystery of his existence choked his throat)[113]

Stephane suffers from the same pain and despair as his young creator; he lived in 'incessante torture de sa vie intérieure' ('incessant torture of his inward life').[114] Laforgue wrote to Sabine Multzer on 5 February 1882:

Je devais être clown. J'ai manqué ma destinée. C'est irrévocablemeni tini.
(I should have been a clown. I missed my destiny. It is irrevocably lost.)[115]

His acute 'metaphysical anguish' ('angoisse metaphysique')[116] and bewilderment in the face of life brought him close to Hamlet, 'our master' ('notre maitre à tous')[117] with whom he identified himself, just as Prufrock is a Hamlet *manqué*. The sentiment that unites Laforgue, Eliot, and the Laforguian Hamlet is succinctly expressed in the epigraph of *Hamlet* in *Moralités Légendaires*: 'C'est plus fort que moi' ('It is too much for me').[118] And all three of them faced the overwhelming question of life in a similar manner by shrugging their shoulders.

When Ad. Van Bever and Paul Léautaud interrogated Laforgue's brother Emile Laforgue, the latter is said to have told them: 'To know him, you must read his *Hamlet*. He is wholly present there. It is himself he has painted. The resemblance is striking'.[119] Laforgue's Hamlet, who like his creator resorts to clowning, distributes cigarettes to the actors, saying, 'Asseyez-vous là et prenez des cigarettes' ('Sit down there, and take some cigarettes').[120] Laforgue's Hamlet actually shrugs his shoulders,[121] just as Eliot's Prufrock seems to shrug off the name of Hamlet by declaring 'I am not Prince Hamlet',[122] in the process only affirming that he is.

Laforgue's Hamlet does not know how to 'play his role with a little decency'[123]—a crisis in his personality, which Eliot highlighted in the eighth Clark Lecture.[124]

Laforgue's auto-irony and shoulder-shrug should not be misconstrued as just a 'literary exercise', as Hugh Kenner tends to think,[125] but a serious way of dealing with a real-life problem, which would otherwise have led to suicide (Laforgue contemplates suicide in *Mélanges Posthumes*[126]). In his moment of despair, Laforgue turned towards Schopenhauer and Hartmann, in whom he found the rationalization he needed:

Much better, according to Hartmann, to deny Nature, to refuse to be duped, to opt out of a system that let one be no more than a pawn in the game.[127]

Laforgue's self-irony, his impersonal approach to art, is possibly part of a well thought out scheme to 'opt out of the system' and turn the tables on life.

His Pierrot is a solution for his hopeless predicament. He is not simply a joker, he is also a sage, an eternal enquirer, he is 'Pierrot-Hamlet', as Valery Larbaud[128] calls him, or the 'metaphysical Pierrot', as Symons believes.[129] 'Adorez-vous le cirque? Les clowns me paraissent arriver à la vraie sagesse'. ('Do you love circus? The clowns seem to reach true wisdom').[130]

T.S. Eliot understood very early the significance and the endless possibilities of the Laforguian *sagesse* based on clowning. Laforgue had a subtle quality of parody, which Pascal Pia links up with the nineteenth century tradition of parody in France, when 'no French poet of some dignity was denied the honour of being pleasantly imitated by a Monselet, a Vermeusch or a Ponchon'.[131] Eliot, an admirer of vaudeville and Groucho Marx,[132] already had an impulse for parody, and did not probably have much difficulty in emulating the Laforguian example. According to Conrad Aiken, 'There was something of the actor in Tom and some of the clown too. For all his liturgical appearance . . . he was capable of real buffoonery'.[133] Therefore, the Laforguian blend of wisdom and buffoonery was definitely his cup of tea.

The constant debate and dialogue between the clown and the sage is encrypted in various texts of Laforgue and Eliot. 'Jonglons avec les entités' ('Let us juggle with the entities')[134] becomes the slogan of the clown-sage. This juggling of identities is crucial to the modernist discourse.

The drollery of Laforgue should not, therefore, detract us from his endemic seriousness. On the other hand, we must understand that Eliot was not merely mimicking Laforgue's poses, as is generally believed, but was desperately trying to comprehend the *philosophy* behind the pose of his favourite poet. The communion seems to be far deeper than the incidental borrowings of images and phrases; it was, in a sense, a conscious and deliberate re-enactment of a somewhat similar predicament in another setting of a poet who may have sincerely believed that Laforgue's particular kind of handling of the problems of existence, his philosophy and aesthetic of poetry worked well for him.

Eliot's views on Laforgue and his 'gift for the emotions of metaphysics' can perhaps be best understood in the light of his eighth Clark Lecture.[135] Since this is his *only* analysis of Laforgue, and presents a highly objective commentary on their relationship, it will be worthwhile to quote at length:

[Laforgue] was a young man of ardent feelings, of *no* cynicism, of active and abstract intellect, and with a singular gift for the emotions of metaphysics. He had an innate craving for order: that is, every feeling should have its intellectual equivalent, its philosophic justification, and that every idea should have its emotional equivalent, its sentimental justification. The one world in which he could have satisfied himself, therefore, was a world such as Dante's. The disintegration of the intellect in Laforgue had reached a much more advanced stage than with Donne: for Laforgue, life was *consciously* divided into thought and feeling; but his feelings were such as required an intellectual completion, a *beatitude,* and the philosophic system which he embraced were so much felt as to require a sensuous completion. They did not fit. Hence the metaphysically of Laforgue reaches in two directions: the intellectualising of the feeling and the emotionalising of the idea. Where they meet, they come into conflict, and Laforgue's irony, an irony always employed against himself, ensues.[136]

Only Laforgue is in revolt, not in acceptance; he is at once the sentimentalist day-dreaming over the *jeune fille* at the piano with her geraniums, and the behaviourist inspecting her reflexes . . . What is interesting and significant is the sacrifice of his art and his mind before an insoluble problem. Here is a poet genuinely occupied with the relation of feeling and thought, not, like Browning and Meredith, playing with their mechanical combinations. Baudelaire had the genius to attempt an insoluble problem and yet be a great artist; if Laforgue was not a great artist, it is not for us, who have dealt no better with the problem to sneer at him.[137]

It is apparent here that Eliot seriously believed that Laforgue had a 'philosophic system', for which he 'sacrificed' his art and his mind. The key-expressions, in my opinion, are 'metaphysicality', 'craving for order', 'beatitude', 'revolt', and 'insoluble', all of which have a bearing on the development of Eliot's own poetry.

What Eliot calls 'the disintegration of the intellect', resulted in what Lawrence Durrell calls a 'semantic disturbance' in Laforgue, Lewis Carroll and Nietzsche—'a new kind of problem', 'the disturbance of meaning within the structure of the langauge'[138] because the reality they tried to express was 'beyond the bounds of the linguistic and conceptual apparatus at their command'. 'They worked language so hard that it fell to pieces'. If for Rimbaud, the absolute lay behind 'un long, immense et raisonné dérèglement de tous les sens' ('a long, immense and reasoned derangement of all senses'),[139] there was the same dislocation of language resulting from a similar anguish in Laforgue. We shall remember Eliot's famous view that 'the poet must be more and more indirect in order to force, to dislocate if necessary language into his meaning'.[140]

Durrell, however, errs in my view when he suggests that the works of Rimbaud and Laforgue are characterized by a matchless 'hysterical subjectivity'[141] which 'surpasses the efforts of the surrealists' and consequently fails to see the conscious element (what Pound calls 'logopoeia' or 'the dance of the intellect among words')[142] in Laforgue, which was so important for Eliot and the modernists.

It is possible that they particularly liked Laforgue's singling out of intellectual understanding as a means of organising one's life-world—which was one of the most radical features of Modernism. As his Clark Lecture on Laforgue and Corbière shows, Eliot could instantly locate in them the terms of awareness, observation and detachment, which according to Fokkema, are 'at the centre of the Modernist Semantic Universe'.[143]

The technique of Laforgue—self-conscious, deliberate, and at times, clever to the point of preciosity—may, therefore, have much to do with Eliot's formulation of his own views and theories on poetry, notably those on impersonality, 'dissociation of sensibility' and the whole concept of metaphysicality (of thought-feeling and feeling-thought).

'L'esthétique', wrote Laforgue, 'doit être chose absolument désintéressée et discrète'. ('The aesthetics should be something absolutely disinterested and discreet.')[144]

In my opinion, Eliot's early readings of Laforgue's highly intelligent and personal impersonal poetry and prose convinced him that one could be both cerebral and emotional at the same time, by employing these two qualities conjointly or for mutual correction. Laforgue and consequently Corbière came to liberate Eliot from certain highly artificial ways of thought; they embodied for Eliot the modern spirit of a new era. 'Laforgue is surprisingly modern', Eliot would re-admit years later during the Turnbull Lectures.[145] I wonder whether without Laforgue's example, Eliot would have ever been able to formulate his crucial statement; 'Poetry is not a turning loose of emotion; it is not the expression of personality, but an escape from personality. But, of course, only those who have personality and emotions want to escape from these things'.[146] This reminds one of Arthur Symons's observation about Laforgue I have quoted earlier on:

Balanced, chill, colloquial style has in the paradox of its intensity, the essential heat of the most obvious emotional prose.[147]

Eliot's theory of impersonality—no doubt aided by Remy de Gourmont's ideas—seems to be primarily a commentary on Laforgue's indigenous method, where an emotional sequence is disfigured with a rigid and unsuitable frame (Laforgue calls this 'comparaisons illegitimes'[148]) so that a powerful emotion is held in check. This seems to explain Eliot's somewhat confusing and deceptive use of the terms 'personal' and 'impersonal', when he calls for an 'impersonal' approach[149] at the same time reminding us of the necessity of a 'personal point of view'.[150] It was probably a Laforguian synthesis of the subjective and the objective that he was pointing at.

It is usually believed that Eliot's idea of transforming ideas into sensations came from Gourmont, but it is quite possible that Gourmont may have had Laforgue in mind when he made this formulation.

Eliot may have been trying to erect as law his experience of the Laforguian poetics. He would admit years later:

It seems to me that these concepts, these generalisations had their origin in my sensibility. They arise from my feeling of kinship with one poet or one kind of poetry rather than another.[151]

So far, I have tried to show how Laforgue and Eliot shared certain characteristics of personality, how the latter partly possessed and developed a similar aesthetic. I shall now try to find out from Laforgue's works how closely intertwined are the tissues of his poetry with Eliot's, how the latter recreated his own texts out of fragments, written in a different language by his young predecessor.

The 'overwhelming question' (or 'the insoluble problem',[152] as Eliot calls it in the eighth Clark Lecture) led Laforgue to a nauseating sense of monotony and boredom: 'Une nausée immense de la vie' ('A huge nausea of life')[153] which appears to have transpired to all of Eliot's works from 'Prufrock' to 'Burbank', *The Waste Land* to *The Hollow Men*. Laforgue found it impossible to escape from this 'solitude de la vie' ('solitude of life'),[154] 'ce train-train sur terre!' ('the humdrum routine on earth!'),[155] those shattered nerves: 'nerfs incompris ou brisés' ('nerves understood or broken'[156]) . . . 'je n'ai fait que souffrir, pour toute la nature . . . /Souffrir par tous mes nerfs, minutieusement' ('I have only suffered, for the whole of nature . . . /suffered through all my nerves minutely').[157]

> Que la vie est une étourdissante foire
> Que toutes sont créature, et que tout est routine
>
> …
>
> Oh! Que nous mourrons
>
> (And life—what a dizzying fair!
> How ordinary they are, and all is so trite
>
> …
>
> Oh and we are dying)[158]

For a man who was 'permanently declassé',[159] the only activity that seemed feasible is

> Défaire et refaire ses tresses
> Broder d'éternels canevas.
>
> (To unmake and remake plaits
> Embroider an eternal canvas.)[160]

which in Eliot becomes 'a hundred visions and revisions' in 'The Love Song of J. Alfred Prufrock'[161] or

> The world revolves like ancient women
> Gathering fuel in vacant lots.[162]

Laforgue's 'Sirote chaque tour ta tasse de néant' ('Sip every day your cup of nothingness')[163] is recreated in Eliot as 'I have measured out my life with coffee spoons'.[164] The boredom in early Eliot seems to be summed up in:

> Allez, stériles ritoumelles,
> La vie est vraie et criminelle

> (Go, sterile rituals
> Life is true and criminal.)[165]

and the anguish and uncertainty of:

> Le bal incessant de nos étranges rues
> (The endless dance of our strange roads)[166]

is reflected in:

> You hardly know when you are coming back[167]

Eliot's 'Birth, copulation and death'[168] seems to merely re-echo word for word Laforgue's lines in 'Litanies de Misére':

> La faim, l'amour, l'espoir . . . la maladie,
> Puis la mort, c'est toujours la même comedie.
>
> (Hunger, love, hope . . . sickness,
> Then death, it's always the same comedy.)[169]

The boredom reflected in lines like

> Ah! jusqu'à ce que la nature soit bien bonne,
> Moi, je veux vivre monotone
>
> (Ah! until nature is really good
> I, I want to live monotonously)[170]

repeated four times by Laforgue like a defiant chant possibly anticipates the agonized cry of *The Waste Land*. The other alternative, the self-imposed 'tobacco trance'[171] in Eliot seems to have come from Laforgue's:

> Allons, fumons une pipette de tabac
>
> (Come on, let us smoke a pipette of tobacco)[172]

The images of futility and absurdity—the 'grimy scraps', to quote from Eliot's 'Preludes'[173]—are remarkably similar. For example, Eliot's image of the madman shaking the dead geranium seems to be a translation of 'La bouche clownesque ensorcèle/Comme un singulier géranium' ('The mouth of a clown bewitches/Like a strange geranium')[174] and even

> Women come and go
> Talking of Michelangelo[175]

could have been wonderfully forged from:

Bouche qui va du trou sans boude
Glacialement désopilé
Au transcendant en-allé
Du sourire vain de la Joconde

(A mouth which goes from an unplugged hole
Of refrigerated levity,
To that winged transcendental aisle
And vain, the Monalisa smile)[176]

since, to Eliot's transforming genius, Leonardo Da Vinci and Michelangelo
may not have been far off. The Beckettian image of the futility of coming
and going is strongly reminiscent of a passage on serious dancing couples
in Laforgue's *Mélanges Posthumes*,[177] if seen in isolation from its immediate
context:

On les voit passer, repasser, serieux . . .
deux femmes causent

(One watches their coming and going
seriously . . . two women talk)'

We find an uncanny similarity between the aural pattern of Laforgue and
Eliot's own: the same objectivity and distance, the same disgust of the
romantic bluster, the same style of phrasing and images characterized by
an elaborate cloaking of emotions:

Un clavecin joue en face
Un chat traverse la place

(A harpsichord plays over there
A cat crosses the square)[178]

This could well have been magically transformed into:

Remark the cat which flattens itself in the gutter
Slips out its tongue . . .[179]

reminding us of the image of the cat in Laforgue, a Baudelairian heritage:

Lissant ton poil
Soyeux de ta langue âpre et rose
Lentement tu venais de ton pas de velours
Devant moi t'allonger en quelque noble pose.
(Licking your silky hair
With your bitter rose-coloured tongue

> Slowly you came on velvet feet
> And stretched yourself before me in some noble pose.)[180]

In the same way, the purulent moon in:

> Et la lune-même (cette amie)
> Salive et larmoie en purulente opthalmie
>
> (And even the moon [our friend]
> With purulent opthalmia sobs and drools)[181]

is transcreated in the wretched picture of the moon, with its smallpox and 'old nocturnal smells'.[182] Similarly, 'Astre de cécité' ('blind star') in Laforgue's *Clair de lune*[183] may have become 'She winks a feeble eye' in Eliot. It is a wretched world where everything gets corrupt, especially the moon. We shall see in chapter on Corbière how these pale images of the moon overlap with those of Corbière.

The powerfully refreshing and destabilizing image of a cigarette-end in Eliot—so startlingly innovative at the turn of the century—would never have been possible without a poem like *La Cigarette* by Laforgue:

> Je fume au nez des dieux de fines cigarettes.
>
> (I smoke on the nose of gods fine cigarettes.)[184]

In *Moralités Légendaires,* Laforgue's Hamlet distributes cigarettes to the actors.[185]

Eliot's obsession with time and hours ('Correct our watches by the public clocks'[186]) is also a typically Laforguian characteristic:

> L'heure sonna à l'horloge du Luxembourg
>
> (Hour struck at the Luxembourg clock)[187]
>
> Le piano clôt la fenêtre
> Quelle heure peut-il bien être?
>
> (The piano closes the window
> What time can it be now?)[188]

Herbert Howarth[189] is probably right when he states that Laforgue's cosmopolitanism (Laforgue called himself a 'prisoner of Paris'[190]) has to be properly highlighted in English. Symons's book, he rightly complains, had not dealt with this aspect of Laforgue. Eliot was quick to realize this, he goes on to say, and 'incorporated the metropolitan vision into his poetry'[191] through Laforgue. Though Baudelaire's contribution in this regard can never be exaggerated, Howarth seems to focus on another very important area of the Laforgue-Eliot relationship, often ignored by the majority of critics. Paul Bourget, Laforgue's friend, advocated in an essay on Turgenev 'a cosmopolitanism which freed the contemporary writer from the particularities of place'.[192] The kind of urban description with which Eliot exploded all the established canons of English poetry, has close resemblances with Laforgue's own. The intrinsic feline urbaneness of Laforgue can be found in the description of Hamlet:

Hamlet quitte la fenêtre, et s'installe devant une table, se met à feuilleter deux cahiers minces.

(Hamlet leaves the window, and settles before a table, starts turning the pages of two thin exercise books.)[193]

Good night, ladies; good night, sweet ladies! good night, good night![194]

The latter used by Eliot in *The Waste Land*.[195]

Sections on city-life in *Mélanges Posthumes* (which was in the third volume of Laforgue's *Oeuvres Complètes* that Eliot had ordered at Harvard in 1908–9) like 'Promenade dans une rue',[196] 'Soir de printemps sur les Boulevards',[197] 'Paysage parisien'. 33),[198] evoke images of cigarettes, housemaids, society women, windows, bedrooms, coffee, beer-mugs, boulevards, street lamps, perfumes, kitchens…transporting us to the world of T.S. Eliot. The soul-less Paris streets on Sundays, the 'soup-smoking roofs' ('les toits fumants de la soupe'[199]), the discordant pianos, and the curtained windows are also raw material for Laforgue's poetry from *Le Sanglot de la Terre* to *Derniers Vers*.

Laforgue's critical and discursive writings, assembled in *Mélanges Posthumes*, have always been ignored by critics, but they can provide some most revealing documents about Eliot's possible debt to Laforgue. Every single entry in the book is important for a better understanding of their fascinating symbiosis. For example, in 'Promenade dans une rue',[200] wandering about ('errer dans la capitale') in the city, Laforgue discovers the monotony ('la quotidenneté') of existence: 'qu'elle' devienne monotone et debonnaire de fatalisme' ('How life becomes monotonous and fatalistically easy-going'). The 'lonely men in shirt-sleeves, leaning out of windows' in 'Prufrock'[201] may have been transcreated from Laforgue's 'accoudé, un je une homme regardant' etc. ('leaning, a young man watches') at the window.[202] 'The cups, marmalade, the tea' may be a more explicit evocation of 'l'ennui de la salle à manger' ('the boredom of the dining room'),[203] just as the 'mésquinerie laborieuse du salon' ('the laborious naughtiness of the salon') and 'le frou-frou de ta robe est le modèle des frous-frous' ('the frou-frou of your dress is the model of frou')[204] are nowhere better illustrated than in the snobbish ladies of 'Prufrock' with their skirts trailing along the floor and 'l'immuable atmosphere de la chambre à coucher' ('stagnant atmosphere of the bedroom') in 'Preludes III'. And who knows if Eliot's housemaids would have ever made their way into English poetry, had there been no 'bonnes' ('housemaids') in Laforgue? The Laforguian housemaids will be seen washing glass panes, and chatting with each other in *Mélanges Posthumes*.[205]

In trying to trace the origin of the startling comparison of the evening with a patient etherized upon a table in 'The Love Song of J. Alfred Prufrock', Grover Smith has drawn attention[206] to Eliot's 'apparent debt' for the table-image to the opening lines of Laforgue's 'Complainte sur certains temps deplacés':[207]

> Le couchant de sang est tâché
> Comme un tablier de boucher
> Oh! qui veut aussi m'écoreher.
>
> (The bloody sunset is stained
> Like the apron of a butcher
> Oh! who wants to skin me.)

Smith has made a serious mistake here: he seems to have taken 'un tablier de boucher' (a butcher's apron) for a butcher's table. However, it is quite possible that Eliot too may have made the same mistake as Grover Smith, thereby gaining from his curious misreading. Yet there are other comparable lines in 'Derniers Vers XII' and Baudelaire's 'Harmonie du Soir':

> Le soleil s'est noyé dans un sang qui se fige
>
> (The sun has drowned in coagulating blood)[208]

In Laforgue this is turned into:

Le soleil couchant qui dans son sang se vautre

(The setting sun which wallows in its blood)[209]

And there is no dearth of references to hospitals and patients in Laforgue. The most obvious example that comes to one's mind is 'Recueillement du soir',[210] where the evening is related to a 'pharmacist on the pale pavement'.[211] In the same poem, at the advent of the evening:

> Au fond des hôpitaux la vieillesse nocturne
> Eclaire le dortoir aux lits numérotés
> (Inside the hospitals the nocturnal oldness
> Lights up the dormitory with its numbered beds)

and

> Le moribond s'accroche, îvre, aux draps de sa couche.
>
> (The moribund drunk clings to his bed-sheets.)

It is quite possible that these highly destabilizing images in Jules Laforgue have fathered the celebrated line of Eliot.

Related to this is Laforgue's deft impressionistic use of colours—a Baudelairian heritage—in evoking city-images, which remind one of Eliot's 'yellow fog', 'yellow soles of feet', and 'blackened street': Laforgue's 'fleuve noir' ('black river'), the 'objective co-relative' of 'quartiers sinistres comme des Morgues' ('quarters as sinister as morgues') has plenty of analogous references in Eliot.

The deeply disturbing self-questionings and metaphysical interrogations in the early and middle-period Eliot, which seem to have upset the reading behaviour in the early decades of this century, appear to have been modelled on the bantering conversations and hyperboles[212] in Laforgue:

> Vous avez bien diné,
> Comment va cette affaire?
>
> (You have dined well,
> How are things?)[213]
>
> Sommes-nous seuls? Pourquoi le Mal?
> (Are we alone? Why this Agony?)[214]
>
> Si nous allions boire un coup?
> (If we went for a drink?)[215]
>
> Si j'avais su, si j'avais su
> (If I had known, if I had known)[216]
>
> Comprenez-vous? Pourquoi ne comprenez-vous pas?
> (Do you understand? Why don't you understand?[217]
>
> Mon Dieu, tout n'est-il pas un cauchemar trompeur?
> (My God, isn't everything a deceptive nightmare?)[218]
>
> C'était done sérieux?
> (Was it then no joke?)[219]

are sought to be transplanted in 'Shall I part my hair behind? Do I dare to eat a peach?';[220] 'Are these ideas right or wrong?';[221] 'Has it begun to sprout? Will it bloom this year?';[222] or 'What are you thinking of? What thinking? What?'.[223] The laborious homework done by Eliot with Laforgue's poems is evident in all this, and shows how Laforgue's verbal habits infiltrated his consciousness.

As for cosmopolitan images, Eliot also uses powerful and thoroughly unconventional images like newspapers and waste paper to express urbane drabness and defilement: 'a litter of Sunday newspapers' where 'many read nothing but race reports';[224] 'Men and bits of paper, whirled by the cold wind'.[225] Presumably, this, too, was culled from his young master, who called himself in his notes 'a prisoner of Paris and newspapers':[226]

> Le sobre et vespéral mystère hebdomadaire
> Des statistiques sanitaires des journaux
>
> (The sober fortnightly evening mystery
> Of sanitary statistics in newspapers)
>
> L'après-midi–à Paris, au mois d'août
> Je veux fuir les journaux . . .
>
> (In August afternoons in Paris
> I often, want to escape from newspapers . . .)[227]

Strong unpoetic words ('cut out the poetry', Eliot told T. S. Matthews, 'That's what I've been trying to do all my life'[228]) like 'foetus' in:

> He laughed like an irresponsible foetus[229]

seem to be summarily borrowed from

> Et vous foetus voûtés glabres contemporains
>
> (And you contemporary hairless stooping foetus)[230]

For many years, critics have tended to limit Eliot's Laforguianisms to his earliest period, when he wrote four pastiche-poems in the *Harvard Advocate* ('Nocturne', 'Humouresque', 'Spleen', 'Conversation Galante'), regarded as practice canters in the hoofprints of Laforgue. And Eliot himself categorized 'Conversation Galante', 'Portrait of a Lady', 'The Love Song of J. Alfred Prufrock', and 'La Figlia Che Piange' as written 'sous le signe de Laforgue'. Yet there is no reason why many of his later works should be left unaccounted for. If Eliot had the boldness to use tricks and gimmicks for many years in order to avoid 'dullness', he had merely taken a leaf out of Laforgue's book. The latter's defiant

> Klip, klip, klop, klop, klip, klop[231]

is echoed in Eliot's

> Drip drop drip drop drop drop drop[232]

Without Laforgue's

> Bonjour poupoupoupou-lette[233]
> Bin bam bin bam[234]

> Hoyotoho!
> Heiaha!
> Hahei! Haiaho! Hoyohai![235]

Eliot would possibly never have cracked the conventional poetic discourse with:

> Co co rico co co rico[236]
>
> Twit twit twit
> Jug jug jug jug jug jug[237]
>
> Weialala leia
> Wallala leialala[238]
>
> Ting a ling ling
> Ting a ling ling[239]
>
> Hoo ha ha
> Hoo ha ha
> Hoo
> Hoo
> KNOCK KNOCK KNOCK[240]

Possibly, it is Laforgue who showed how 'words strain, crack, and sometimes break, under the burden'.[241] Even Eliot's masterly use of nursery rhyme in *The Waste Land*:

> London Bridge is falling down falling down falling down[242]

could well have been inspired by Laforgue's bold use of a nursery rhyme in 'Complainte du pauvre jeune homme':

> Quand on est mort, c'est pour de bon
> Digne dondaine, digne dondaine
> Quand on est mort, c'est pour de bon
> Digne dondaine, digne dondaine
>
> (When you are dead, it's for so long
> Ding dong ding-a-ling
> When you are dead, it's for so long
> Ding dong ding-a-ling)[243]

Eliot scholars have failed to tell us that his love of the cryptogrammatic was in all probability a heritage of Laforgue and Corbière. The above examples of exciting parallels should prove beyond doubt that Laforgue may have cast a much longer spell on Eliot's psyche than is usually believed. These Laforguian diversions never degenerated into a surrealist *poésie en jeu* of Apollinaire and Breton in the hands of T.S. Eliot.

It should be equally interesting to note that one of the most powerfully evocative images of Laforgue, woven presumably from the texts of Baudelaire and Corbière, and used by Eliot at the end of 'Prufrock', gradually assumed great importance in the latter's works—that of drowning:

> Heard the mermaids singing each to each . . .
> I have seen them riding seawards on the waves
> Combing the white hair of the sea blown back
> When the wind blows the water white and black.
> We have lingered in the chambers of the sea
> By sea-girls wreathed with seaweed red and brown
> Till human voices wake us, and we drown.[244]

I suggest that this sudden expansiveness came from Laforgue's 'Préludes autobiographiques' (the opening poem of *Les Complaintes)* in the last stanza of which he transcended the contradictions of his world in an identical manner:

> Je m'en vais flottant aux orgues sous-marins
> Par les coraux, les oeufs, les bras verts, les écrins
> Dans la tourbillonnante éternelle agonie
> D'un Nirvana des Danaïdes du génie
> Lacs de syncopes esthétiques! Tunnels d'or!
> ...
> Maintenant, tu n'as pas cru devoir rester coi
> Eh bien, un cri humain s'il en reste un pour toi.

> (I float away with underwater organs
> Through the coral, the eggs, green hands, caskets
> In the whirlpool of eternal agony
> Lakes of aesthetic forgetfulness! Tunnels of gold!
> ...
> Now you thought, you should not keep silent.
> Well then, a human cry, if you can still do so.)[245]

It is legitimate to think that Laforgue's 'tunnels of gold' gave birth to Eliot's 'chambers of the sea', just as 'human cry' became 'human voices' in Eliot.

In my opinion (although Eliot had always been spiritually attached to water, being familiar with the 'moods and rhythms of the great Mississippi' in his childhood) it may be Laforgue who opened up for the American an indefinite variety of associations, contiguities and cross-references. Of course, there was also the irresistible lure of the sea in Baudelaire and Corbière, but Laforgue's marine metaphors like:

> Mais l'idéal c'est ces éponges, ces astérics, ces plasmas dans le silence opaque et frais, tout au rêve, de l'eau.
>
> (But the ideal are these sponges, these asterisks, the plasma in the opaque and fresh dreamy silence of water.)[246]
>
> Plûtot une éponge passive, un corail au fond de lamer, incrusté à la même place, voir le défilé de la nature sous-marine . . .
>
> (Rather a passive sponge, a coral at the bottom of the sea, incrusted at the same place, watching the parade of underwater nature . . .)[247]

or a rather liberating description of the seawaters in 'Persée et Andromède',[248] in retrospect strangely Eliotic, appear to have sparked off a series of analogous reconstructions in Elliot's poetry:

> His laughter was submarine and profound
> Like the old man of the sea's
> Hidden under coral islands
> Where worried bodies of drowned men drift down in the green silence
> Dropping from fingers of surf.[249]

Then, there are those two brilliant passages on the drowned Phoenician in 'Dans le Restaurant' and *The Waste Land* with the 'cry of gulls', 'cargaison d'etain' ('cargoes of tin'), underwater current picking the bones in whispers and the whirlpool,[250] once again bringing back memories of Laforgue. But, if this water-motif in Laforgue and early and middle-period Eliot is somewhat surrealistic, we can notice a tendency in later Eliot to gradually see it as a timeless symbol. It acquires a new philosophic depth in 'Marina', where 'all the water meet'[251] in *Ash-Wednesday*, where he invokes the 'spirit of the river, spirit of the sea'.[252] Although Laforguian resonances can still be heard in:

> Out at sea the dawn wind
> Wrinkles and glides.[253]
>
> The houses are all gone under sea.[254]
>
> The wave cry, the wind cry, the vast waters
> Of the petrel and the porpoise.[255]

he speaks much more reflectively of 'the trial and the judgement of the sea',[256] knowing well that 'The river is within us, the sea is all about us' and 'The sea has many voices,/Many gods and many voices'.[257]

While Laforgue wished to 'plunge [his head] in the seas' ('plonger mon front dans l'eau des mers'),[258] Eliot, hovering among seaweed, foam, sea-mists, currents, and the Gulf Stream for thirty years, finally seems to have found the truth, the 'stillness', 'between the two waves of the sea' in the last lines of *Four Quartets*.[259]

Laforgue has always been branded as an adolescent and derided for his 'shallowness of roots' and 'lack of a ground bass'. It was believed that he 'hastens across abysses, he has no taste for exploring'.[260] This, of course, is wholly untrue. Interaction with Laforgue was so supremely decisive for Eliot that it may help us not only to understand the latter's early poetry, but also his more profound later developments.

In *Mélanges Posthumes*, Laforgue jots down the theme of his ultimate book:

Et alors mon grand livre de *prophétie,* la Bible nouvelle qui va faire déserter les cités. La vanité de tout, le déchirement de l'Illusion, *l'Angoisse* des temps, *le renoncement,* l'Inutilité de l'Univers, *la misère et l'ordure de la terre perdue* dans les vestiges d'apothéoses éternellcs de

soleils.

(And then my great book of *prophecy,* the new Bible which is going to empty the cities. The vanity of everything, the disintegration of illusion, *the Anguish* of the times, *renouncement,* inutility of the universe, *the misery and the rubbish of the land lost* in the vestiges of the eternal glory of the sun.)[261]

The key words and expressions here are *prophecy*, *anguish*, *renouncement*, *misery*, *rubbish*, and *lost land.*

In a letter to his friend Gustave Kahn, Laforgue divided 'the macabre adventure of humanity' in three great panels, corresponding to Hartmann's three stages of illusion. 'I'll write a prologue describing the first days of humanity, and an epilogue imagining the last, when illusion is dead, the cities deserted and man, his head shaved and covered with ashes, awaits Nothingness'.[262] This apocalyptic vision of Laforgue leads us inevitably to the predicament of *The Waste Land* and *The Hollow Men*, and dispels any doubt about his seriousness.

Hugh Kenner calls the Laforguian impasse between self-sufficiency and art 'a dead end'.[263] Though the other Eliot critics have not said as much, they, too, seem to believe the same. Undoubtedly, this is a very convenient way of dismissing the cross with Laforgue as a temporary phase. But in reality, the latter was the last man to be pigeonholed. 'Mon clavier est perpétuellement changeant' ('my keyboard is always changing'), he said.[264] His later works *Derniers Vers* and *Mélanges Posthumes*, testify to this restlessness to find some kind of an order in chaos, a great inner urge to spread to a larger life.

I suggest that in the crucial second phase of Eliot, when he crossed Laforgue's age, he fulfilled many of the possibilities and promises of his 'admired elder brother'. As B. Rajan explains:

Seen in the symbolic continuum, the waste land is Prufrock's world more full realised, a world where prophecy has fallen to fortune-telling, where love has hardened into the expertise to lust, where April is the cruellest month, and where the dead are no longer buried but planted in gardens . . .[265]

This tallies with Laforgue's own book of prophecy quoted earlier.

Laforgue's deep pessimism is particularly evident in a fragment called 'Le Mai, destine du monde' ('Evil, destiny of the world'),[266] which seems to be written under the influence of Schopenhauer, and in many other passages in his correspondences and articles. 'La vie est trop triste, trop sale. L'histoire est un vieux cauchemar bariolé.' ('Life is too sad, too dirty. History is an old multicoloured nightmare.')

It may be interesting to look up Laforgue's poem 'Enfer', which may have suggested to an imaginative reader like Eliot the vision of *The Waste Land*. It speaks of impotence, exile, incapacity for dreams, nausea, horror, anguish, pity, and asphyxiation in the mud.

Un flot de vieux dégoûts me fait lever le coeur.

(Waves of old tilth make me vomit.)

This poem[267] is, indeed, very different from our received opinion about Laforgue, the image of a frivolous man that has been carefully built on an obviously incomplete reading of his works.

As a way out of the impasse ('Absurdity of remedies'[268]) Laforgue showed an inclination towards Indian religious philosophy, especially Buddhism. He had two solutions before him:

Deux solutions proposées: Bouddha, l'Inde vénérable—
Schopenhaüer. Hartmann.

(Two solutions proposed: Buddha, venerable India—
Schopenhauer, Hartmann.)[269]

He spoke of 'renouncement', 'Nirvana':

Résignons-nous à nos misères

(Let us resign to our misery)[270]

and discerned, like the later Eliot, that 'material suicide' and 'renouncement' can take man towards an awareness of the 'principe mystérieux, insaisissable qui circule partout' ('intractable, mysterious principle which is everywhere').[271]

If Eliot's position is not clear enough at the end of *The Waste Land*, Laforgue's following statement can possibly help us to understand his mind:

Il faut se hâter de multiplier le remède du renoncement, entretenir l'homme de l'éternel pour qu'il ne fasse pas attention à sa misère ephémère.

(One must make haste and multiply the remedies of renouncement, to keep alive the eternal in man so that he does not pay attention to In. ephemeral misery.)[272]

One such remedy for Laforgue was Buddhism ('Impassibles Bouddhas, je vous admire fort': 'Impassive Buddhas, I admire you so much'[273]) to which there are several references in his works. He wrote to Gustave Kahn on 12 September 1882: 'Avant j'étais bouddhiste tragigue et maintenant je suis bouddiste dilettante'. ('In the past, I was a tragic Buddhist, now I am a dilettante Buddhist'.)[274]

Although Irving Babbitt's *Buddha and the Occident* and Sir Edwin Arnold's long epic poem on the life of Buddha, *The Light of Asia*, may also have played an important role, it would be legitimate to speculate that Laforgue was the chief inspiration behind Eliot's brush with Buddhism. And this is particularly illuminating for Eliot's readers, because *The Waste Land* has indeed been called 'a Buddhist poem'.[275] According to T.S. Matthews, Eliot borrowed from the Buddha the red rock and the thunder.[276] Edmund Wilson had thought that, 'like Buddha, Eliot saw the world as 'an arid conflagration'[277] and found Buddhist renunciation in the poem. Spender has recorded how he overheard Eliot recounting to Gabrielle Mistrale that he had 'seriously considered becoming a Buddhist' while writing *The Waste Land*.[278] My contention is that Laforgue's own unusual interest in Buddhism—the authoritative *Dictionnaire de littérature française* of Larousse calls him a 'confirmed Buddhist'[279]—may have resulted in Eliot's brush with it. I know of no critic who has highlighted the strong possibility of Laforgue's influence on Eliot in this regard. (The latter admitted his awareness of Laforgue's 'pseudo-Buddhism' in his eighth Clark Lecture).[280]

If, as T.S. Matthews claims, two years' study of Sanskrit and Pali 'nearly made a Buddhist of him' and left him in a state of 'enlightened mystification',[281] that may perhaps be indirectly attributed to Laforgue; for Eliot enrolled in the classes of Indic philosophy and Buddhism in Harvard *after* he returned from Paris in 1911.[282]

Unfortunately, Eliot scholars have also failed to note that Laforgue, too, sometimes burst into a discourse of the East (like Eliot in *The Waste*

Land) and spoke of the 'rites végétatifs de l'Inde' ('the vegetative rituals of India').[283] And what is infinitely important for Eliot, he showed a surprisingly deep awareness of the Indian philosophic world view:

> . . . les passions des grappes cosmiques,
> O Robe de Maïa
>
> (. . . The passion of cosmic grapes,
> O Robe of Maïa)[284]
>
> Maïa—l'Illusion—l'Illusion[285]
> Quoi qu'il en soit
> O Maïa
> Tout pour toi
>
> (Whatever it may be O Maïa
> Everything for you)[286]

and even invoked Brahma, the All-in-Oneself.[287]

There is a wistful inclination in Laforgue for the great Indian spiritual tradition embodied in the Ganges:

> Dans les Indes du Rêve, aux pacifiques Ganges,
> Que j'en ai des comptoirs, des hamacs de rechanges
>
> (In India of Dream where peaceful Ganges curve,
> I've plenty of rocking chairs and hammocks in reserve)[288]

The resonance of this could have come back in Eliot: 'Gangawas sunken',[289] suggesting how firm Laforgue's grip was on Eliot's psyche.

Now I shall focus on another feature of Laforgue shared by Eliot, briefly broached by G.M. Turnell[290]: his 'half-heartedness about sex and his recoil from physical love'[291]—something which appears to have deeply influenced his world view. Since Eliot's texts, too, display an unusual suspicion of the opposite sex, and his biographers have unanimously referred to his 'inhibition, distrust of women, and a certain physical queasiness',[292] it may be worth examining his mentor's strong views on women and sex.

Laforgue wrote in a letter to Charles Henry:

You tell me: love. I am unable. From my heart, I no longer can, and that alone would not be love. In my head, yes. But that would not be love either, and where is the woman who could inspire in me that cerebral love? With the senses? Less than the rest. With me, desires do not come with bodily substance; when I pass away the hours, I imagine to myself I have desires but they are false desires.[293]

Je puis mourir demain et je n'ai pas aimé.

(I may die tomorrow and I haven't loved.)[294]

and he made an extraordinary confession to Charles Henry:

La Femme ne m'excite ni le coeur, ni la tête, ni les sens—peut-être, les sens, mais cinq minutes toutes deux semaines à peu près.

(Women don't excite my heart, nor my head, nor the senses—perhaps the senses, but may be five minutes every two weeks.)[295]

This dichotomy between dream and reality led to occasional ferocious misogyny in Laforgue: 'O panthère caline/Griffant nos mousselines' ('O cuddly panther/Clawing our muslin'),[296] and 'j'ai craché sur l'amour et j'ai tué la chair' ('I have spat on love and killed the flesh'.[297] There is uncompromising hatred in 'vierges d'hier…traîneuses de foetus' ('Virgins of yesterday…carriers of foetus')[298] or 'La femme est cramponne' ('The woman is a leech').[299] In 'Le Concile féerique', the chorus cries:

> Ah! Saignons, tandis qu'elles déballent
> Leurs serres de beauté, pétale par pétale.
>
> (Ah! Let's bleed, while the girls
> Unpack their greenhouses of beauty, petal by petal.)[300]

Laforgue uses a familiar verb like 'déballer' (to unpack, expose) to show his disgust for women, who dress up and use make-up to attract men. He will bleed while the ladies will continue their relentless aggression; the contrast is made clearer by the use of the conjunction 'tandis que'. For Laforgue, the adult woman is 'before everything else a symbol of carnal love', which is against the cherished ideals of Pierrot. Eroticism is visible in 'Complainte du vent',[301] where the woman who shares the room is ravaged by repentance: this room is 'le miroir de (son) tombeau' ('the mirror of [his] tomb'), which reminds us of the prostitute's room in Eliot's 'Preludes III' (a parallel that escaped the notice of Grover Smith, who regards Charles-Louis Philippe's *Marie Donadieu* and *Bubu de Montparnasse* as chief sources of Eliot's poem).[302]

No doubt, apart from his own preconceived ideas about sex and women, Laforgue seems to have been doubly biased by his favourite philosopher Edouard Hartmann's ('my Hartmann': letter to Charles Henry[303]) swashbuckling attacks on the pleasures of sex. According to Hartmann, 'These vices soil the aesthetic sense, blunt the delicacy of mind. They unsettle the health and only too often sow the seeds of ruin for the following generation'.[304] As for Schopenhauer, Laforgue's other model, Frank Kermode has focused on his 'depressing views on sex'.[305] When Laforgue says, 'J'ai peur de la vie comme d'un mariage' ('I'm afraid of life, like marriage'),[306] it is much more than a joke, it is a revelation of his inmost self, perplexed, intellectually over-refined, but emotionally immature, like Eliot.

On the other hand, this nihilism seems to match perfectly with Eliot's own revulsion (is 'queasiness' a better word?) for sex. In 'Conversation Galante', written as early as in 1909, Eliot had already indicted the woman as 'the eternal enemy of the Absolute'. Peter Ackroyd, who deals with the subject at great length, records how he trembled at the 'feeling of being engorged by a woman'.[307] Generations of Eliot readers have shivered at his limitless hatred for 'those who suffer the ecstasy of the animals, meaning Death'.[308] I would like to relate this to the ferocious misogyny in the manuscript of *The Waste Land*. Eliot is possibly one poet who never wrote a single true love poem in his life. Indeed, everything that he wrote about women in his poetry, in 'Prufrock', 'Portrait of a Lady', 'Preludes', 'Hysteria', and *The Waste Land* (cf. the story of the typist) betray his brooding dislike, and his own nervous sexual instincts, with feelings of guilt and self-disgust, his fear of 'the murky facts of life'.[309] To quote F.R. Leavis, sex in Eliot is 'sterile, breeding not life and fulfilment, but disgust, accidia and unanswerable questions',[310] like, for example, in the 'Ode' which deals with a man's horror of his partner who seems to him to be a 'succuba eviscerate'.[311]

It is strange that no Eliot critic has noticed the almost uncanny similarity between Laforgue's attitude to love, and that of his disciple. It is quite likely that the latter's disastrous experience of married life, coupled with his own mental and moral dilemmas and family background, was responsible for his recoil from women, but on a literary level (which is really literary-moral), Laforgue's compelling influence on Eliot cannot be ruled out.

Yet, in a sense, both Laforgue and Eliot were ceaselessly aware of femininity, which paradoxically still held 'promises of pneumatic bliss'. (The Pierrots in Laforgue make fools of themselves; 'Afin d'avoir des seins/pis-aller de coussins': 'In order to have breasts,/The last resort of cushions',[312] which Eliot transforms into 'promises of pneumatic bliss'.) Despite their inability to think uninhibitedly of women, their works remain strewn with references to them. There is not a page without them in Laforgue, and Eliot remains, despite a sense of guilt and sin, obsessed with women: this shows their cruel need for love. Probably Laforgue and Eliot still believed that a lady of silences could open the door to the rose garden. But apparently, neither Laforgue nor Eliot could develop this feeling into a stable commitment. At least, this is what Eliot admitted to Martin Browne.[313]

Writing about the Symbolists' feel for the language, their 'îvresse verbale' ('verbal drunkenness',[314] Remy de Gourmont felt:

> Les mots out peut-être donné plus de joie que les idées, et de plus délicieuses.
>
> (Perhaps words have given me more joy than ideas, more delicious joy.)[315]
>
> J'aime les mots en eux-mêmes, pour leur esthétique personnelle.
>
> (I love words themselves, for their own aesthetics.)[316]
>
> J'ai vu naître un mot; c'est voir naître une fleur.
>
> (I have seen the birth of a word; it is like watching a flower blossom.)[317]

Indeed, Laforgue himself (like Mallarmé) would have said much the same thing. Like Gourmont, he seems to be infatuated with the physical beauty of words. This can be sensed in the creation of a word like 'éternullité'.[318] No wonder, then, that Mallarmé held him in high esteem.

Linguistically, Eliot seems to be deeply indebted to Laforgue's abundant lexical virtuosity. Earlier on I referred to Eliot's intelligent use of Laforgue's cryptograms and polyglot texts.

Laforgue had gradually discarded, after initial hesitations, the Baudelairian alexandrine in favour of an extremely varied 'free verse' in *Derniers Vers,* which Eliot seems to have consciously used as his model in 'Prufrock' and which seems to be the basis of his later style. The rhyme is unimpaired by prosaic elements and free-verse paragraphs of varying length determined by semantic connections. Laforgue seems to anticipate Eliot's technique of musicalized composition 'charged with meaning and emotive suggestions, fusing the prosaic and the poetic'.[319]

Eliot imbibed Laforgue's audacious tendency to flout traditional syntax with a highly individual alchemy of vocabulary. To quote the French critic Pierre Raboul:

> Le mot n'est plus l'équivalent de la touche du peintre, mais déjà une synthése l'équivalent de toute une proposition, voire une phrase, l'expression d'une impression ou d'une idée complexe.
>
> (The word is no longer the equivalent of the painter's touch but already a synthesis which is equivalent to a whole proposition, even a sentence, the expression of a complex impression or idea.)[320]

Laforgue's vocabulary was the result of a complex laboratory-work as much as Eliot's own: his language has an astonishingly large arsenal of familiar words, neologism, scientific, and philosophic jargon. There are choric interpolations (reminding us of 'Women come and go/Talking of Michelangelo'), hyperboles, repetitions, different manipulations of repeated words, which I have touched upon. To take a closer look at Laforgue's use of words:[321]

1. Scientific words (derived from science, medicine, arts, religion, mythology, philosophy, and ancient history): Alme, bizarrant, écarquiller, ilote, interlope, sédentaire, ululer, condimenter, hypogée, plénipotentaire, zaimph, anthropomorphe, Hippone, Hypocondrie, pactole, tuf, vivapare, chlorose, cruor, solfatare, Alphée, Corybante, Cydalise, Lusiade, Phoebus, Cosmogénie, Néant, Nirvâna, substratum, etc.

2. Popular vocabulary and slangs: S'amener, corbleu, lupanar, cuver, déballer, dégringoler, gargouiller, guilledou, hure, pot-au-feu, talonner, sucer, vanné, bastringue, turne, s'engueuler, se larder, flanquer, grabuge, crevasion, vache enragée, etc.

3. Neologism (archaisms, borrowings, and real neologism): Angéluser, arguital, sangsuel, voluptial, se substanter, spleenuosité, tumulter, vortex-nombril, etc.

Most of these daring uses were new in French, and typically Laforguian. We can well imagine how much Eliot gained from all this when he quietly forged his own language with words like (to give a few examples): phthisic, protozoic, water-stair;[322] velleities;[323] anfractuous, polypheme, broadbottomed;[324] inflexious, miasmal;[325] pneumatic, marmoset, circumambulate, arboreal;[326] polypiloprogentive, sapient, sutlers, superfetation, presbyters, piaculative, staminate, pistillate, polymath;[327] Apeneck, maculate, mocha, wistaria;[328] laquearia;[329] etc.

Sure enough, Laforgue's intrepid use of a word like 'cold cream' ('une face imberbe au cold cream': 'a beardless face with cold-cream'[330]) was sufficient to give Eliot the fillip he needed.

So far, we have tried to show how Eliot's debt to Laforgue seems to have operated on multiple levels—personality, temperament, language, style—and how he wished to express a similar predicament in a queerly identical manner. If Eliot's career is divided into three phases—the early, middle, and the later Eliot—not only did he try to emulate Laforgue's 'metaphysical' qualities in the first phase, but went on to work out the implications of Laforgue even in the subsequent phases as well. We note the movement from 'Vanité, vanité, tout n'est que vanité' ('Vanity, vanity, everything is only vanity') to a tentative solution ('Absurdity of remedies, nothing can cure the universal malady'[331]) proposed by Laforgue: 'Résignons-nous à nos misères' ('Let us resign to our miseries'[332]) mirrored in Eliot's 'Shantih, Shantih, Shantih'. I have pointed out how Eliot is able to partially 'demolish the discourse of the West petitioning the East for solace and recovery',[333] following the footsteps of his master, who had recommended 'renonciation totale et douce' ('total and sweet renouncement').[334]

Eliot complained in a book review[335] that although in many ways Laforgue seems to express 'more clearly than Baudelaire the difficulties of his own age, he speaks to us, or spoke to my generation, more intimately than Baudelaire seems to do', he did not foreshadow 'an issue from these difficulties like Baudelaire'. While Eliot's debt to Baudelaire's moral vision cannot be overestimated, I have little doubt that Laforgue anticipated the final movement in Eliot's works: the *issue* from his difficulties. I consider this to be one of the most important findings of my research and I do not think any Eliot critic has highlighted this vital point.

However, it is Eliot himself who provided us with a clue to the puzzle of his great final phase, beginning from *Ash-Wednesday*, in the eighth Clark Lecture in 1926. There he emphasized Laforgue's 'craving for order', which he identified as the central driving force operating in him.

Eliot mentioned how Laforgue transformed Baudelaire's prayer for strength and courage into the following in *Derniers Vers XII*.

> O Nature, donne-moi la force et le courage
> De me croire en age
> O Nature, relève-moi le front
>
> (O Nature, give me courage and strength
> To believe I am old enough
> O Nature, lift up my head)[336]

Here Baudelaire's words ('la force el le courage') are softened with humility. Gone is the old self-deprecation in Laforgue, who now prays for courage and strength to live life's dizzying fair—a final release from his 'monomaniac exile'.[337] This new sustained seriousness in the later Laforgue anticipates well Eliot's own enlightened discourse in the final Christian phase of *Ash-Wednesday* and *Four Quartets*:

> Teach us to care and not to care
> Teach us to sit still
> Even among these rocks[338]

Laforgue did not live long but Eliot knew his texts so intimately that they still 'directed [his] steps'[339] even as friends and critics erroneously thought that he had left Laforgue far behind.

The latter wrote to a friend that he was a 'mystic' ('je suis un pessimiste mystique', letter to Mme Mültzer, 1882).[340] In his childhood, the only subject in which he did remarkably well was religious instruction. And in the controversy about his plagiarism of Corbière's poetry, Laforgue had steadfastly defended himself by saying that he had a *faith* and a *mission*—'je suis d'une philosophic absolue' ('I have an absolute philosophy')[341] which he believed his predecessor had not.

In his moments of contemplation, Laforgue wanted to forget the 'vices' of Paris:

> Oubliant Paris, ses vices, ses cris
> Seul au fond d'une église
>
> (Forgetting Paris, its vices, its cries
> Alone deep inside a Church)[342]

and most significantly for Eliot, retire in a church. Deeply moved by the Sunday mass, he scribbled in his notes: 'Les cloches de la messe du dimanche sonnent a toute volée—*Dieu est présent partout*' ('The belles of the Sunday mass were peeling out—*God is present everywhere.*').[343] His book of poems *Le Sanglot de la Terre* has as epigraph Heine's line:

> Douter de Dieu, c'est douter de la vie elle-même, ce n'est pas moins que la mort.
>
> (To be sceptic about God is to be sceptic about life itself, which is no less than death.)[344]

There is a passage of enlightenment in Laforgue's *Mélanges Posthumes* where the poet speaks of liberation from oneself, from time and space; of the death of the individual consciousness, of the reaching towards a 'great liberty', at the end of illusions.[345] 'Le vouloir est souffrance', he wrote, 'trêve à la souffrance, non-être, Dieu' ('To want is to suffer; at the end of suffering, non-being, God').[346] In one poem in *Le Sanglot de la Terre*, which has Pascal's call for renunciation as epigraph, he described this transcendence:

> Mon être se dissout . . . je me liquéfie
> Je circule à travers l'universelle vie,
> Je suis illimité, je suis Dieu, je suis Tout.
>
> (My soul dissolves . . . I turn into liquid,
> Move across the universal life,
> I become limitless, I become God, Everything.)[347]

Laforgue shows a profound awareness of 'la Force universalle' ('the universal Force') and 'éternité' ('eternity').[348]

Thus, it was not merely Dante who 'passed into a larger life', but Laforgue, too, desperately wanted to do likewise—a message that could not have missed Eliot's eager attention.

Although I do not wish to underplay the towering influences of Dante and Baudelaire on one level, and those of Lancelot Andrewes, Charles Maurras, and Jacques Maritain on another, I would like to draw attention to the fact that Jules Laforgue, who once 'directed [Eliot's] first steps' seems to absorb much of the richness and variety, bends and curves of Eliot's poetry, and foreshadows many of his outstanding qualities. Alain-Fournier, who once initiated him to a more serious study of Laforgue in 1910–11, wrote to Jacques Rivière, 'Quant à Laforgue, il vous tire par la veste à tous les tournants' ('As for Laforgue, he pulls you by your vest at every turning point').[349] Eliot's own texts would one day prove the veracity of this statement.

Laforgue died at 27, but to regard him as merely an 'adolescent' poet, as very often done by Eliot scholars, would be an injustice. He wrote his poetry seriously and it was not his fault that he would not cross young age. As I pointed out earlier, Remy de Gourmont called his works 'the prelude to an oratorio that ended in silence'.[350] One of the few to understand this prelude was T.S. Eliot.

The 'liberating light'[351] (Valery Larbaud's words) of Laforgue enlightened others like Larbaud, Gide, Claudel, Saint-John Perse, Pound, and Aldous Huxley (significantly, Eliot had once attacked Huxley later for mechanically copying Laforgue, without being able to assimilate him 'into a perfect language of his own'[352]) but none of them seem to have come so tantalizingly close to him as the New Englander.

It is Laforgue who incited him to write a new kind of poetry and in some ways anticipated his development and ultimate transcendence, although, it must be admitted, with F.R. Leavis, that 'to learn as Eliot learnt in general from Laforgue is to be original to the point of genius'.[353] The practice canters in the hoof prints of Laforgue took him far.

Eliot confided to Lawrence Durrell that 'he had spent years dreaming of a Laforgue translation',[354] and actually, set about to translate *Hamlet* into English,[355] but found it 'impossible': 'the language was so elliptical and so impacted'.[356] Yet, in a sense, he paid homage to his admired elder brother by translating his dreams throughout his career.

NOTES

1. *Jules Laforgue* (1860–87): Born in Montevideo, Uruguay, he came to France at the age of six; became the Empress Augusta's Reader in Berlin; married an English woman Leah Lee in 1886 in St. Barnabas' Church (London) where, curiously, seventy-one years later, his disciple Eliot would tie the knot with Valerie Fletcher in 1957. They moved to Paris, where Laforgue died of tuberculosis in August 1887.

   One of the leading innovators of poetic form at the time of his sudden death at the age of 27, he was considered to be 'one of the principal poets' of the Symbolist movement by Mallarmé (letter to J. Huret, 1891, quoted in the introduction to Jules Laforgue, *Oeuvres Complètes* [hereafter referred to as *OC*], ed. Jean-Louis Debauve, Lausanne: L'Age d'Homme, 1986, p. 68). He was held in the highest esteem by such luminaries of French poetry as Valéry, Gide, Claudel, Larbaud, Breton, Eluard, and Saint-John Perse. He was also the favourite of Eliot's dearest literary critic Remy de Gourmont, who regarded him as 'l'incontestable maître de la jeunesse…notre adorable frère aîné ('the incontestable master of youth…our adorable elder brother') (Remy de Gourmont, *Le Livre des Masques*, Paris: Mercure de France, 1896, p. 136). In the words of Pierre Seghers, 'Laforgue remains one of the fathers of modern poetry' (*Le Figaro Littéraire,* 15 October 1960). His poetical works include: *Les Complaintes* (1885), *L'Imitation de Notre-Dame la lune* (1886), *Des Fleurs de Bonne Volonté* (1888), and *Derniers Vers* (1890); he wrote a novelette, *Stéphane Vassiliew* (1881), and a volume of short stories *Moralités Légendaires* (1887). His reflective and critical works are compiled in *Mélanges Posthumes* (1903).

2. T.S. Eliot, *To Criticize the Critic* (hereafter referred to as *TCC*), London: Faber and Faber, 1978, p. 126.

3. T.S. Eliot, 'Reflections on Contemporary Poetry', *The Egoist*, July 1919, p. 9.

4. T.S. Eliot, *Letters of T.S. Eliot,* ed. Valerie Eliot, vol. I, London: Faber and Faber, 1988, p. 317.

5. Bernard Bergonzi, *T.S. Eliot*, London: Macmillan, 1972, p. 9.

6. Peter Ackroyd, *T.S. Eliot*, London: Hamish Hamilton, 1984, p. 319.

7. Erik Svarney, *The Men of 1914: T.S. Eliot and Early Modernism*, Philadelphia: Open University Press, Milton Keynes, 1988, p. 46.

8. E.J.H. Greene, *T.S. Eliot et la France*, Paris: Boivin, 1951, p. 52.

9. Laforgue to his sister Marie, 14 May 1883; see Jules Laforgue, *OC*, ed. Jean-Louis Debauve, Lausanne: L'Age d'Homme, 1986, p. 821.

10. Jules Laforgue, *Textes et Critique d'art*, ed. Mireille Dottin, Lille: Presse Universitaire de Lille, 1988, p. 157.

11. Gourmont, *Le Livre des Masques*, p. 206.

12. T.S. Eliot, Review, '*Baudelaire and the Symbolists*, by Peter Quennell', *The Criterion*, January, 1930, p. 359.

13. T.S. Eliot, *The Use of Poetry and the Use of Criticism* (hereafter referred to as *UPUC*), London: Faber and Faber, 1980, p. 34.

14. Eliot, 'Reflections on Contemporary Poetry', p. 39.

15. Ibid.

16. Robert Sencourt, *T.S. Eliot: A Memoir*, ed. Donald Adamson, London: Garnstone Press, 1971, p. 34.

17. Eliot, 'Reflections on Contemporary Poetry', p. 39.

18. Eliot, *TCC*, p. 22.

19. Ibid., p. 23.

20. Ibid., p. 126.

21. Ibid.

22. Ibid., p. 22.

23. Ibid.

24. T.S. Eliot, *Selected Essays* (hereafter referred to as *SE*), London: Faber and Faber, 1951, p. 292.

25. Letter to Théophile Thoré, quoted in Louis Seylaz, *Edgar Poe et les premiers Symbolistes français* [1923], Geneva: Slatkine Rpts., 1979, p. 46.

26. Ibid.

27. Ibid., p. 47.

28. Eliot, *TCC*, p. 126.

29. Ibid., p. 127.

30. René Wellek, *History of Modern Criticism 1750–1950*, vol. V, London: Jonathon Cape, 1986, p. 18. Eliot said in the eighth Clark lecture that the first note about Laforgue in English was by Sir Edmund Gosse (T.S. Eliot, *The Varieties of Metaphysical Poetry* [hereafter referred to as *VMP*], ed. Ronald Schuchard, London: Faber and Faber, 1993, p. 212).

31. Herbert Howarth, *Notes on Some Figures Behind T.S. Eliot*, London: Chatto & Windus, 1965, p. 103.

32. Eliot, Review, '*Baudelaire and the Symbolists*, by Peter Quennell', p. 357.

33. Arthur Symons, *The Symbolist Movement in Literature*, London: Archibald Constable, 1908, p. 105.

34. Ibid., p. 102.

35. Ibid., p. 104.

36. Ibid.

37. Ibid., p. 108.

38. Ibid., p. 111.

39. Ibid., p. 107–8.

40. Ibid., p. 108.

41. Eliot, *SE*, p. 32.

42. Remy de Gourmont, *Le Problème du style*, Paris: Mercure de France, 1902, p. 165.

43. Remy de Gourmont, *Promenades littéraires*, vol. I, Paris: Mercure de France, 1904, p. 105.

44. Gourmont, *Le Livre des Masques*, p. 206.

45. Ibid., p. 208.

46. Gourmont, *Promenades littéraires*, vol. I, p. 110.

47. Ibid., p. 109.

48. Gourmont, *Le Problème du style*, p. 107.

49. Remy de Gourmont, 'La Sensibilité de Jules Laforgué', *Promenades littéraires*, vol. I, Paris: Mercure de France, 1904, p. 106.

50. Gourmont, *Le Livre des Masques*, p. 136.

51. Alain-Fournier and Jacques Rivière, *Correspondance*, 2 vols., Paris: Gallimard, 1991.

52. Howarth, *Some Figures Behind T.S. Eliot*, p. 167.

53. Index of proper names, Fournier and Rivière, *Correspondance*.

54. Fournier to Rivière, 13 September 1905, in Alain-Fournier and Jacques Rivière, *Correspondance*, vol. I, Paris: Gallimard, 1991, p. 141.

55. Fournier to Rivière, 22 January 1906, quoted in Howarth, *Some Figures Behind T.S. Eliot*, p. 155.

56. Fournier to Rivière, 21 March 1906, in Alain-Fournier and Jacques Rivière, *Correspondance*, vol. I, Paris: Gallimard, 1991, pp. 334–5.

57. Fournier's letter to Rivière, in Fournier and Rivière, *Correspondance*, vol. I, p. 381.

58. Eliot, *TCC*, p. 126.

59. Ibid., p. 127.

60. Fournier's letter to Rivière, in Fournier and Rivière, *Correspondance*, vol. I, p. 380.

61. Rivière finally wrote to Fournier on 28 August 1906: 'Sur Laforgue, nous nous croisons, je commence à l'adorer' ('As far as Laforgue is concerned, we cross each other, I begin to adore him'). See Fournier and Rivière, *Correspondance*, vol. I, p. 492.

62. Fournier to Rivière, 13 August 1905, in Alain-Fournier and Jacques Rivière, *Correspondance*, vol. I, Paris: Gallimard, 1991, p. 88.

63. 'Now you can understand the quality of love that warms me towards you, so that I forget our vanity, and treat the shadows like the solid thing'. This translation from the *Purgatorio* (Dante, *Purgatorio*, vol. II, canto XXI, pp. 133–6) is Eliot's own. See T.S. Eliot, 'Dante' [1929], *SE*, London: Faber and Faber, 1951, p. 255.

64. Many years later, Eliot reminisced about his friend Jean Verdenal in T.S. Eliot, 'A Commentary', *The Criterion*, April 1934, p. 452:

I am willing to admit that my own retrospect is touched by a sentimental sunset, the memory of a friend coming across the Luxembourg Gardens in the later afternoon, waving a branch of lilac, a friend who was later (so far I could find out) to be mixed with the mud of Gallipoli.

65. Eliot, *Letters of T.S. Eliot*, vol. I, p. 20, fn.

66. Ackroyd, *T.S. Eliot*, p. 42.

67. Eliot, *Letters of T.S. Eliot*, vol. I, p. 29.

68. A fascinating account of the early days of the *NRF* can be found in Auguste Anglès, *André Gide et le premier groupe de la Nouvelle Revue Française*, 2 vols., Paris: Gallimard, 1978–86.

69. Ibid., vol. II, 1986, p. 110.

70. T.S. Eliot, 'Rencontre', *La Nouvelle Revue Française* (hereafter referred to as *NRF*), 1 March 1925, pp. 657–8.

71. André Gide to Paul Valéry, 23 June 1891, quoted in Jean-Louis Debauve, *Laforgue en son temps*, Neuchâtel: A la Baconnière, 1972, p. 185.

72. Valery Larbaud, 'A propósito de la publicación de un libro inédito de Julio Laforgue', *La Nación*, 15 April 1923.

73. T.S. Eliot, *Notes Towards the Definition of Culture* (hereafter referred to as *NTDC*), London: Faber and Faber, 1948, p. 115.

74. Howarth, *Some Figures Behind T.S. Eliot*, p. 105.

75. Eliot himself drew attention to this point in his lecture at the Italian Institute in 1950:

   Such early influences, the influences which so to speak, first introduce one to oneself, are, I think, due to an impression which is in one aspect, the recognition of a *temperament akin to ones own*. (Eliot, *TCC*, p. 126; my italics)

76. Jules Laforgue, *Poésies Complètes*, ed. Pascal Pia, Paris: Le Livre de Poche, 1970, p. 147.

77. Stephen Spender, *Eliot*, Glasgow: Fontana Press, 1986, p. 48.

78. Quoted in Sencourt, *T.S. Eliot: A Memoir*, p. 168.

79. François Ruchon, *Jules Laforgue, sa vie, son oeuvre*, Geneva: Albert Ciana, 1924, p. 38.

80. 'Manners', wrote Conrad Aiken, 'is an obsolete word nowadays, but he had them. He did things with an enviable grace'. See *Life*, 15 January 1965, p. 92, quoted in Lyndall Gordon, *Eliot's Early Years*, Oxford: Oxford University Press, 1977, p. 31.

81. Ackroyd, *T.S. Eliot*, p. 279.

82. Ruchon, *Jules Laforgue, sa vie, son oeuvre*, p. 38.

83. Quoted in Ronald Bush, *T.S. Eliot: A Study in Character and Style*, New York: Oxford University Press, 1984, p. 104.

84. Ruchon, *Jules Laforgue, sa vie, son oeuvre*, p. 16.

85. Jules Laforgue, 'Albums, *Des Fleurs de Bonne Volonté*, XIX', in *Poésies Complètes*, ed. Pascal Pia, Paris: Le Livre de Poche, 1970, p. 219.

86. Ruchon, *Jules Laforgue, sa vie, son oeuvre*, p. 15.

87. Quoted in Ruchon, *Jules Laforgue, sa vie, son oeuvre*, p. 16.

88. Lyndall Gordon, *Eliot's New Life*, Oxford: Oxford University Press, 1988, p. 92.

89. Frank Kermode, *An Appetite for Poetry*, Glasgow: Fontana Press, 1989, pp. 109–10.

90. Laforgue to his sister Marie, 14 May 1883, in Laforgue, *OC*, p. 821.

91. Laforgue, *Textes et Critique d'art*, p. 157.

92. Laforgue, *OC*, p. 685–7.

93. Ibid., pp. 720–2, 728–9, 740–1, 745–6, 781–2, 830–1.

94. Ibid., p. 798.

95. Michael Collie, *Jules Laforgue*, London: University of London Press, 1977, p. 8.

96. Laforgue to Mme Mültzer, 5 February 1882, in Jules Laforgue, *OC*, ed. Jean-Louis Debauve, Lausanne: L'Age d'Homme, 1986, p. 753.

97. Collie, *Jules Laforgue*, p. 1.

98. *Dictionnaire de la littérature française et francophone*, vol. II, Paris: Librairie Larousse, 1988, p. 772.

99. Francis Scarfe, 'Eliot and Nineteenth Century French Poetry', in *Eliot in Perspective*, ed. Graham Martin, London: Macmillan, 1970, p. 53.

100. Greene writes: 'Sa passion pour Laforgue est exclusive: it voit les Elisabéthains à travers Laforgue'. ('His passion for Laforgue was exclusive: he saw the Elizabethans through Laforgue.') See Greene, *T.S. Eliot et la France*, p. 19.

101. Laforgue, *Poésies Complètes*, p. 33.

102. Laforgue, *OC*, pp. 685–7.

103. T.S. Eliot, 'The Love Song of J. Alfred Prufrock', *The Complete Poems and Plays of T.S. Eliot* (hereafter referred to as *CPP*), London: Faber and Faber, 1990, p. 15.

104. Jules Laforgue, 'Avis, je vous prie', in *Poésies Complètes*, ed. Pascal Pia, Paris: Le Livre de Poche, 1970, p. 177.

105. Paul Valéry writes: 'Le plus grand poète possible—c'est ce système nerveux. L'inventeur de tout—mais plutôt le seul poète'. ('The biggest possible poet—is the nervous system. Inventor of everything—rather the only poet). See Paul Valéry, *Oeuvres de Paul Valéry*, vol. I, Paris: Bibliotheque de la Pleiade, 1957, p. 335.

106. F.R. Leavis, *New Bearings in English Poetry*, London: Chatto & Windus, 1971, p. 115.

107. T.S. Eliot to Richard Aldington, 26 October 1921, quoted in the introduction to T.S. Eliot, *The Waste Land: A Facsimile and Transcript*, ed. Valerie Eliot, London: Faber and Faber, 1971, pp. xxii, xxxiii.

108. Jules Laforgue, *Mélanges Posthumes* [1903], Geneva: Slatkine Reprints, 1979, p. 7.

109. Collie, *Jules Laforgue*, p. 3.

110. Laforgue, *Mélanges Posthumes*, p. 9.

111. Jules Laforgue, 'Stéphane Vassiliew', in *OC*, ed. Jean-Louis Debauve, Lausanne: L'Age d'Homme, 1986, p. 478.

112. Laforgue, *Moralités Légendaires*, ed. Pascal Pia, Paris: Gallimard, 1977, p. 49.

113. Laforgue, 'Stéphane Vassiliew', p. 462.

114. Laforgue, *OC*, p. 463.

115. Ibid., p. 753.

116. Laforgue, *Moralités Légendaires*, p. 9.

117. Ibid., p. 204.

118. Ibid., p. 22.

119. Pascal Pia, 'Notes', in Jules Laforgue, *Moralités Légendaires*, ed. Pascal Pia, Paris: Gallimard, 1977, p. 236.

120. Laforgue, *Moralités Légendaires*, p. 30.

121. Ibid., p. 31.

122. T.S. Eliot, *CPP*, London: Faber and Faber, 1990, p. 16.

123. Laforgue, *Moralités Légendaires*, p. 45.

124. Indeed, Eliot quotes Laforgue's 'Hamlet'. See Eliot, *VMP*, pp. 212–13.

125. Hugh Kenner, *The Invisible Poet,* London: Methuen, 1985, p. 16.

126. Laforgue, *Mélanges Posthumes*, p. 9.

127. Collie, *Jules Laforgue*, p. 13.

128. Larbaud, 'A propósito de la publicación de un libro inédito de Julio Laforgue', *La Nación*, 15 April 1923.

129. Symons, *Symbolist Movement in Literature*, p. 109.

130. Laforgue, *OC*, p. 753.

131. Pascal Pia, 'Foreword', in Jules Laforgue, *Moralités Légendaires*, ed. Pascal Pia, Paris: Gallimard, 1977, p. 9.

132. Eliot wrote fan letters to Groucho Marx. See Gordon, *Eliot's Early Years*, p. 32.

133. *Life*, January 1965, p. 92, quoted in Gordon, *Eliot's Early Years*, p. 32.

134. Jules Laforgue, 'Complainte de Lord Pierrot', in *Poésies Complètes*, ed. Pascal Pia, Paris: Le Livre de Poche, 1970, p. 84.

135. Now published in Eliot, *VMP*, these lectures should bring a new perspective to Eliot's poetic and critical philosophy.

136. Eliot, *VMP*, pp. 212–13.

137. Ibid., p. 216–17.

138. Lawrence Durrell, *A Key to Modern Poetry*, Norman: University of Oklahoma Press, 1972, p. 39.

139. Quoted in Durrell, *Key to Modern Poetry*, p. 39.

140. Eliot, *SE*, p. 289.

141. Durrell, *Key to Modern Poetry*, p. 39.

142. James Hiddleston, ed., *Laforgue Aujourd'hui*, Paris: Lib. José Corti, 1988, p. 180.

143. D. Fokkema, *Issues in General and Comparative Literature*, Calcutta: Papyrus, 1987, p. 103.

144. Laforgue, *Textes et Critique d'art*, p. 166.

145. Eliot, *VMP*, p. 283.

146. T.S. Eliot, *The Sacred Wood* (hereafter referred to as *SW*), London: Methuen, 1982, p. 58.

147. Symons, *Symbolist Movement in Literature*, p. 105.

148. Jules Laforgue, 'Nuages', in *Poésies Complètes*, ed. Pascal Pia, Paris: Le Livre de Poche, 1970, p. 370.

149. Eliot, *SW*, p. 53.

150. Eliot, *SW*, p. 117.

151. Eliot, *TCC*, p. 19.

152. Even in 1926, Eliot spoke with equal verve about Laforgue's predicament before this 'insoluble problem', which still haunted him as it did in his early years of creativity (See Eliot, *VMP*, p. 217).

153. Jules Laforgue, 'Bouffée de printemps', in *Poésies Complètes*, ed. Pascal Pia, Paris: Le Livre de Poche, 1970, p. 406.

154. Laforgue, *Mélanges Posthumes*, p. 20.

155. Jules Laforgue, 'Préludes autobiographiques, *Les Complaintes*', in *Poésies Complètes*, ed. Pascal Pia, Paris: Le Livre de Poche, 1970, p. 30.

156. Jules Laforgue, 'Complainte des pianos', in *Poésies Complètes*, ed. Pascal Pia, Paris: Le Livre de Poche, 1970, p. 30.

157. Jules Laforgue, 'Pour le livre d'amour, *Le Sanglot de la Terre*', in *Poésies Complètes*, ed. Pascal Pia, Paris: Le Livre de Poche, 1970, p. 337.

158. Jules Laforgue, 'Derniers Vers', XII, in *Poésies Complètes*, ed. Pascal Pia, Paris: Le Livre de Poche, 1970, p. 312.

159. Collie, *Jules Laforgue*, p. 3.

160. Jules Laforgue, 'Rabâchages, *Le Sanglot de la Terre*', in *OC*, ed. Jean-Louis Debauve, Lausanne: L'Age d'Homme, 1986, p. 367.

161. Eliot, *CPP*, p. 14.

162. T.S. Eliot, 'Preludes', *CPP*, London: Faber and Faber, 1990, p. 23.

163. Jules Laforgue, 'Complainte du sage, de Paris', in *Poésies Complètes*, ed. Pascal Pia, Paris: Le Livre de Poche, 1970, p. 129.

164. Eliot, 'The Love Song of J. Alfred Prufrock', p. 16.

165. Laforgue, 'Complainte des pianos', p. 47.

166. Ibid.

167. T.S. Eliot, 'Portrait of a Lady', *CPP*, London: Faber and Faber, 1990, p. 20.

168. T.S. Eliot, 'Fragment of an Agon', *CPP*, London: Faber and Faber, 1990, p. 125.

169. Jules Laforgue, 'Litanies de Misère, *Le Sanglot de la Terre*', in *OC*, ed. Jean-Louis Debauve, Lausanne: L'Age d'Homme, 1986, p. 423.

170. Jules Laforgue, 'Complainte d'un certain dimanche', in *Poésies Complètes*, ed. Pascal Pia, Paris: Le Livre de Poche, 1970, p. 52.

171. Eliot, 'Portrait of a Lady', p. 19.

172. Jules Laforgue, 'Complainte de l'automne monotone', in *Poésies Complètes*, ed. Pascal Pia, Paris: Le Livre de Poche, 1970, p. 66.

173. Eliot, *CPP*, p. 22.

174. Jules Laforgue, 'Pierrots, *L'Imitation de Notre-Dame la lune*', in *Poésies Complètes*, ed. Pascal Pia, Paris: Le Livre de Poche, 1970, p. 145.

175. Eliot, 'The Love Song of J. Alfred Prufrock', p. 13.

176. Laforgue, 'Pierrots, *L'Imitation*', p. 145.

177. Laforgue, *Mélanges Posthumes*, p. 32.

178. Jules Laforgue, 'Complainte de la lune en province', in *Poésies Complètes*, ed. Pascal Pia, Paris: Le Livre de Poche, 1970, p. 61.

179. T.S. Eliot, 'Rhapsody on a Windy Night', *CPP*, London: Faber and Faber, 1990, p. 25.

180. Jules Laforgue, 'A la mémoire d'une chatte naine', in *Poésies Complètes*, ed. Pascal Pia, Paris: Le Livre de Poche, 1970, p. 410.

181. Jules Laforgue, 'Petites misère de juillet, *Le Concile Féerique*', in *Poésies Complètes*, ed. Pascal Pia, Paris: Le Livre de Poche, 1970, p. 202.

182. Eliot, 'Rhapsody on a Windy Night', p. 25.

183. Jules Laforgue, 'L'Imitation', in *Poésies Complètes*, ed. Pascal Pia, Paris: Le Livre de Poche, 1970, p. 140.

184. Laforgue, *OC*, p. 443.

185. Laforgue, *Moralités Légendaires*, p. 30.

186. Eliot, 'Portrait of a Lady', p. 19.
187. Laforgue, *Mélanges Posthumes*, p. 28.
188. Laforgue, 'Complainte de la lune en province', p. 61.
189. Howarth, *Some Figures Behind T.S. Eliot*, p. 107.
190. Laforgue, *OC*, p. 655.
191. Howarth, *Some Figures Behind T.S. Eliot*, p. 107.
192. Collie, *Jules Laforgue*, p. 9.
193. Jules Laforgue, 'Hamlet', *Moralités Légendaires*, Paris: Gallimard, 1977, p. 28.
194. Laforgue, *Moralités Légendaires*, p. 46.
195. Eliot, *CPP*, p. 66.
196. Laforgue, *Mélanges Posthumes*, p. 30.
197. Ibid., p. 32.
198. Ibid., p. 33.
199. Laforgue, 'Complainte d'un certain dimanche', p. 53.
200. Laforgue, *Mélanges Posthumes*, pp. 30–1.
201. Eliot, *CPP*, p. 15.
202. Laforgue, *Mélanges Posthumes*, p. 31.
203. Ibid.
204. Jules Laforgue, 'Derniers Vers', VII, in *Poésies Complètes*, ed. Pascal Pia, Paris: Le Livre de Poche, 1970, p. 299.
205. Laforgue, *Mélanges Posthumes*, pp. 30–1.
206. Grover Smith, *T.S. Eliot's Poetry and Plays: A Study in Sources and Meaning*, Chicago: University of Chicago Press, 1961, p. 305.
207. Laforgue, *Poésies Complètes*, p. 101.
208. Charles Baudelaire, *Oeuvres Complètes*, vol. I, Paris: Bibliothèque de la Pléiade, 1990, p. 47.
209. Laforgue, 'Derniers Vers', XII, in *Poésies Complètes*, p. 311.
210. Laforgue, *OC*, pp. 359–61.
211. Ibid., p. 360.
212. These metaphysical questionings are a characteristic of Laforgue's poetry. No other French poet shows this trait.
213. Jules Laforgue, 'Complainte de l'oubli des Morts', *Poésies Complètes*, ed. Pascal Pia, Paris: Le Livre de Poche, 1970, p. 104.
214. Jules Laforgue, 'Noël Résigné, *Le Sanglot de la Terre*', in *OC*, ed. Jean-Louis Debauve, Lausanne: L'Age d'Homme, 1986, p. 370.
215. Jules Laforgue, 'Derniers Vers', II, in *Poésies Complètes*, ed. Pascal Pia, Paris: Le Livre de Poche, 1970, p. 283.
216. Laforgue, 'Derniers Vers', VII, in *Poésies Complètes*, p. 296.
217. Ibid.
218. Laforgue 'Rabâchages, *Le Sanglot de la Terre*', p. 368.
219. Jules Laforgue, 'Autre complainte de Lord Pierrot', in *Poésies Complètes*, ed. Pascal Pia, Paris: Le Livre de Poche, 1970, p. 85.
220. Eliot, 'The Love Song of J. Alfred Prufrock', p. 16.
221. Eliot, 'Portrait of a Lady', p. 20.
222. T.S. Eliot, 'The Waste Land', I, *CPP*, London: Faber and Faber, 1990, p. 63.

223. Ibid., II, p. 65.
224. T.S. Eliot, 'The Rock', *CPP*, London: Faber and Faber, 1990, p. 154.
225. T.S. Eliot, 'Burnt Norton', III, *CPP*, London: Faber and Faber, 1990, p. 174.
226. Laforgue, *OC*, p. 655.
227. Jules Laforgue, 'A Saint-Cloud, *Le Sanglot de la Terre*', in *OC*, ed. Jean-Louis Debauve, Lausanne: L'Age d'Homme, 1986, p. 366.
228. T.S. Matthews, *Great Tom: Notes Towards the Definition of T. S. Eliot*, London: Wiedenfeld and Nicholson, 1974, p. 159.
229. T.S. Eliot, 'Mr. Apollinax', *CPP*, London: Faber and Faber, 1990, p. 31.
230. Jules Laforgue, 'Climat, faune et flaure de la lune, *L'Imitation*', in *Poésies Complètes*, ed. Pascal Pia, Paris: Le Livre de Poche, 1970, p. 55.
231. Jules Laforgue, 'Derniers soupirs', in *Poésies Complètes*, ed. Pascal Pia, Paris: Le Livre de Poche, 1970, p. 407.
232. Eliot, 'The Waste Land', V, *CPP*, p. 73.
233. Jules Laforgue, 'Pierrot fumiste', in *OC*, ed. Jean-Louis Debauve, Lausanne: L'Age d'Homme, 1986, p. 511.
234. Jules Laforgue, 'Complainte des cloches', in *Poésies Complètes*, ed. Pascal Pia, Paris: Le Livre de Poche, 1970, p. 97.
235. Laforgue, *Moralités Légendaires*, p. 163.
236. Eliot, 'The Waste Land', I, *CPP*, p. 74.
237. Eliot, 'The Waste Land', III, *CPP*, p. 67.
238. Ibid., p. 169.
239. T.S. Eliot, 'Sweeney Agonistes', *CPP*, London: Faber and Faber, 1990, p. 116.
240. Eliot, 'Fragment of an Agon', p. 126.
241. Eliot, 'Burnt Norton', V, *CPP*, p. 175.
242. Eliot, 'The Waste Land', V, *CPP*, p. 74.
243. Laforgue, *Poésies Complètes*, p. 108.
244. Eliot, *CPP*, pp. 16–17.
245. Laforgue, 'Préludes autobiographiques, *Les Complaintes*', p. 33.
246. Jules Laforgue, 'L'Aquarium de Berlin', *Mélanges Posthumes*, Geneva: Slatkine Reprints, 1979, p. 35.
247. Jules Laforgue, 'Après-dîner torride et stagnant', *Mélanges Posthumes*, Geneva: Slatkine Reprints, 1979, p. 39.
248. Laforgue, *Moralités Légendaires*, pp. 77–8.
249. Eliot, 'Mr. Apollinax', p. 31.
250. Eliot, *CPP*, pp. 57, 71.
251. Ibid., p. 109.
252. Ibid., p. 99.
253. T.S. Eliot, 'East Coker', *CPP*, London: Faber and Faber, 1990, p. 178.
254. Ibid., p. 179.
255. Ibid., p. 183.
256. T.S. Eliot, 'The Dry Salvages', *CPP*, London: Faber and Faber, 1990, p. 188.
257. Ibid., p. 184.
258. Jules Laforgue, 'Complainte d'une convalescence en mai', in *Poésies Complètes*, ed. Pascal Pia, Paris: Le Livre de Poche, 1970, p. 126.

259. T.S. Eliot, 'Little Gidding', *CPP*, London: Faber and Faber, 1990, p. 198.
260. Kenner, *The Invisible Poet*, p. 19.
261. Laforgue, *Mélanges Posthumes*, p. 9; my italics.
262. Laforgue to Gustave Kahn, 12 or 19 December 1880, in Jules Laforgue, *OC*, ed. Jean-Louis Debauve, Lausanne: L'Age d'Homme, 1986, p. 685.
263. Kenner, *The Invisible Poet*, p. 34.
264. Laforgue, *Mélanges Posthumes*, p. 14.
265. B. Rajan, 'The Overwhelming Question', in *T.S. Eliot: 'Prufrock', 'Gerontion', 'Ash-Wednesday' and Other Shorter Poems*, ed. B.C. Southam, London: Macmillan, 1993, p. 115.
266. Laforgue, *Mélanges Posthumes*, pp. 19–20.
267. Laforgue, *Poésies Complètes*, p. 460.
268. Laforgue, *Mélanges Posthumes*, p. 10.
269. Ibid.
270. Ibid., p. 13.
271. Ibid., p. 10.
272. Ibid.
273. Laforgue, *OC*, p. 365.
274. Ibid., p. 800.
275. Craig Raine, 'The Waste Land as a Buddhist Poem', *Times Literary Supplement*, May 4, 1973.
276. Matthews, *Great Tom*, p. 35.
277. Excerpt in Michael Grant, ed., *T.S. Eliot: The Critical Heritage*, vol. II, London: Routledge and Kegan Paul, 1982, pp. 140–1.
278. Stephen Spender, 'Remembering Eliot', in *T.S. Eliot: The Man and his Work*, ed. Allen Tate, London: Chatto & Windus, 1967, p. 40.
279. *Dictionnaire de la litterature française et francophone* vol. II, p. 772.
280. Eliot, *VMP*, p. 216.
281. Matthews, *Great Tom*, p. 35; Ackroyd, *T.S. Eliot*, p. 47.
282. Ackroyd, *T.S. Eliot*, p. 47; Gordon, *Eliot's Early Years*, p. 57.
283. Laforgue, *Poésies Complètes*, p. 205.
284. Laforgue, 'Préludes autobiographiques, *Les Complaintes*', p. 33.
285. Jules Laforgue, 'Lettres à un ami', in *Laforgue Aujourd'hui*, ed. James Hiddleston, Paris: Lib. José Corti, 1988, p. 39.
286. Laforgue, *Mélanges Posthumes*, p. 15.
287. Laforgue, 'Préludes autobiographiques, *Les Complaintes*', p. 33.
288. Laforgue, 'Complainte d'une convalescence en mai', p. 125.
289. Eliot, 'The Waste Land', p. 74.
290. G.M. Turnell, 'The Poetry of Jules Laforgue', *Scrutiny*, September 1936, pp. 128–49.
291. Ibid., p. 130.
292. Gordon, *Eliot s Early Years*, p. 75; also Ackroyd, *T.S. Eliot*, p. 31.
293. Quoted in Collie, *Jules Laforgue*, p. 27.
294. Laforgue, 'Pour le livre d'amour, *Le Sanglot de la Terre*', p. 337.

295. Laforgue to Charles Henry, on 15 May 1882, in Jules Laforgue, *OC*, ed. Jean-Louis Debauve, Lausanne: L'Age d'Homme, 1986, p. 781.

296. Jules Laforgue, 'Dimanches, *Des Fleurs de Bonne Volonté*', in *Poésies Complètes*, ed. Pascal Pia, Paris: Le Livre de Poche, 1970, p. 266.

297. Laforgue, 'Pour le livre d'amour, *Le Sanglot de la Terre*', p. 425.

298. Laforgue, *Poésies Complètes*, p. 64.

299. Jules Laforgue, 'Locution des Pierrots, *L'Imitation*', in *Poésies Complètes*, ed. Pascal Pia, Paris: Le Livre de Poche, 1970, p. 157.

300. Laforgue, *Poésies Complètes*, p. 186.

301. Ibid., p. 90.

302. Grover Smith, 'Charles-Louis Philippe and T.S. Eliot', *American Literature*, November 1950, pp. 254–9.

303. Laforgue, *OC*, p. 741.

304. Collie, *Jules Laforgue*, p. 15.

305. Frank Kermode, *Continuities*, London: Routledge and Kegan Paul, 1968, p. 62.

306. Laforgue, 'Avis, je vous prie', p. 177.

307. Ackroyd, *T.S. Eliot*, p. 66.

308. T.S. Eliot, 'Marina', *CPP*, London: Faber and Faber, 1990, p. 109.

309. Matthews, *Great Tom*, p. 22.

310. Leavis, *New Bearings*, p. 93.

311. T.S. Eliot, *Inventions of the March Hare*, ed. Christopher Ricks. London: Faber and Faber, 1996, p. 383.

312. Jules Laforgue, 'Pierrots II, *L'Imitation*', in *Poésies Complètes*, p. 146.

313. Gordon, *Eliot's New Life*, p. 49.

314. Remy de Gourmont, *Le Chemin de velours*, Paris: G. Crès, 1923, p. 239.

315. Ibid.

316. Ibid., p. 240.

317. Remy de Gourmont, *Esthétique de la langue française*, Paris: Mercure de France, p. 92.

318. Laforgue, *Poésies Complètes*, p. 392.

319. A.C. Partridge, *The Language of Modern Poetry*, London: André Deutsch, 1976, p. 179.

320. Pierre Raboul, *Laforgue*, Paris: Hatier, 1960, p. 62.

321. For this part of my chapter, I am indebted to Madeleine Betts, *L' Univers de Laforgue à travers les mots*, Paris: la Pensee Universelle, 1978.

322. T.S. Eliot, 'Burbank with a Baedeker', *CPP*, London: Faber and Faber, 1990, p. 40.

323. Eliot, 'Portrait of a Lady', p. 18.

324. T.S. Eliot, 'Sweeney Erect', *CPP*, London: Faber and Faber, 1990, pp. 42–3.

325. T.S. Eliot, 'The Hippopotamus', *CPP*, London: Faber and Faber, 1990, pp. 49–50.

326. T.S. Eliot, 'Whispers of Immortality', *CPP*, London: Faber and Faber, 1990, pp. 52–3.

327. T.S. Eliot, 'Mr. Eliot's Sunday Morning Service', *CPP*, London: Faber and Faber, pp. 54–5.
328. T.S. Eliot, 'Sweeney among the Nightingales', *CPP*, London: Faber and Faber, p. 56–7.
329. Eliot, 'The Waste Land', p. 64.
330. Laforgue, 'Pierrots II, *L'Imitation*', in *Poésies Complètes*, p. 145.
331. Laforgue, *Mélanges Posthumes*, p. 10.
332. Ibid., p. 13.
333. I have borrowed Ellmann's words from Maud Ellmann, *The Poetics of Impersonality*, Sussex: The Harvester Press, 1987, p. 107. Ellmann does not see the possible Laforgue connection.
334. Jules Laforgue, 'L'Oubli, *Le Sanglot de la Terre*', in *OC*, ed. Jean-Louis Debauve, Lausanne: L'Age d'Homme, 1986, p. 363.
335. Eliot, Review, '*Baudelaire and the Symbolists*, by Peter Quennell', p. 357.
336. Laforgue, *Poésies Complètes*, p. 312.
337. Jules Laforgue, 'Derniers Vers', III, in *Poésies Complètes*, ed. Pascal Pia, Paris: Le Livre de Poche, 1970, p. 285.
338. T.S. Eliot, '*Ash-Wednesday*', *CPP*, London: Faber and Faber, 1990, p. 98.
339. Eliot, *TCC*, p. 126.
340. Laforgue, *OC*, p. 763.
341. 'I live by an absolute philosophy and not in fits and starts. . . . I am a good soul who amuses himself as best as he can, but who has a faith and believes in his mission, just as you say'—quoted in Jean-Louis Debauve, *Laforgue en son temps: Langages et documents*, Neuchâtel: A la Baconnière, 1972, p. 199.
342. Jules Laforgue, 'Apotheose', in *Poésies Complètes*, ed. Pascal Pia, Paris: Le Livre de Poche, 1970, p. 400.
343. Jules Laforgue, *Feuilles Volantes*, ed. Daniel Grojnowski, Paris: Sycamore, 1981, p. 82.
344. Jules Laforgue, *Le Sanglot de la Terre*, in *OC*, ed. Jean-Louis Debauve, Lausanne: L'Age d'Homme, 1986, p. 265.
345. Laforgue, *Mélanges Posthumes*, p. 11.
346. Ibid., p. 66.
347. Laforgue, 'L'Oubli', p. 365.
348. Laforgue, *Poésies Complètes*, p. 392.
349. Fournier and Rivière, *Correspondance*, vol. I, p. 112.
350. Gourmont, *Le Livre des Masques*, p. 206.
351. See note 128.
352. T.S. Eliot, 'London Letter', *The Dial*, April 1921, p. 452; quoted in Greene, *T.S. Eliot et la France*, p. 21.
353. Leavis, *New Bearings*, p. 79.
354. Durrell gives this significant information in Laforgue, *OC*, p. 18.
355. T.S. Eliot to Conrad Aiken, 21 August 1916, in T.S. Eliot, *Letters of T.S. Eliot*, ed. Valerie Eliot, vol. I, London: Faber and Faber, 1988, p. 143.
356. T.S. Eliot to Durrell, see note 338.

2

Baudelaire and Eliot
Damnation and the Necessity
of Christianity

WE HAVE NO REASON TO quarrel with the noted French critic and poet Pierre-Jean Jouve, who claims:

Baudelaire[1] est le premier poète malheureux et conscient de porter une malédiction, ce par quoi devait commencer une poésie française qui ne fut ni un discours ni un jeu de rimes. Baudelaire est par son malheur et son intrépidité, par son pouvoir aussi, le fondateur d'un acte de poésie qui devait se continuer avec Mallarmé, Rimbaud, Verlaine et même Apollinaire.

(Baudelaire is the first poet who was at the same time unhappy and conscious of bearing a curse, heralding a French poetry that was neither a discourse nor a game of rhymes. Baudelaire is—because of his unhappiness and intrepidity, and also his power—the founder of an act of poetry which continued with Mallarmé, Rimbaud, Verlaine and even Apollinaire.)[2]

It was 'un chemin de sacrifice' ('a way of sacrifice')[3] reminding us of the sentence repeated several times in *Journaux Intimes:* '*Avant tout*, être un grand homme et un saint pour soi-même' ('*Before everything*, to be a great man and a saint for oneself').[4] Eliot's 1930 essay on Baudelaire reveals that he had instinctively understood this fundamental tortuous paradox of Baudelaire, his excesses, complications and subversions. As the latter confessed to his lawyer Narcisse-Désiré Ancelle in a letter, he put into his 'atrocious' book, *Les Fleurs du Mal*, 'tout mon coeur, toute ma tendresse, toute ma religion (travestie), toute ma haine. Il est vrai que j'écrirai le contraire, que je jurerai mes grands dieux que c'est un livre d'art pur, de singerie, de jonglerie. . .' ('my whole heart, all my tenderness all my religion (travesty), all my hate. It is true that I shall write the opposite, that I shall swear by all my gods that this is a book of pure art, of antics, of jugglery. . .').[5] This offers a useful conspectus on the problem of modernity, which can be a secret language, a cipher, a ritual dance that precludes any satisfactory classification. It was a siege against the cliché.

Few, with the possible exception of Dante, expressed the whole range of human emotions of his time in such a ruthlessly uncompromising manner. Baudelaire's poetry redefines the moral position of the poet in a world of suffering. It was no doubt he who pioneered and doctored the metaphysics of modernity in French poetry, while 'the pattern was yet incomplete',[6] thus becoming, in Rimbaud's words, the 'premier voyant, le roi des poètes' ('first seer, the king of poets').[7] To Eliot, he was 'a fragmentary Dante'[8] whose 'true claim as an artist' is that he was searching not for a 'superficial form' but 'a form of life'.[9] Eliot believed that Baudelaire was 'the human prototype of new experience'.[10]

Always the finest critic of his own works, Eliot never felt tired of reiterating that he belonged to the tradition which starts with Baudelaire and without which his own poetry 'would hardly be conceivable'.[11] 'The currency of French poetry which sprang from Baudelaire', he wrote in *The Criterion*[12] 'is one which has affected all English poetry that matters'. The tremendous impact of the vision and structural practice of Dante and Laforgue notwithstanding Baudelaire's influence on Eliot's moral consciousness was seminal, although an unbiased assessment of their relationship has rarely been attempted.

The trend to ignore Baudelaire as a possible influence on Eliot was probably set by Richard Aldington in 1922, when he placed the latter's works in a tradition of French poetry that ran through Laforgue and Verlaine, Rimbaud and Corbière, and Villon and the goliards, but made no mention of Baudelaire.[13] René Taupin's pioneering study on the influence of symbolism on American poetry between 1910 and 1920 has small sections on Gautier, Laforgue, and Corbière, but nothing at all on Baudelaire. The trend continues till today. But, in all fairness, one must recognize the estimates of Edward Greene, Herbert Howarth, and, more recently, Kerry Weinberg. However, they have not shown the binary vision to gauge the historicity of the relationship and separate the essential from the contingent.

A random survey, I believe, would show that English critical attention has been a little tendentiously riveted on Eliot's debt to Baudelaire's 'fourmillante cité, cité pleine de rêves' ('swarming city, city full of dreams')[14] which he specifically acknowledged in the notes appended to *The Waste Land*. In my opinion, this has etiolated Eliot criticism by tending to overlook the moral aspect of the relationship.

Before we move on to Baudelaire's cosmopolitanism, let us examine what may be considered a more vital point of contact between two great poets.

Eliot is said to have confessed to Edward Greene[15] that he took up Baudelaire as early as in his second year at Harvard in 1907 or 1908, when it made a 'great impact' on him. We guess it was the end of his Swinburnian sojourn. He learnt that 'life is not a system of gig-lamps systematically arranged',[16] which could lead to a 'transmutation de la réalité naturelle en surréalité poétique' ('transmutation of the natural reality into a surrealist poetics'),[17] an exploration of the 'matière inconsciente' ('unconscious matter').[18] This was an entry into a world of correspondences, 'the forest of symbols'. In Eliot's words, it showed 'the possibility of the fusion between the sordidly realistic and the phantasmagoric, the possibility of the juxtaposition between the matter-of-fact and the fantastic'.[19] 'From him, as from Laforgue', Eliot would admit, 'I learnt that the sort of material I had, the sort of experience that an adolescent had had, in an industrial city in America, could be the material for poetry; and that the source of new poetry in what had been regarded hitherto as the impossible, the sterile, the intractably unpoetic'.[20] It is Baudelaire who seems to have taught young Eliot that anguish, boredom, and sordidness could be the theme of the new poetry, that the stereotyped rhetoric could be replaced by living associations. Charles Baudelaire was the first to create (in Victor Hugo's words) 'un frisson nouveau' ('a new shiver')[21] in French poetry, to 'break the neck of eloquence',[22] and almost singlehandedly cast aside the old discourse to reconstruct the new. He was possibly the first to feel the need to purify the speech of the tribe; the first to realize well before Eliot that 'words will not stay in place,/Will not stay still'.[23] This was the beginning of an 'intolerable wrestle/With words and meanings'[24] in French poetry.

Eliot could have found an echo of his own impressions in Remy de Gourmont, the critic he trusted most:

Toute la littérature actuelle et surtout celle que l'on appelle symboliste est Baudelairienne, non sans doute par la technique extérieure, mais la technique interne et spirituelle, par le sens du mystère, par le souci d'écouter ce que disent les choses, par le désir de correspondre, d'ame à âme, avec l'obscure pensée répandue dans la nuit du monde.

The whole literature of today and especially what one calls symbolist literature is Baudelairian, surely not because of its external technique, but the sense of mystery, the anxiety to listen to what the things say, the desire to correspond, soul to soul, with the obscure thought spread over the night.[25]

Gourmont's statement throws light on Eliot's debt to others (especially Laforgue and Corbière) discussed in the present book.

Although he was soon to come under the 'daemonic spell'[26] of Laforgue, which in my opinion, was to be lifelong, Eliot never underestimated Baudelaire's importance. He always acknowledged his debt to the 'current of poetry *which sprang from Baudelaire*'.[27] Referring to what he called 'metaphysical' poetry of the nineteenth century, he said: 'Its parent is Baudelaire'.[28] Significantly, of all French poets, Baudelaire is the only one he actually wrote about, and that too, at least four times: 'The Lesson of Baudelaire' (1922),[29] 'Poet and Saint' (1927),[30] 'Baudelaire in Our Time' (1927),[31] and 'Baudelaire' (1930),[32] which was the preface to Baudelaire's *Intimate Journals*.[33]

Despite his earlier identification with Jules Laforgue, his 'kin' and 'brother', Eliot seemed to know in his heart of hearts that Laforgue was, after all, no more than Baudelaire's 'minor successor'.[34] This growing reverence for Baudelaire, 'by far the greatest of the French symbolists',[35] is evident in his essays on Baudelaire, as well as his review of Peter Quennell's *Baudelaire and the Symbolists in The Criterion*,[36] not to speak of the other numerous references at other places. In one of the most illuminating asides on Baudelaire, Eliot observed that he should be considered (along with Donne and Marvell) 'the inventor of an attitude, a system of feelings or of morals'.[37] This I would like to regard as a seminal proposition, which could help us to contextualize Eliot's creative responses to the French poet in the right historical perspective.

In his attempt to overhaul the poetic discourse, Eliot did not fail to see that the amalgamation of the material with the spiritual, the finite with the infinite (Baudelaire himself recognizes the 'perpetual and simultaneous rapport of the ideal and the real' as his objective in his personal notes[38]) seemed more clearly discernible in Baudelaire than in either Laforgue or Corbière. In Baudelaire's words:

La modernité, c'est le transitoire, le fugitif, le contigent, la moitié de Tart, dont l'autre moitié est l'éternel et l'immuable.

(Modernity is the transitory, the fugitive, the contingent, the half of art, the other half being eternal and immutable.)[39]

This, I believe, is 'the attitude, the system of feeling or of morals'[40] that Eliot hinted at. Eliot may have also realized that Baudelaire had revived the problem of Good and Evil and thus succeeded in recombining thought and feeling and establishing a moral order. Eliot would come to regard Baudelaire's tormented outcry as a consequence of his Christianity: to him, he was 'essentially a Christian, born out of his due time'.[41]

It would be interesting to remember that Eliot would not even hesitate to attack Arthur Symons, whose book, *The Symbolist Movement in Literature,* had once changed his life, for his hopeless inability to understand 'notre' ('our') Baudelaire, his Christianity, and his aspiration for order.[42] In his 1930 essay on Baudelaire, Eliot seemed to mellow a little, and expressed reservations about his own earlier view that Baudelaire was essentially Christian, but still considered him, despite a dose of romantic detritus, the first counter-Romantic in poetry,[43] whose hallmark was 'his sense of Sin in the permanent Christian sense'.[44] Baudelaire's blasphemy, he thought, was a way of affirming his belief: 'the sense of Evil implies the sense of Good'.[45]

Christianity, in Eliot's view, with its system of feelings or morals, as represented in Baudelaire's poetic texts, is the point of departure. It would be useful to read closely Eliot's 1930 essay, bearing in mind the latter's repeated reminders that his was essentially a 'workshop criticism' which revealed his own temperament. At the outset, Eliot refers to Baudelaire's 'theological innocence':

He is discovering Christianity for himself; he is not assuming it as a fashion or weighing social or political reasons or any other accidents. He is beginning, in a way, at the beginning, and, being a discoverer, is altogether certain what he is exploring and to what it leads; he might almost said to be beginning again, as one man, the effort of scores of generations . . . His business was not to practise Christianity, but—what was much more important for his time—to assert its *necessity*.[46]

In this pursuit he was alone in the solitude which is only known to saints. To him the notion of Original Sin came spontaneously, and the need for prayer.[47]

This would almost seem to be a succinct comment on Eliot's own poetry of unrelieved agony since his Harvard days till the time of *The Waste Land* and *The Hollow Men*. He privately admitted to Edward Greene[48] in 1940 that he re-read Baudelaire with renewed interest in 1919–20 during the composition of *The Waste Land,* which likewise asserts the *necessity* of Christianity.

Eliot draws our attention to the fact that Baudelaire 'exploited'[49] his weaknesses, which was a way to 'liberate his mind'; it was 'the legacy and lesson that he has left'.

He was one of those who have great strength, but strength merely to *suffer*. He could not escape suffering, and could not transcend it, so he attracted pain to himself. But what he could do with that immense passive strength and sensibilities which no pain could impair, was to study his suffering . . . Such suffering as Baudelaire's implies the possibility of a positive state of beatitude.[50]

I believe that Baudelaire's aesthetics of suffering, 'a true form of *acedia,* arising from the unsuccessful struggle towards the spiritual life'[51]—

eventually leading to beatitude (but not quite)—is also the primary characteristic of Eliot's poetry in *The Waste Land*. Going through his works in the early and middle periods, or reading his biographies, one learns how Eliot, too, had great strength to suffer, and being unable to transcend it, how he exploited his suffering to create great poetry. As for the notion of beatitude, Eliot never failed to emphasize this aspect of Baudelaire, which is also evident in his review of Peter Quennell's book (mentioned earlier) in *The Criterion*:

One difference between Baudelaire and the later poets—Laforgue, Verlaine, Corbière, Rimbaud and Mallarmé—is that Baudelaire not only reveals the troubles of his own age and predicts those of the age to come, but also *foreshadows some issue from these difficulties*. [Emphasis mine]

This reminds one of Baudelaire's evaluation by Charles du Bos, the Baudelaire critic Eliot admired the most and whom he quotes at length:

Cet incoércible besoin de prière au sein même de l'incredulitè—signe majeur d'une âme marquée de christianisme, qui jamais ne lui échappera tout à fait. La notion du péché, et plus profondément encore le besoin de prière, telles sont les deux réalités souterraines qui paraissent appartenir à des gisements enfouis bien plus avant que ne l'est la foi elle-même.

(This irrepressible need for prayer even in the midst of incredulity is a sure indication of a soul influenced by Christianity, which he will never be able to escape. The notion of Sin, and at a still deeper level, the need for prayer—these are the two subterranean realities which seem to be deeply buried in the mind even before faith itself.)[52]

This is best exemplified in the last part of *The Waste Land*, and a Baudelairian resonance in it is nowhere more convincing.

Writing about the excellence of form of Baudelaire's poems, their perfection of phrasing, Eliot concludes, 'In reality, they seem to me to have external but not internal form of Classic art',[53] which in turn concealed an 'inner disorder'. This illuminates us as much about the paradox of Eliot's own predicament as Baudelaire's and helps us to figure out the implications of their interaction. If Eliot desperately craved for order and beatitude, he found an identical moral anguish in Baudelaire's tortured self, whose role as 'a great poet, a great landmark in poetry', 'indeed the greatest exemplar in *modern* poetry in any language', he never fails to emphasize. Eliot goes on to declare that Baudelaire's 'renovation of an attitude towards life' is no less 'radical' than 'the complete renovation' he effected in verse and language. To him, Baudelaire's poetry was 'a reminder of the duty, of the consecrated task of sincerity. From a fundamental sincerity he could not deviate.'[54]

'Le cas Baudelaire' seems to have formed a substratum of moral influence, more especially in 1920–2, when Eliot was composing *The Waste Land*. But he was in a sense always indebted to Baudelaire because he knew instinctively that 'Baudelaire . . . plus certain other influences produced Laforgue and Corbière'.[55] He was conscious that Laforgue merely repeated the theme of Baudelaire: 'Ne suis-je pas un faux accord/Dans la divine symphonie?' ('Am I not a faulty chord/In this divine symphony?')[56] and 'Donnez-moi la force et le courage/De contempler mon corps et mon coeur sans dégoût' ('Give me the force and the courage/To contemplate my body and my heart without disgust';[57] and in spite of his undoubted allegiance to Laforgue, the former remained for him a greater poet than the latter.[58] As for Tristan Corbière, Eliot had no doubt that his redoubtable 'ironic terseness'[59] came from Baudelaire.

In the crucial 1930 essay, Eliot also highlighted the importance of Baudelaire's language, its variety and resourcefulness: 'he gave new possibilities to poetry in a new stock of imagery of contemporary life'.[60] Not only did he 'elevate' the sordid imagery to a level of 'first intensity', but he 'made it represent something much more than itself.[61] This makes clear Eliot's own eventual approach to imagery, for 'Baudelaire has created a mode of release and expression for other men'.[62] His invention of language was thus a landmark: 'his verse and language is the nearest thing to a complete renovation we have experienced'.[63]

While this renovated imagery has great historical significance, we shall not miss the implications of what Eliot calls 'the real problem of Good and Evil', where 'the sense of Evil implies the sense of Good'[64] and it is this knowledge which, according to him, distinguishes the relationship of man and woman from the copulation of beasts. About this morality, Eliot wrote in 1922, the year *The Waste Land* was published:

All first-rate poetry is occupied with morality: this is the lesson of Baudelaire.

. . . As for [English] verse of the present time, the lack of curiosity in technical matters, of the academic poets of today (Georgian etc.) is only an indication of their lack of curiosity in *moral* matters.[65]

This reminds us of what Baudelaire wrote to his advocate: 'Le livre doit être jugé en sa totalité. Et alors il en ressort *une terrible moralité*.' ('The book should be judged in its totality. And then emerges *a terrible morality*')[66] and shows how correct Eliot's assessment of Baudelaire was.

It would, therefore, be quite logical and profitable to find out in Eliot's poetry echoes of Baudelairian morals, which seem to have played a fundamental role in Eliot's development. In Baudelaire, he found corroboration of his own perception that true civilization is neither in the gas nor in the vapour, but in the 'diminution des traces du péché originel',[67] that damnation provided some hope for salvation from the boredom of man, that damnation itself is not far from bliss. This, as we know, is also the story of Eliot in the early and the middle period. No doubt, this could be one reason why Eliot singled out 'L'Invitation au voyage' as one of Baudelaire's best poems; it represents the same longing for order and calmness: 'Là, tout n'est qu'ordre et beauté/Luxe, calme et volupté.' ('There, everything is only order and beauty/Luxury, calmness and voluptuousness').[68] In a life of misery and wretchedness, the French poet's yearning for order was intricately associated with his tortuous sense of Sin and Redemption, to which Eliot attached so much importance. After all, Baudelaire is perhaps the only French master of Eliot who wrote categorically: 'It n'y a rien d'intéressant sur la terre que les religions'. ('On earth, there is nothing as interesting as the religions').[69]

What is worth noting is that, even as critics, Baudelaire and Eliot shared their consciousness of Original Sin: the former expressed disapproval of Victor Hugo for 'closing his eyes' to spirituality: 'l'oeil fermé à la spiritualité'.[70] Eliot's own beliefs, the twenties onwards, were alike. 'Literary criticism', he observed, 'should be completed by criticism from a definite ethical and theological standpoint . . . The "greatness" of literature cannot be determined solely by literary standards alone'.[71]

The new 'act of poetry', as Jouve called it, appears to have stuck to Eliot's mind, and produced irresistible results. He may have been guided, even deeply biased, by Jules Laforgue's views on Baudelaire in 'Notes sur Baudelaire' in the 1903 edition of the *Mélanges Posthumes.* It is astonishing that Eliot critics have not shown interest in Laforgue's text, which is likely to have influenced Eliot's outlook in his early years at Harvard and Paris. Laforgue described Baudelaire as 'le premier, il se raconta sur un mode modéré de confessionnel et ne prit pas l'air inspiré' ('the first to speak about himself in the moderate tone of confession without taking an inspired air').[72] According to Laforgue, Baudelaire was the first to refuse to cater to the public.[73] In this context, we shall remember Eliot's repeated references to Baudelaire's sincerity ('the duty, consecrated task of sincerity'[74]). To Laforgue, Baudelaire was 'le premier qui ne soit pas triomphant mais s'accuse, montre ses plaies, sa paresse, son inutilité ennuyée au milieu de ce siècle travailleur et devoué' ('the first who is not triumphant but one who accuses himself, shows his wounds, his laziness, his bored inutility in the midst of an active and devoted century')[75] . . . 'Le premier qui ait apporté dans notre littérature l'ennui dans la volupté et son décor bizarre . . . le spleen et la maladie (non la phtisie poétique mais la névrose) sans en avoir écrit une fois le mot. Et la damnation icibas.' ('The first to bring in our literature the boredom of voluptuousness and its strange ways . . . the spleen and the sickness [not the poetic pleurisy but the neurosis] without ever using these words. And here is damnation.')[76] We at once realize that both Laforgue, and subsequently, his disciple Eliot, could make out where they belong; it was a heritage of damnation they had to bear ruefully.

To Laforgue, Baudelaire broke the harmony of a period, known for its wild romanticism, with his 'comparaisons crues' ('crude comparisons'),[77] giving birth no doubt to Laforgue's own 'comparaisons illégitimes'.[78] He could be cynical, but there was nothing fake about his expressions: 'Jamais il n'a eu un pli canaille, un faux pli aux expressions dont il se vêt.' ('He never had any coarse crease in the expression with which he drapes himself'.)[79] According to Laforgue, Baudelaire was never lazy, he never insisted, never charged because of his anti-democratic attitude and hatred of the bourgeois imbecile, he was an unctuous and wily *spiritualist*, satanic like an irreligious Jesuit.[80] Laforgue's repeated references to Baudelaire's spirituality is extremely important; it guided Eliot's response as a reader.

What Eliot regarded as Baudelaire's beatific vision had also struck Laforgue: 'cette noblesse immuable qui annoblit les vulgarités intéressantes, captivantes'. ('This immutable nobility which ennobles the interesting, captivating vulgarities').[81]

Laforgue also drew attention to the strange and individual music of Baudelaire's verse. He had sounded (noted Laforgue) a new and poignant note in modern writing, which resembled the lonely complaint of a vagrant cat, a lost spirit which knows that it would never find the refuge it seeks.[82]

Laforgue's conclusion was, one would like to believe, much like Eliot's own: 'Ni grand coeur, ni grand esprit; mais quels nerfs plaintifs! Quelles narines ouvertes à tout! Quelle voix magique!' ('Not a great heart, nor a grand spirit like Dante! But what plaintive nerves! What nostrils for everything! What a magical voice!')[83] It was a voice that neither Laforgue nor Eliot could got away from.

Laforgue would have been delighted to know that Baudelaire stuck Delacroix's lithographs of Hamlet on his hotel wall in Paris. And no critic of Laforgue or Eliot seems to have noticed Baudelaire's sketch of Hamlet, which has great importance for the Baudelaire-Laforgue-Eliot tradition I am trying to establish. In Baudelaire's words:

> Contemplons à loisir cette caricature
> Et cette ombre d'Hamlet imitant sa posture,
> Le regard indécis et les cheveux au vent.
>
> N'est-ce pas cette grand-pitié de voir ce bon vivant,
> Ce gueux, cet histrion en vacances, ce drôle,
> Parce qu'il jouait artistement son rôle. . .

(This parody of Hamlet, take this measure,
And contemplate this travesty at leisure.
It is not sad to see the puzzled stare,

The halting gait, and the dishevelled hair,
With which this clownish actor, on half-pay.
Because he is an artist in his way. . .)[84]

In a captivating essay, Yves Bonnefoy has shown how Hamlet, the loving and sceptic actor-artist-poet in Baudelaire's poem, anticipates Laforgue's Hamlet.[85]

Eliot (like Laforgue, one would guess) also read Baudelaire's pages on laughter and caricature, 'De l'essence de rire', from which he quoted in the 'London Letter' in *Dial* (June 1921), adding in French that it is 'as important as Bergson's'.[86] Historically, it places Laforgue, Corbière, and Eliot in the same tradition with Baudelaire—an aspect Eliot highlighted again in the eighth Clark Lecture in 1926 when he claimed that the ironists derived from Baudelaire. It is interesting to remember that Eliot considered Baudelaire's sardonic, bathetic vein as 'strictly "modern"'.[87]

Laughter, says Baudelaire, has a 'satanic' origin; therefore, it is profoundly human. It is the expression both of man's sense of superiority to animals and his anguished consciousness of insignificance in relation to the Absolute. Since it is essentially human, laughter is essentially contradictory. Baudelaire makes a clear distinction between laughter and joy. For him, joy is a *unity,* whereas laughter is the revelation of a double, not to say, a self-contradictory, statement. That is the reason why laughter is convulsive.

In my opinion, Baudelaire's analytic discourse on laughter may have great bearing on Laforgue and Eliot: in a sense, they were possibly born out of it. For example, Baudelaire states:

Ils (le rire et les larmes) sont également les enfants de la peine, et ils sont venus parce que le corps de l'homme énervé manquait de force pour les contraindre. Au point de vue de mon philosophe chrétien (Philippe de Chennevières), le rire de ses lèvres est signe d'une aussi grande misère que les larmes de ses yeux . . . Remarquez que c'est aussi avec les larmes que l'homme lave les peines de l'homme, que c'est avec le rire qu'il adoucit quelquefois son coeur et l'attire; car les phénomènes engendrés par la chute deviendront les moyens de rachat.

(They [laughter and tears] are both children of suffering, and occur only when the human body is unable to restrain them. From the point of view of my Christian philosopher [Philippe de Chennevières] the laughter on his lips denotes no less misery than do the tears in his eyes . . . Note, too, that with tears a man may wash away men's sufferings, and with laughter sometimes soften men's hearts and draw them to him. For the phenomena engendered by the Fall can become the means of salvation).[88]

To Baudelaire, therefore, laughter can be 'l'explosion perpetuelle' ('the perpetual explosion') of anger and suffering: it is necessarily the result of man's 'double nature contradictoire' ('contradictory double nature').[89] It can help man to establish his superiority over nature: 'Le rire est l'expression de l'idée de supériorité, non plus de l'homme sur l'homme, mais de l'homme sur la nature.' ('The laughter is the expression of the idea of superiority, not of man to man, but of man to nature'). This would almost seem to be a justification of Laforgue's ironic laughter, or perhaps even Eliot's who wanted to 'bite off' the matter with a smile. Curiously, Baudelaire deals with Pierrot at great length, and it seems unlikely that Laforgue, the great admirer of Pierrot, was unaware of it. Baudelaire's views seem hardly different from Laforgue's who believed: 'Les clowns me paraissent arriver à la vraie sagesse' ('Clowns seem to attain true wisdom').[90]

Sure enough, all this would have thrilled Eliot who would agree ('Prufrock', the quatrain poems, and *The Waste Land* bear witness to this) with Baudelaire that laughter bore the symptom of weakness ('il y avait symptôme de faiblesse dans le rire': 'there were symptoms of weakness in laughter'), that there was no better sign of debility and nervous convulsion than its involuntary spasm.[91] I propose that this shows how far the debt to Baudelaire goes back, a debt which could either have helped Eliot directly or infiltrated through the poetry of Laforgue and Corbière.

Baudelaire used his theories of laughter quite abundantly in his poetry—even Tsémégiste dreams of gallows, smoking a pipe, and prepares to swallow the world in one gaping yawn in the opening poem of *Les Fleurs du Mal*—but the texts which stand out are his savage 'Salon Caricatural de 1846' in collaboration with Theodore de Banville and Vitu in an album sketched by Bertall,[92] and *'Bouffonneries'*.[93] Both have the characteristics of ironic humour, which make Eliot so stridently original in English poetry:

> Il me dit qu'il était très riche,
> Mais qu'il craignait le choléra;
> —Que de son or il était chiche,
> Mais qu'il goûtait fort l'Opéra.

> (He told me that he was very rich,
> Though he panicked about cholera;
> —That though he was niggardly about money,
> He simply loved Opera.)[94]

These recognizable Laforguianisms, which are, in all fairness, Baudelairian in origin, Eliot found scattered in *Les Fleurs du Mal* in Pierrotesque lines like 'Ils trottent, tous pareils à des marionnettes' ('They trot like puppets'),[95] or poems like 'L'Héautontimorouménos'.

It may be equally interesting to note Baudelaire's lines on the painter Watteau (with whom Arthur Symons compared Laforgue[96]) in his 'Les Phares':

> Watteau, ce carnaval où bien des coeurs illustres,
> Comme des papillons, errent en flamboyant,
> Décors frais et légers éclairés par des lustres
> Qui versent la folie à ce bal tournoyant . . .
>
> (Watteau, carnival where many a distinguished soul
> Flutters like a moth, lost in the brilliance
> Of chandeliers shedding frivolity on the cool,
> Clear decors enclosing the changes of the dance . . .)[97]

This shows the Laforguian traits latent in Baudelaire, and possibly establishes him as the real precursor of Eliot's Laforguian heritage.

Baudelaire's poetry was a kind of prism which could enlighten an eager apprentice in a thousand ways. What he said of Delacroix is applicable to him as well: 'Ces malédictions, ces blasphèmes, ces plaintes/Ces extases, ces cris, ces pleurs, ces *Te Deum*,/Sont un écho redit par mille labyrinths . . .' ('These curses, blasphemies, and lamentations,/These ecstasies, tears, cries and soaring psalms—/Through endless mazes reverberate. . .')[98]

Stephen Spender makes a very important point when he says unwittingly of Prufrock: 'He *suffers*, which means that he is one of those who know that he is in a Baudelairian Hell'.[99] Prufrock's predicament can surely be traced back to Baudelaire's 'pauvre âme solitaire' ('the solitary poor soul'), 'dans la nuit et dans la solitude' ('in the night and in the solitude'), and 'dans la rue et dans la multitude' ('in the road and in the multitude'). The arresting metaphor of the evening spread against the sky, compared to a patient étherized upon a table, has Laforguian resonances (see chapter on Laforgue); but it may, after all, have originated from Baudelaire's reference to the hospitals ('L'Hôpital se remplit de leurs soupirs': 'Their groans overflow the hospital') in his poem on evening.[100] The evocative and revolutionary image of 'the yellow fog' in Eliot's 'Prufrock'[101] is a more direct translation of Baudelaire's 'un brouillard sale et jaune inondait tout l'espace' ('a dirty and yellow fog flooded the whole space').[102] Eliot seems to have learnt from Baudelaire how the outside erupts into the inside, and erodes the parameters of life.

For example, 'female smells' in Eliot may have been welded from Baudelaire's 'Parfum Exotique', where in a hot autumn evening he breathes the sensuous smell of his lover's breasts: 'Je respire l'odeur de ton sein chaleureux' ('I breathe the fragrance of your warm breast').[103] 'Her strange synthetic perfumes'[104] would possibly never have found a place in English poetry without Baudelaire's 'ta chevelure profonde/Aux acres parfums. . .' ('Your tresses dark and deep/Where acrid perfumes drown. . .')[105] or the 'feline smell' in 'Whispers of Immortality'[106] without the impact of the cat-smell in 'Le Chat' ('un dangereux parfum': 'a dangerous perfume'[107]) and expressed the same revulsion from the flesh.

The Baudelairian surprises—the unusual elements, the combination of vital and unexpected images, even the occasional shrill notes—stud the poetry of Eliot. There is a startling similarity of phrasing in the two poets. Eliot's ability to create a mood through an image, lines, or phrases, which have become magical touchstones, inevitably brings to mind Baudelaire's

> Comme un visage en pleurs que les brises essuyent
>
> (Like a face in tears which the wind dries)[108]
>
> comme un oeil sanglant qui palpite et qui bouge
>
> (like a bleeding eye that throbs and moves)[109]
>
> Le violon frémit comme un coeur qu'on afflige
>
> (The violin shudders like a tortured heart)[110]

There is the same newness of imagery, the same kind of evocative impressionism, the same rhythmic, melodious effect. It would almost seem that Eliot had deliberately and labouriously worked out the *style* of imagery from *Les Fleurs du Mal*, although, to be sure, much of it dovetails with and is overshadowed by Laforguian pyrotechnics.

While Laforgue, Dante and Corbière were still his trusted guides during the composition of *The Waste Land*, Eliot could realize how useful would be Baudelaire's stupendous gift to create poetry out of the unexplored resources of the unpoetical. This gave him courage and confidence.

He shared with Baudelaire his deep distrust of the meaningless automata of the crowd of the metropolis, and learnt to employ the infernal flitting, jaundiced images with deadly effect. In short, he learnt from Baudelaire to symbolize the city.

Interestingly, Eliot always openly acknowledged his special debt to the urban imagery of Baudelaire: he quoted four lines from 'Les Sept Vieillards' in *Tableaux Parisiens*[111] as the source of the vision of the Unreal City in *The Waste Land* and acknowledged his debt to 'half a dozen lines in Baudelaire', presumably from the same section.[112] While the weight of such an assertion cannot be ignored, it seems quite likely that Eliot started off from this point and gradually delved deep into the *oeuvre*, trying to unravel the mystery of Baudelaire's mind.

Baudelaire was the first poet of the modern, industrial city in all its ruthless, faceless anonymity. The tides Baudelaire initially chose for his *Spleen de Paris* were *Le Rôdeur parisien* (*The Parisian Prowler*) and *Le Promeneur solitaire* (*The Solitary Walker*), and he separated twenty-one poems in *Les Fleurs du Mal* in a section called *Tableaux Parisiens* (*Parisian Pictures*). As Philippe Soupault[113] has pointed out, if Poe was a great influence on Baudelaire, so was Paris, where he was born and passed most part of his life. It is well known and he always boasted of it, that all his life he walked the roads of Paris by night and day, often as a lucid observer, and sometimes, as a dreamer who regularly haunted the artificial paradises. It was not as a historian that he wanted to penetrate the mysteries of the city, which he did not leave without regret, but as a lover who cherished even the defects of his mistress. Obviously, he preferred the 'landscapes' of Paris to the Parisians, whom he often despised and hated. In the streets of Paris, Baudelaire searched for solitude in settings which seemed convenient to him. Frequently, he was a spectator and had memories of meeting people who mattered much. He met, for instance, Jeanne Duval,[114] who was found in a third-rate theatre, possibly tired of streetwalking in Paris. One can imagine the couple, Baudelaire and Jeanne Duval, straying across the lanes, looking at the shadows and nocturnal mysteries of deserted districts. These explorations are reflected in *Les Fleurs du Mal*: memories and evocations of hospitals, palaces, beggars, old men and women, prostitutes and the underworld, pictures, old books, suburbs, maisons de jeu . . . These are often the points of departure for meditations and allusions. In the words of Philippe Soupault, 'Il ne décrit pas. Il évoque. Il suggère plus qu'il ne dépeint'. ('He does not describe. He evokes. He suggests more than he paints').[115]

It is difficult to locate the exact itineraries of this Parisian walker. One can ascertain only one, to which he alludes most freely: the promenades down the banks of the Seine (Baudelaire complained that Brussels was insipid, for it had no river[116]) he undertook every day 'comme un pelérinage' ('like a pilgrimage'):

> Flairant dans tous les coins les hasards de la rime,
> Trébuchant sur les mots comme sur les pavés,
> Heurtant parfois des vers depuis longtemps rêvés.
>
> (Stalking, in all the nooks, the odds of rhyme,
> Tripping on words like cobbles as I go.
> And bumping into lines dreamed long ago.)[117]

He dedicates to Paris poems of unique sombre beauty, ending with these verses:

L'aurore grelottane en robe rose et verte
S'avançait lentement sur la Seine déserte,
Et le sombre Paris, en se frottant les yeux,
Empoignait ses outils, vieillard laborieux.

(Morning, shivering in her robe of rose and green
Made her hesitant way along the deserted Seine,
While Paris rubbing tired eyes in its dark,
Woke like an ancient drudge to another day's work.)[118]

Baudelaire was, as it were, under a spell, which enabled him, in Rimbaud's words, to 'see the invisible and hear the unheard' (letter to Ernest Delahaye on 15 May 1871).[119] In his dedication of *Le Spleen de Paris*, Baudelaire said that he wanted to adapt to 'the lyrical movements of the soul, the undulations of the dream, the crises of conscience'. And he gave a strange reason for writing poems in prose: 'C'est surtout la fréquentation des villes énormes, e'est du croisement de leurs innombrables rapports que naît cet idéal obsédant.' ('It is specially the frequentation of the big cities, the intersection of their countless similarities that this obsessive ideal is born').[120] Apart from Brussels, where he lived for two years from 1864, the only city Baudelaire knew was Paris, but he was conscious how symbolic and allegoric his urban experience was. The city, to Baudelaire, was both a city of the mind and of the external world.

Walter Benjamin has noted in 'Baudelaire ou les rues de Paris' in his *Paris, Capitale du XIXe Siecle*:

Pour la première fois chez Baudelaire, Paris devient objet de poésie lyrique. Cette poésie locale est à l'encontre de toute poésie de terroir. Le regard que le génie allégorique plonge dans la ville trahit bien plutôt le sentiment d'une profonde aliénation. C'est là le regard d'un flâneur dont le genre de vie dissimule derrière un mirage bienfaisant la détresse des habitants futurs de nos métropoles. Le flâneur cherche ou refuge dans la foule. La foule est le voile à travers lequel la ville familière se meut pour le flâneur en fantasmagorie. Cette fantasmagorie, où elle apparait comme un paysage, tantôt comme une chambre, semble avoir inspiré par la suite le décor des grands magasins, qui mettent ainsi la flânerie même au service de leur chiffre d'affaires.

(For the first time in Baudelaire, Paris becomes the object of his poetry. This local poetry runs counter to all poetry of the soil. The look that the allegoric genius casts at the city betrays the feeling of a profound alienation. It is the observation of a walker, whose life hides behind a mirage the distress of the future inhabitants of our big cities. The walker looks for a refuge in the crowd. The crowd is the veil across which the familiar city moves into phantasmagoria for the walker. This phantasmagoria, where it appears as a landscape, sometimes in the form of a bedroom, seems to have subsequently inspired the decor of big shops, which thus utilise the stroll in the service of business).[121]

Benjamin uses as epigraph a quote from Maxime du Camp:

L'histoire est comme Janus, elle a deux visages: qu'elle regarde le passé, ou le présent, elle voit les mêmes choses.

(History is like Janus, it has two faces: it looks at the past, or the present, it finds the same things.)[122]

His reading should make clear that any mechanical comparison of Eliot's city with those of other contemporaries like James Thomson (as done by Robert Crawford)[123] is far from adequate. Only Baudelaire can possibly provide us with vital clues to decipher the plural character of the city-motif in Eliot's poetic texts.

The city was the same as Baudelaire's *Civitas Dei* and symbolized his struggle with the unknown, the intractable, and the infinite across the decrepitude that no one else in French (or in English, for that matter) literature had dared to encounter. The projection of the city is itself a raid on the inarticulate. No one before Baudelaire ripped through the outer layers and smelt the city: 'On dit que chaque ville, chaque pays a son odeur.' ('One says that every city, every country has its odour.'). Paris smelt 'chou aigre', Le Cap smelt mutton, and the tropical islands *reeked* of rose, musk, or coconut oil, Brussels of black soap.[124] Eliot uses these 'smells'—new constructions in European poetic discourse—with lethal effect.

Eliot's Unreal City reconstructs and restates, as far as the changing times permitted, the Baudelairian experience. The brown fog and the crowd flowing over the London bridge undone by death (reminding one of Baudelaire's 'Les Foules', *Le Spleen de Paris*[125]), the dull canal (which seems to transplant 'less canaux étroits' ['the narrow canals'] in Baudelaire[126]) and the pleasant whining of the mandolin are an astonishing example of intertextual transportation. The total perspective of Baudelaire's theme is brought alive in a few cryptic lines—a classic example of Eliot's art of absorption at its best, where Baudelaire becomes part of his own search for the *Civitas Dei*.

It is true that Eliot had always lurked about the smoky, sinuous folds of the *fourmillante cité* from the days of 'Prufrock', but then it was possibly closer to Laforgue, with its cyclic structure of a hundred indecisions of evenings, mornings, afternoons. Nevertheless, Baudelaire's *coeur nu* remains the nerve centre of his metropolitan experience, which comes to the fore in the 'half-deserted streets', in the 'yellow fog' that rubs its back and muzzle upon the window panes, and slides along the streets and rises from the pipes. The yellow fog and smoke may have originated not only from 'un brouillard sale et jaune inondait tout l'espace' ('a dirty and yellow fog flooded the whole space'),[127] as mentioned earlier, but also from 'une mer de brouillard baignait les édifices' ('a sea of fog bathed the buildings').[128] A thoroughly self-conscious, typically Laforguian poem of Eliot, like 'Rhapsody on a Windy Night', flashes a Baudelairian surprise: 'Remark the cat which flattens itself in the gutter, slips out its tongue/And devours a morsel of rancid butter. . .'. Even the child and his toy that come after appear to be transported from 'Le Joujou du pauvre' in Le Spleen de Paris: 'A côté de lui les gisait sur l'herbe un joujou splendide' ('Beside him lay on the grass a splendid toy').[129]

The powerful feline symbol in the double version of 'Le Chat' could have inspired Eliot to use the image 'with subtle effluence of cat'.[130] Likewise, the references to 'chat mystérieux, chat séraphique, chat étrange' ('the mysterious cat, the seraphic cat, the strange cat') may have generated a whole range of affiliative poems in *Old Possum's Book of Practical Cats*. The former scribbled in his diary:

Pourquoi les démocrates n'aiment pas les chats, it est facile de le deviner. Le chat est beau; il lui révèle des idées de luxe, de propreté, de volupté, etc. . . .

(It is easy to guess why the democrats are not fond of cats. The cat is beautiful; it reveals to him ideas of luxury, cleanliness, voluptuousness, etc. . . .)[131]

Eliot, himself often accused of misogyny, has drawn our attention to Baudelaire's 'constant vituperations of the female'.[132] This is explained by the latter's letter to Apollonie Sabatier:

Vous voyez, ma bien belle chérie, que j'ai d'odieux préjugés à l'endroit des femmes. Bref, je n'ai pas la foi. Vous avez l'âme belle, mais en somme, e'est une âme féminine.

(You see, my darling, that I have odious prejudices about women. In short, I don't have faith. You have beautiful soul, but, on the whole, it is a feminine soul.)[133]

Even in his most intense love-poems, Baudelaire betrayed a revulsion: 'Je le hais autant que je t'aime' ('I hate you as much as I love you'),[134] which served the counter-Romantics, Corbière and Laforgue, in a big way. He abhorred 'la froide majesté' ('the cold majesty') of women; their velvet looks were 'infernal et divin' ('infernal and divine'),[135] they walked on the dead ('Tu marches sur les morts'),[136] they are stupid and indifferent,[137] their breasts have the coolness of tombs ('trouver sur ton sein la fraîcheur des tombeaux'),[138] their enjoyment had a bitter sterility ('L'âpre stérélité de votre jouissance'),[139] which troubled one's peace ('pour troubler le repos';[140] they were full of pus ('toute pleine dc pus')[141] and sucked the marrow from the bones of men ('elle eut de mes os sucé toute la moelle'),[142] who were as attractive as they were shocking,[143] they were often no more than carcasses ('Ta carcasse a des agréments');[144] the uncorseted sirens of nightmare pulled the saintly robe of the poet or his wise man's beard and offered him the poison of bold love ('Cauchemar de mes nuits, sirène sans corsage,/Qui me tirez, toujours debout à mon côté/Par ma robe de saint ou ma barbe de sage/Pour m'offrir le poison d'un amour effronté').[145] Without this heritage of misogyny in recent poetry, Eliot would not have probably dared to construct his woman with her bruised, defiled flesh in *The Waste Land*—the typist with her carbuncular caresses.

There are more straightforward accounts of women in *Mon coeur mis à nu*, where he tries to explain and rationalize his hatred:

La femme est le contraire du Dandy.
Done elle doit faire horreur.
La femme a faim et elle veut manger. Soif, et elle veut boire.
Elle est en rut et elle veut être foutue.
Le beau mérite!
La femme est *naturelle*, e'est-à-dire abominable.
Aussi-est-elle toujours vulgaire, c'est-à-dire le contraire du Dandy.

(Woman is the opposite of the Dandy.
That is why she should be so fearsome.
Woman is hungry, and she wants to eat. Thirsty, and she wants to drink.
She is ready and wants to be—.
Fine qualities!
Woman is 'natural', that is to say, abominable.
Therefore, she is always vulgar, that is to say, the opposite of the Dandy.)[146]

Yet, ironically, the sensual charm of women remains unsurpassed in Baudelaire's poetry. This, I believe, is linked with the theme of damnation, the inevitable attraction of the flowers of evil, which is man's destiny. Anyone acquainted with Eliot's life would know how similar was his own perception of women: his uncorseted experience in France and his love-hate relationship (there was probably more hate than love) with Vivienne and the inevitable sense of damnation that entailed it in his poetry seem to re-enact Baudelaire's precarious position: there is a similar sense of brooding sexuality and a revulsion from the flesh—a predicament also visible in Laforgue (see chapter on Laforgue). This is what Laforgue called Baudelaire's 'l'ennui dans la volupté' ('boredom in voluptuousness')[147] which both he and Eliot inherited. And this compulsive bifocal attitude to love is perfectly compatible with the notion of impersonality which is so crucial to modernist aesthetics.

If Baudelaire was constantly torn between two extremes, the desire for spirituality and the pull towards sensuality, and his poetry reveals the torment of guilt and despair, this is equally true of Eliot. In fact, much of Eliot's poetry is an expiation of this guilt. What is striking is Baudelaire's daring assertion in his diary that the woman is the 'opposite of the Dandy'.

To Baudelaire, the Dandy is one who can morally fight out a lone battle of survival, who is a non-conformist and a hero, who censures all conformism, and who is not to be perturbed in all temptation, not to be cowed down in the struggle towards keeping his wholeness and composure. Baudelaire defends 'l'éternelle superiorité du Dandy' ('the eternal superiority of the Dandy').[148] 'En vérité', says he, 'je n'avais pas tout à fait tort de considérer le dandysme comme une espèce de religion'. ('Indeed, I was not far wrong in regarding dandysm, as a sort of religion'.) For him, 'le dandysme est un soleil couchant; comme l'astre qui décline, il est superbe, mais sans chaleur et plein de mélancolie' ('The dandysm is a setting sun. Like the great sinking star, it is superb, cold and melancholic').[149] Clearly, as his numerous references to the Dandy in his correspondence show, he was less interested in the external attributes of the Dandy, the cult of elegance, than in the significance of the doctrine:

C'est avant tout le besoin ardent de se faire une originalité, contenu dans les limites extérieures des convenances. C'est une espèce de culte de soi-même, qui peut survivre à la recherche du bonheur à trouver dans autrui, dans la femme, par exemple; qui peut survivre même à tout ce qu'on appelle les illusions. C'est le plaisir d'etonner et la satisfaction orgueilleuse de ne jamais être étonné. Un dandy peut être un homme blasé, peut être un homme souffrant; mais dans ce dernier cas, il sourira comme le Lacédémonien sous la morsure du renard . . .

(It is above all a burning need to acquire originality, within the apparent bounds of convention. It is a sort of cult of oneself, which can dispense even with what are commonly called illusions. It is the delight in causing astonishment, and the proud satisfaction of never oneself being astonished. A Dandy may be indifferent, may be a man who suffers, but in the latter case, he will smile like a Spartan under the muzzle of fox.)[150]

Le caractère de beauté du dandy consiste surtout dans l'air froid qui vient de l'inébranlable résolution de ne pas être ému . . .

(The quality of beauty of the Dandy consists especially in the cold air which comes from the unshakable resolution not to be moved emotionally . . .)[151]

To be sure, there is no clear line of demarcation between the Dandy and the Saint in Baudelaire's *Journaux Intimes*, 'Mon coeur mis à nu', and 'Fusées'.

This is made particularly clear when Baudelaire scribbles: 'Le Dandy doit aspirer à être sublime sans interruption; il doit vivre et dormir devant un miroir' ('The Dandy must endlessly aspire for sublimity; he must live and sleep in front of a mirror').[152]

Baudelaire—like his successors, Corbière and Laforgue, and through them, the early Eliot—desperately wanted to be a Dandy, because it seemed to him (them) the only mode of survival in a world of decadence, the only way of being different from those who are *sans personalité* and *sans originalité* and born for 'la domesticité publique' ('the public slavery'); but, at the same time, they could perceive how difficult it was to be different from others in a world of mutation. The Dandy, nevertheless, remained an ideal for Baudelaire, as it remained an irrealizable ideal for Corbière, Laforgue, and the Eliot of 'Prufrock'. As for Eliot, if he could somehow maintain the composure of the Dandy till his Sweeney poems in 1920, all hell broke loose at the advent of the twenties while he composed *The Waste Land*. He complained about Baudelaire in 1930 that 'the content was constantly bursting out of the receptacle',[153] which was probably also the case with Eliot himself in his celebrated work.

I think it is very significant that Eliot actually suggested *La Terre mise à nue* as the title for the first French translation of *The Waste Land*, an obvious reminder of Baudelaire's 'Mon coeur mis à nu'.[154] While Dante, Laforgue, Larbaud, and the sacred Indian texts played significant roles in the making of Eliot's great poem, Baudelaire's presence is discernible everywhere. And, I would like to point out that this is so not merely in the vision of the Unreal City, but also perhaps in the myth of the Fisher King, which Eliot used as a scaffold to hold the poem together. I want to especially draw attention to a solemn poem called 'Spleen' by Baudelaire, which likewise deals with the landscape of barrenness, recounted by an impotent king:

Spleen

Je suis le roi d'un pays pluvieux,
Riche, *mais impuissant, jeune etpourtant très vieux,*
Qui, de ses précepteurs méprisant les courbettes.
S'ennuie avec ses chiens comme avec d'autres bêtes,
Rien ne peut l'égayer, ni gibier, ni faucon,
Ni son peuple mourant en face du balcon.
Du bouffon favori de la grotesque ballade
Ne distrait plus le front de ce cruel malade
Son lit fleurdelisé *se transforme en tombeau,*
Et les dames d'atour, pour qui tout prince est beau,

Ne savent plus trouver d'impudique toilette
Pour tirer un souris de ce jeune *squelette*.
Le savant qui lui fait de l'or n'a jamais pu
De son être êxtirper l'élément corrompu,
Et dans ces bains de sang qui des Romains nous viennent,
Et dont leurs vieux jours les puissants se souviennent,
Il n'a su réchauffer ce *cadavre* hébété
Où coule au lieu de sang l'eau verte du Léthé. [emphasis mine]

(*I am like the king of a* rainy *land,*
Wealthy, but *impotent, young and very old,*
Scorning his tutors, fawning, plausible,
Weary of dogs, and of other animals.
Nothing can cheer him, game of falconry,
His dying people by the balcony.
The monstrous ballad of the favourite fool
No longer makes him smile, cruel and ill.
His bed, with lilies decked, *is now a tomb.*
Tire-women who to a prince succumb
Can improvise no new and daring dress
To give this *skeleton* some happiness.
The sage who makes gold for him never could
Cut out the canker which his soul endued
And in those blood-baths which gave Rome content.
And which great men recall when youth is spent,
He never could revive this *corpse* obtuse
In whom not blood but Lethe's water flows.) [emphasis mine]¹⁵⁵

It is possible that herein lies the germ of the anthropological myth which
will eventually replace the aesthetic myth in *The Waste Land*. What if we
mix with it the obsessive vision of the desolate country in Baudelaire's 'De
Profundis Clamavi'?

C'est un universe morne à l'horizon plombé,
Où nagent dans la nuit l'horreur et le blasphème;

Un soleil sans chaleur plane au-dessus six mois,
Et dans les six autres mois la nuit comme la terre;
C'est un pays plus nu que la terre polaire;
—Ni bêtes, ni ruisseaux, ni verdure, ni bois!

Or il n'est pas d'horreur au monde qui surpasse
La froide cruauté de ce soleil de glace
Et cette immense nuit semblable au vieux Chaos;

Je jalouse le sort des plus vils animaux
Qui peuvent se plonger dans un sommeil stupide,
Tout l'écheveau du temps lentement se dévide!

(A barren land hemmed in by leaden skies
Where horror flies at night, and blasphemy.

For half the year the sickly sun is seen,
The other half thick night, lies on the land,
A country bleaker than the polar strand;
—No beasts, no brooks, nor any shade of green.

There never was a horror which surpassed
This icy sun's cold cruelty, and this vast
Night like primeval chaos; would I were

Like the dumb brutes, who in a secret lair
Lie wrapt in stupid slumber for a space . . .
Time creeps at so burdensome a pace!)[156]

Thematically, I venture to say, the result would not be far off from the apocalyptic, nightmarish experience of the complete collapse of the civilization in *The Waste Land*, though understandably there are, at the same time, complex feedbacks, overlappings, and intertwining of various other texts too. But there is unmistakably the same Eliot-like hollowness at the centre of Baudelaire's poem. It will be instructive to know, as Claude Pichois points out, that the latter poem made a clear reference to Dante: 'De Profundis Clamavi' was first published as 'La Béatrix'.[157] So, the Dante connection of Eliot does not prove that Baudelaire did not influence him.

E.J.H. Greene[158] has identified Baudelaire's 'Un Voyage à Cythère' as a possible source of Eliot because of lines like 'Quelle est cette île triste et noire?' ('What is this sad and dark island?')[159] and phrases like 'un désert rocailleux' ('a rocky desert'), 'pauvre terre' ('infertile land').[160] But more interesting is 'Le Cygne' where an escaped swan (exiled from Eden, it seems), lost in the dust and stones of the city, reaches a dry stream-bed, finds no water, looks up at the cruel sky and asks, 'When will it rain again? When will there be thunder?'—much like the ironic question raised at the end of *The Waste Land*. The pattern of thought in Baudelaire has echoes and cross-references in Eliot's poem. (Interestingly, Eliot quotes from both these poems of Baudelaire in 'Baudelaire in Our Time').[161]

Another very important similarity between *The Waste Land* and *Les Fleurs du Mal* to which I would like to draw attention is their *architecture*. In the Clark Lectures in 1926,[162] Eliot spoke about Dante's 'architechtonic ability, power of organisation and structure', but he must have known that

Baudelaire's was no less. In an article sent to *Pays* in July 1857, Barbey d'Aurevilly had refused to quote from Baudelaire's volume of poems because:

une pièce citée aurait sa valeur individuelle, il ne faut pas s'y méprendre, dans le livre de M. Baudelaire, chaque poésie a. de plus que sa réussite, des détails ou la fortune de sa pensée, une valeur très importante d'ensembles et de situations qu'il ne faut pas lui faire perdre en détachant. Les artistes qui voient sous le luxe et l'efflorescence de la couleur percevront très bien qu'il y a ici *une architecture secrète*, un plan calcule par le poète, méditatif et volontaire . . . Elles sont moins de poésies *qu'une oeuvre poétique de la plus forte unité.*

(one poem quoted would have individual value but there is no mistaking in it that in Mr Baudelaire's book, each poem has, despite its success, details and richness of thought, a very important structural value which must not be lost by detaching them. The artists who can see through the richness and efflorescence of the colour will be able to perceive very well that here there is *a secret architecture*, a plan schemed by the poet which is meditative and voluntary . . . These are less poems than a *poetical work of the strongest unity*).[163]

He added that if Baudelaire's poems are not read in the proper order, they lose their 'moral effect'.[164] This was no doubt also the opinion of Baudelaire himself. He sent to Alfred de Vigny along with a copy of the second edition of *Les Fleurs du Mal*: 'Le seul éloge que je sollicite pour ce livre est qu'on reconnaisse qu'il n'est pas un pur album et qu'il a un commencement et une fin'. ('The sole eulogy that I solicit for this book is the recognition that it is not a pure album and that it has a beginning and an end'). And in the introduction to *Articles justificatifs* published during the case of *Les Fleurs du Mal*, Baudelaire wrote that his book had to be appreciated 'dans son ensemble et *par sa conclusion*' ('in its whole and *by its conclusion*'[165]). Though the book does have an order and apparently projects the same individual crossing different steps on his way to a spiritual itinerary, like in *The Waste Land*, it is quite likely that the architectural design was determined a *posteriori* in both cases, once the poems were written. Like *The Waste Land*, *Les Fleurs du Mal* is divided into five sections of unequal sizes: 'Spleen et Idéal', 'Fleurs du Mal', 'Révolte', 'Le Vin' et 'La Mort'. The last poems of the book, however, find even in death the blossoming of new flowers of hope, which is also more or less the emotional pattern of Eliot's *tour de force.*

The Waste Land shows a similarity with the five-part structure of *Les Fleurs du Mal*: despite the sketchiness, there is the same notion of architectural unity. One of the two things (the other is no doubt the *moral* vision) that harmonizes these two works is the inner music, the approximation of the pattern of modern musical composition. We know of Baudelaire and Eliot's fascination for music: 'La musique me prend comme une mer' ('Music sways me like the sea'), wrote Baudelaire; 'This music crept by me upon the waters', echoed Eliot.[166] Baudelaire was one of the earliest admirers of Wagner and a large number of his poems have been set to music by great musicians such as Debussy and Duparc. As for Eliot, Helen Gardner speaks of the symphonic richness of *The Waste Land*, which is also true of *Four Quartets*. It may be worthwhile to remember Eliot's writing on this:

There are possibilities of transitions in a poem comparable to the different movements of a symphony or a quartet; there are possibilities of a contrapuntal arrangement of a subject-matter. It is in the concert-room, rather than the opera-house, that the germ of a poem is quickened . . .[167]

where even 'the less intense' matter could be 'structurally vital'.[168] This, I think, is very close to what Barbey d'Aurevilly stated, or Baudelaire wrote to Vigny.

It is important to remember once again Eliot's clarification to Greene[169] that he was indeed re-reading Baudelaire at the time of writing *The Waste Land*. His proposal of a distinctly Baudelairian title for the French version of the poem, the debate between the soul and the flesh, the vision of the Unreal City and the beatific vision (which helped Eliot to 'find an issue from the difficulty' and the route to Redemption) confirm a profound communion with Baudelaire. Certainly, the above poems help us to get one more crossword clue to the generative multiplicity of Eliot's text.

Interestingly, Eliot singles out Baudelaire's poetry as 'a poetry of flight'—or the 'reaching out towards something'[170] by citing a 'beautiful passage' from 'Mon coeur mis à nu', where Baudelaire imagines the vessels in harbour saying 'Quand partonsnous vers le bonheur?' ('When do we leave for happiness?') The symbol of water and sea plays a liberating role in Eliot's poetry, which may have enriched itself by following the plurality of the water-motif in the poetry of Baudelaire, Laforgue, Corbière, and of Paul Claudel in *Four Quartets*. His wonderful exploitation of Baudelairian material is evident in lines like:

This form, this face, this life
Living to live in a world of time beyond me; let me
Resign my life for this life, my speech for that
    unspoken—
The awakened, lips parted, the hope, the new ships.[171]

I wish to draw attention to Baudelaire's poem 'L'Homme et la mer':

Homme libre, toujours tu chériras la mer
La mer est ton miroir, tu contemples ton âme
Dans le déroulement infini de sa lame . . .

(Free man, you will for ever love the sea!
The sea's your mirror; you observe your soul
Perpetually as its waves unroll . . .)[172]

There is another revealing passage in 'Mon coeur mis à nu' which focuses more clearly on Baudelaire's relation with the sea:

Pourquoi le spectacle de la mer est-il infiniment et si éternellement agréable?

Parce que la mer offre à la fois l'idée de l'immensité et du mouvement. Six ou sept lieues représentent pour l'homme le rayon de l'infini. Voilà un infini dimunitif. Qu'importe s'il suffit à suggérer l'idée de l'infini total? Douze ou quatorze lieues (sur le diamètre), douze ou quatorze de liquide en mouvement suffisent pour donner la plus haute idée de beauté qui soit offerte à l'homme sur son habitacle transitoire.

(Why is the sight of the sea so infinitely and eternally attractive?

Because the sea simultaneously provides the idea of immensity and of movement. To mankind, six or seven leagues represent the radius of the infinite. A diminutive infinite, certainly—but what matter, if it suffices to suggest the idea of total infinity? Twelve or fourteen leagues of moving liquid suffice to provide the noblest idea of beauty that is offered to man in his transitory habitation.)[173]

I have suggested in the chapters on Laforgue, Corbière, and Claudel that Eliot may have learnt the infinite possibilities of the water-symbol from them, as he may have from others too, but this aspect of their poetry—like many other aspects, one presumes, could have originated from Baudelaire.

The fact of Baudelaire's 'impact' (Eliot's own word quoted earlier) on Eliot is reconfirmed in the latter's own declaration in a French article in *Chroniques* III in 1927, where he considered 'Dante in the absolute scale, and Baudelaire in modern times' as the two greatest artisans who helped in the 'expansion de la réalité' ('expansion of reality') in poetry. 'J' avoue 'J'avoue que ce sont ceux qui m'intéressent le plus . . .', he added ('I admit that these are the ones who interest me most').[174] Eliot's bracketing of Dante and Baudelaire is all the more interesting because Baudelaire himself submitted an article by Edouard Thierry in his self-defence during the prosecution of *Les Fleurs du Mal*, in which the latter had compared him with Dante and his book with *The Divine Comedy*.

If, in the final analysis, Eliot was to consider Baudelaire's Christianity as 'rudimentary'[175] and incomplete, and apparently sought to complement it with Dante's more well-integrated one (Eliot believed that very few succeeded 'as did Dante in expressing the complete scale from negative to positive'[176]), Baudelaire's

> Ah! Seigneur! donnez-moi la force et le courage
> De contempler mon coeur et mon corps sans dégôut!
>
> (Ah! Lord! Give me force and courage
> To contemplate my heart and my body without disgust!)[177]

(used by Laforgue in *Derniers Vers*, which, as I said in the first chapter, was probably Eliot's immediate model) or

> Soyez béni, mon Dieu, qui donnez la souffrance
> Comme un divin remède a nos impuretés
> Comme la meilleure et la pure essence
> Qui prépare les forts aux saintes voluptés! . . .
>
> Je sais que la douleur est la noblesse unique
> Où ne mordront jamais la terre et les enfers,
> Et qu'il faut pour tresser ma couronne mystique
> Imposer tous les temps et tous les univers.
>
> (Blessed be thou, my God, who gives pain
> As divine remedy for our folly
> And as the highest and purest essence
> Which makes us long for thy felicities! . . .
>
> I know that grief is the one human strength
> On which neither earth nor hell can impose.
> And that all the universe and all time's strength
> Must be wound into the mystic crown for my brows.)[178]

nevertheless, adequately foreshadows Eliot's own half-constructed spiritual discourse during the time of *The Waste Land*, aspiring more to the conditions of a ritual than a prayer. Indeed, it may even be said to anticipate the humility of *Ash-Wednesday* and *Four Quartets*. To quote from Eliot's first essay on Dante: 'We are not here studying the philosophy, we see it'.[179]

It seems that both Baudelaire and Eliot (till *The Waste Land*) wanted basically to build an aesthetic of suffering, where finally suffering itself seems to acquire a strangely redeeming quality. I discovered the following lines scribbled in English by Baudelaire in his diary, apparently quoting from Emerson's *The Conduct of Life*:

> Great men . . . [are] perceivers of *the terror of life* . . .
> [Baudelaire's italics]

We acquire the strength we have overcome.
The hero is he who is immovably centred.
No honest seeking goes unrewarded.[180]

'Prie, prie sans cesse', he wrote, 'La prière est réservoir de force' ('Pray, pray incessantly. Prayer is the reservoir of force').[181]

The quiet conviction in these lines seems to indicate why Eliot believed that Baudelaire succeeded (with Laforgue) in establishing a moral order. This Baudelairian moral framework—which, for Eliot, was an assertion of the necessity of order and institutions[182]—suited him well at that moment of crisis in his life just before the composition of *The Waste Land*. If Eliot was able to extend the framework in his later works, he nevertheless always paid homage to Baudelaire for going as far as he could possibly go.

Eliot had come to know Baudelaire *before* he met Laforgue and Corbière, who 'prolonged his work in the domain of self-consciousness'.[183] His identification with the last two may have forced him to temporarily forget Baudelaire's impact, but he had the necessary historic sense to realize that it was Baudelaire who was responsible for the new 'system of feelings' of his successors. Eliot went back to re-read him in 1919–20, and it now seems obvious that with all his 'imperfections and delinquencies',[184] Baudelaire ('notre' Baudelaire: 'our'[185] Baudelaire, Eliot reminded us) became an essential part of his discourse, helped him to know and moralize his predicament, and, consequently, transform 'slime into gold'.[186]

NOTES

1. *Charles Baudelaire* (1821–67): French poet, one of the pioneers of modern poetry, who, in Victor Hugo's words, brought 'a frisson nouveau' ('a new shiver') into literature.

   His poetical works include *Les Fleurs du Mal* (1857) *and Le Spleen de Paris* (1869); his reflective writings, *Les Paradis artificiels* (1860); his translations of the works of Edgar Allan Poe, *Histoires extraordinaires and Nouvelles Histoires extraordinaires* (1856–7); his literary and art criticism *Curiosités esthétiques* (1868), his personal notes, *Fusées and Mon coeur mis à nu* (1917). All his works are now collected in *Oeuvres Complètes*.

2. Pierre-Jean Jouve, 'Le Secret de Baudelaire', in René Huyghe et al., *Baudelaire*, Paris: Hachette, 1966, p. 57.

3. Ibid.

4. Charles Baudelaire, *Oeuvres Complètes* (hereafter referred to as *OC*), vol. I, Paris: Bibliothèque de la Pléiade, 1990, p. 691; Baudelaire's italics.

5. Jouve, 'Le Secret de Baudelaire', p. 58.

6. T.S. Eliot, *Selected Essays* (hereafter referred to as *SE*), London: Faber and Faber, 1951, p. 382.

7. Arthur Rimbaud to Ernest Delahaye, 18 May 1871, quoted by Philippe Soupault, in Jouve, 'Le Secret de Baudelaire', p. 134.

8. Eliot, *SE*, p. 382.

9. T.S. Eliot, 'Baudelaire', *SE*, London: Faber and Faber, 1951, p. 386.

10. T.S. Eliot, Review, '*Baudelaire and the Symbolists*, by Peter Quennell', *The Criterion,* January 1930, p. 359.

11 T.S. Eliot, *Notes Towards the Definition of Culture*, London: Faber and Faber, 1948, p. 115.

12. Eliot, Review, '*Baudelaire and the Symbolists*, by Peter Quennell', p. 359.

13. Richard Aldington, 'The Poetry, of T.S. Eliot', in *T.S. Eliot: A Selected Critique*, ed. Leonard Unger, New York: Rinehan & Co., 1948, p. 7.

14. Baudelaire, *OC*, vol. I, p. 87.

15. E.J.H. Greene, *T.S. Eliot et la France*, Paris: Boivin, 1951, p. 18.

16. Virginia Woolf, *The Common Reader*, London: Hogarth Press, 1951, p. 189. For the relevance of this remark to modern poetry, see Lawrence Durrell, *A Key to Modern Poetry*, Norman: University of Oklahoma Press, 1972, p. 26.

17. Henri Lemaître, *La Poésie depuis Baudelaire*, Paris: Armand Colin, 1978, p. 27.

18. Quoted in Daniel Leuwers, *Introduction à la poésie moderne et contemporaine*, Paris: Bordas, 1990, p. 72.

19. T.S. Eliot, *To Criticize the Critic* (hereafter referred to as *TCC*), London: Faber and Faber, 1978, p. 126.

20. Ibid.

21. Victor Hugo on Baudelaire, quoted by Claude Pichois in the introduction to Charles Baudelaire, *OC*, vol. I, Paris: Bibliothèque de la Pléiade, 1990, p. xliii.

22. 'Prends l'éloquence et tords-lui le cou' ('Take eloquence and break its neck')— Verlaine's line in 'Sagesse VI' is more applicable to Baudelaire.

23. T.S. Eliot, 'Burnt Norton', *The Complete Poems and Plays of T.S. Eliot* (hereafter referred to as *CPP*), London: Faber and Faber, 1990 p. 175.

24. T.S. Eliot, 'East Coker', *CPP*, London: Faber and Faber, 1990, p. 179.

25. Remy de Gourmont, *Le Livre des Masques*, Paris: Mercure de France, 1896, pp. 57–8.

26. T.S. Eliot, *The Use of Poetry and the Use of Criticism*, London: Faber and Faber, 1980, p. 34.

27. Eliot, Review, '*Baudelaire and the Symbolists*, by Peter Quennell', p. 359; emphasis mine.

28. T.S. Eliot, 'Clark Lecture I', in *The Varieties of Metaphysical Poetry* (hereafter referred to as *VMP*), ed. Ronald Schuchard, London: Faber and Faber, 1993, p. 59.

29. T.S. Eliot, 'The Lesson of Baudelaire', *The Tyro*, no. 1, 1922, cited in Greene, *T.S. Eliot et la France*, p. 108.

30. The Dial, May 1927, quoted in René Taupin, *L'Influence du symbolisme français sur la poésie américaine (de 1910 à 1920)*, 1929; Geneva: Slatkine Rpts, 1979, p. 222.

31. T.S. Eliot, *For Lancelot Andrewes* [1928] (hereafter referred to as *FLA*), London: Faber and Faber, 1970, pp. 68–78; also, T.S. Eliot, *Essays Ancient and Modern* (hereafter referred to as *EAM*), London: Faber and Faber, 1947, pp. 63–75.

32. Eliot, *SE*, pp. 381–92.

33. Charles Baudelaire, *Intimate Journals*, tr. Christopher Isherwood, London: Blackmore Press, 1930.

34. Eliot, *SE*, p. 376.

35. Eliot, Review, '*Baudelaire and the Symbolists*, by Peter Quennell', p. 357.

36. Ibid.

37. T.S. Eliot, 'Andrew Marvell', *SE*, London: Faber and Faber, 1951 p. 292.

38. Baudelaire, *OC*, vol. I, p. 785.

39. Charles Baudelaire, 'La Modernite', *OC*, vol. II, Paris: Bibliothèque de la Pléiade, 1990, p. 695.

40. Eliot, 'Andrew Marvell', *SE*, p. 292.

41. Eliot, *EAM*, p. 73.

42. Ibid., p. 71.

43. Eliot, *SE*, p. 372.

44. Ibid., p. 389.

45. Ibid.

46. Ibid., p. 384; Eliot's italics.

47. Eliot, *EAM*, p. 73.

48. Greene, *T.S. Eliot et la France*, p. 108.

49. Eliot, *SE*, p. 384.

50. Ibid., p. 385.

51. Ibid.

52. T.S. Eliot, 'Baudelaire in Our Time', *EAM*, London: Faber and Faber, 1947, p. 74.

53. Eliot, *SE*, p. 386.

54. All citations are from Eliot, 'Baudelaire', *SE*, p. 388.

55. T.S. Eliot, 'Clark Lecture VIII', in *VMP*, ed. Ronald Schuchard, London: Faber and Faber, 1993, p. 210.

56. Charles Baudelaire, 'L'Héautontimorouménos, *Les Fleurs du Mal*', *OC*, vol. I, Paris: Bibliothèque de la Pléiade, 1990, p. 78.

57. Charles Baudelaire, 'Un voyage à Cythère', *OC*, vol. I, Paris: Bibliothèque de la Pléiade, 1990, p. 119.

58. Eliot, 'Clark Lecture VIII', p. 220.

59. Eliot, *SE*, p. 388.

60. Ibid., p. 387.

61. Ibid., p. 388.

62. Ibid.

63. Ibid.

64. Ibid., p. 389.

65. Eliot, 'The Lesson of Baudelaire', quoted in Greene, *T.S. Eliot et la France*, p. 108.

66. Baudelaire, *OC*, vol. I, p. 193; emphasis mine.

67. Charles Baudelaire, 'Mon coeur mis à nu', *OC*, vol. I, Paris: Bibliothèque de la Pléiade, 1990, p. 697.

68. Baudelaire, *OC*, vol. I, p. 53.

69. Baudelaire, 'Mon coeur mis à nu', p. 696.

70. Charles Baudelaire, 'Eugene Delacroix', *OC*, vol. II, Paris: Bibliothèque de la Pléiade, 1990, p. 593.

71. T.S. Eliot, 'Religion and Literature', in *Selected Prose of T.S. Eliot*, ed. Frank Kermode, London: Faber and Faber, 1975, p. 97.

72. Jules Laforgue, *Mélanges Posthumes*, 1903; Geneva: Slatkine Rpts, 1979, p. 111.

73. Ibid., p. 115.

74. Eliot, *SE*, p. 388.

75. Laforgue, *Mélanges Posthumes*, p. 112.

76. Ibid.

77. Ibid., p. 113.

78. Laforgue, 'Nuages', *Poésies Complètes*, Paris: Le Livre de Poche, 1970, p. 370.

79. Laforgue, *Mélanges Posthumes*, p. 114.

80. Ibid., p. 115.

81. Ibid., p. 117.

82. Ibid., p. 114.

83. Ibid., p. 119.

84. Charles Baudelaire, 'La Béatrice', *OC*, vol. I, Paris: Bibliothèque de la Pléiade, 1990, p. 117.

85. Yves Bonnefoy, 'Hamlet et la couleur', in *Laforgue Aufourd'bui*, ed. James Hiddleston, Paris: Librairie José Corti, 1988, p. 168.

86. T.S. Eliot, 'London Letter', *The Dial*, June 1921, p. 686.

87. Eliot, *FLA*, p. 96.

88. Charles Baudelaire, 'De l'Essence de Rire', *OC*, vol. II, Paris: Bibliothèque de la Pléiade, 1990, p. 528.

89. Ibid., p. 531.

90. Laforgue's letter to Sabine Mültzer, in Jules Laforgue, *Oeuvres Complètes*, Lausanne: L'Age d'Homme, 1986, p. 753.

91. Baudelaire, *OC*, vol. II, p. 530.

92. Baudelaire, *OC*, vol. II, notes, pp. 1326–7.

93. Baudelaire, *OC*, vol. I, pp. 175–8.

94. Charles Baudelaire, 'Bouffonneries', *OC*, vol. I, Paris: Bibliothèque de la Pléiade, 1990, p. 176.

95. Charles Baudelaire, 'Les petites vieilles', *OC*, vol. I, Paris: Bibliothèque de la Pléiade, 1990, p. 89.

96. Arthur Symons, *The Symbolist Movement in Literature*, London: Archibald Constable, 1908, p. 107.

97. Charles Baudelaire, 'Les Phares', *OC*, vol. I, Paris: Bibliothèque de la Pléiade, 1990, p. 13.

98. Ibid., p. 14.

99. Stephen Spender, *T. S. Eliot*, Glasgow: Fontana Press, 1986, p. 39.

100. Charles Baudelaire, 'Le Crépuscule du soir', *OC*, vol. I, Paris: Bibliothèque de la Pléiade, 1990, p. 95.
101. Eliot, *CPP*, p. 13.
102. Charles Baudelaire, 'Les Sept Vieillards', *OC*, vol. I, Paris: Bibliothèque de la Pléiade, 1990, p. 87.
103. Baudelaire, *OC*, vol. I, p. 25.
104. T.S. Eliot, 'The Waste Land', *CPP*, London: Faber and Faber, 1990, p. 64.
105. Charles Baudelaire, 'Le Serpent qui danse', *OC*, vol. I, Paris: Bibliothèque de la Pléiade, 1990, p. 29.
106. Eliot, *CPP*, p. 53.
107. Baudelaire, *OC*, vol. I, p. 35.
108. Charles Baudelaire, 'Le Crépuscule du matin', *OC*, vol. I, Paris: Bibliothèque de la Pléiade, 1990, p. 103.
109. Ibid.
110. Charles Baudelaire, 'Harmonie du soir', *OC*, vol. I, Paris: Bibliothèque de la Pléiade, 1990, p. 47.
111. Baudelaire, *OC*, vol. I, p. 87.
112. T.S. Eliot, 'What Dante Means to Me', *TCC*, London: Faber and Faber, 1978, p. 127.
113. Philippe Soupault, 'Fourmillante cité, cité pleine de rêves', in René Huyghe et al., *Baudelaire*, Paris: Hachette, 1966, p. 131.
114. Ibid., p. 132.
115. Ibid., p. 133.
116. Charles Baudelaire, 'Pauvre Belgique', *OC*, vol. II, Paris: Bibliothèque de la Pléiade, 1990, pp. 823, 827.
117. Charles Baudelaire, 'Le Soleil', *OC*, vol. I, Paris: Bibliothèque de la Pléiade, 1990, p. 83.
118. Baudelaire, 'Le Crépuscule du matin', p. 103.
119. Jouve, 'Le Secret de Baudelaire', p. 134.
120. Baudelaire, *OC*, vol. I, pp. 275–6.
121. Walter Benjamin, *Ecrits Français*, Paris: Gallimard, 1991, p. 301.
122. Ibid., p. 315.
123. Robert Crawford, *The Savage and the City in the Work of T.S. Eliot*, Oxford: Clarendon Press, 1990, pp. 36–52.
124. Baudelaire, *OC*, vol. II, pp. 822–3.
125. Baudelaire, *OC*, vol. I, p. 291.
126. Ibid., p. 87.
127. Baudelaire, 'Les Sept Vieillards', p. 87.
128. Baudelaire, 'Le Crépuscule du matin', p. 104.
129. Baudelaire, *OC*, vol. I, p. 304.
130. T.S. Eliot, 'Whispers of Immortality', *CPP*, London: Faber and Faber, 1990, p. 52.
131. Charles Baudelaire, 'Journaux Intimes', *OC*, vol. I, Paris: Bibliothèque de la Pléiade, 1990, p. 662.
132. Eliot, *SE*, p. 391.

133. Alain-Fournier and Jacques Rivière, *Correspondance*, vol. I, Paris: Gallimard, 1991, p. 425.

134. Charles Baudelaire, 'A celle qui est trop gaie', *OC*, vol. I, Paris: Bibliothèque de la Pléiade, 1990, p. 21.

135. Charles Baudelaire, 'Hymne à la Beauté', *OC*, vol. I, Paris: Bibliothèque de la Pléiade, 1990, p. 24.

136. Ibid., p. 25.

137. Charles Baudelaire, 'L'Amour du Mensonge', *OC*, vol. I, Paris: Bibliothèque de la Pléiade, 1990, p. 98.

138. Charles Baudelaire, 'Les Epaves', *OC*, vol. I, Paris: Bibliothèque de la Pléiade, 1990, p. 154.

139. Ibid., p. 155.

140. Charles Baudelaire, 'Les Bijoux', *OC*, vol. I, Paris: Bibliothèque de la Pléiade, 1990, p. 158.

141. Charles Baudelaire, 'Les Métamorphoses du vampire', *OC*, vol. I, Paris: Bibliothèque de la Pléiade, 1990, p. 159.

142. Ibid.

143. Charles Baudelaire, 'Le Monstre', *OC*, vol. I, Paris: Bibliothèque de la Pléiade, 1990, p. 165.

144. Ibid., p. 164.

145. Charles Baudelaire, 'Bises', *OC*, vol. I, Paris: Bibliothèque de la Pléiade, 1990, p. 189.

146. Baudelaire, 'Mon coeur mis à nu', p. *677*.

147. Laforgue, *Mélanges Posthumes*, p. 112.

148. Baudelaire, 'Mon coeur mis à nu', p. *682*.

149. Charles Baudelaire, 'Le Dandy', *OC*, vol. II, Paris: Bibliothèque de la Pléiade, 1990, p. 712.

150. Ibid., p. 710.

151. Ibid., p. 712.

152. Baudelarie, 'Mon coeur mis à nu', p. 678.

153. Eliot, *SE*, p. 386.

154. Robert M. Adams in A. Walton Litz, ed., *Eliot in His Time*, Oxford: Oxford University Press, 1973, p. 143. The translation was done by Jean-André Moise de Menasce.

155. Baudelaire, *OC*, vol. I, p. 74.

156. Ibid., pp. 32–3.

157. Ibid., p. 796, notes.

158. Greene, *T.S. Eliot et la France*, p. 122.

159. Baudelaire, *OC*, vol. I, p. 118.

160. Ibid.

161. Eliot, *EAM*, pp. 72, 74.

162. Eliot, 'Clark Lecture I', p. 58.

163. Baudelaire, *OC*, vol. I, p. 798; d'Aurevilly's italics.

164. Ibid.

165. Ibid., p. 793; Baudelaire's italics.

166. Eliot, 'The Waste Land', p. 69.
167. T.S. Eliot, *On Poetry and Poets*, London: Faber and Faber, 1969, p. 38.
168. Ibid., p. 32.
169. Greene, *T.S. Eliot et la France*, p. 108.
170. Eliot, *SE*, p. 428.
171. T.S. Eliot, 'Marina', *CPP*, London: Faber and Faber, 1990, p. 109.
172. Baudelaire, *OC*, vol. I, p. 19.
173. Baudelaire, 'Mon coeur mis à nu', p. 696.
174. T.S. Eliot, 'Deux Attitudes Mystiques: Dante et Donne', *Le Roseau d'or, Chroniques III*, Paris: Plon, 1927, pp. 149–50.
175. Eliot, *SE*, p. 384.
176. T.S. Eliot, *The Sacred Wood* (hereafter referred to as *SW*), London: Methuen, 1982, p. 169.
177. Baudelaire, 'Un Voyage à Cythère', p. 119.
178. Charles Baudelaire, 'Bénédiction', *OC*, vol. I, Paris: Bibliothèque de la Pléiade, 1990, p. 9.
179. Eliot, *SW*, p. 170.
180. Baudelaire, 'Journaux Intimes', pp. 673–5.
181. Ibid., p. 653.
182. Eliot, *SE*, p. 392.
183. T.S. Eliot, 'Turnbull Lecture III', in *VMP*, ed. Ronald Schuchard, London: Faber and Faber, 1993, p. 281.
184. Eliot, *SE*, p. 391.
185. Eliot, 'Baudelaire in Our Time', p. 71.
186. Baudelaire's assessment of his own achievements in poetry:

J'ai fait mon devoir
Comme un parfait chimiste et comme une âme sainte.
Car j'ai de chaque chose extrait la quintessence,
Tu m'as donné ta boue et j'en ai fait de l'or.

(I have done my duty
Like a perfect chemist and a saintly soul.
Because I have extracted the quintessence from everything,
You gave me your slime and I transformed it into gold.)

(Project of an epilogue for the 1861 edition of *Les Fleurs du Mal*, in Baudelaire, *OC*, vol. I, p. 192).

3

Tristan Corbière and Eliot
'Mélange Adultère'

IN HIS DESPERATE BID TO create a new poetic discourse, T.S. Eliot also needed the help of the most macabre of the *poètes maudits*, Tristan Corbière (1845–75),[1] who had died of tuberculosis thirteen years before he was born. In 1923, Eliot acknowledged Corbière as one of his masters,[2] a stand he would maintain throughout his life. Yet, if Laforgue has provided some grist for source-hunters, critics[3] have shown no real desire to understand Eliot's interaction with the dark horse of Symbolism.

To the readers of French poetry, Corbière is a poet of dissent, of negation, of refusal; in other words, an anti-poet, who wished to reject the security and conformism of 'mensonges littéraires' ('literary lies') and of 'la larme écrite' ('the written tear')[4] of stereotyped poetic texts. His feelings were never set, literary ones: possibly the reason why he 'fell into Limbo'.[5] One of the strangest poets of the late nineteenth century France, his works remind us of a lullaby in one of his own poems:

> J'entends le renard, le lièvre
> Le lièvre, le loup chanter.
>
> (I hear the fox, the hare
> The hare, the wolf sing.)[6]

Despite sporadic attentions from poets like Apollinaire, Breton, and Eliot, and a handful of adventurous French critics like Jean Rousselot, E. Noulet, and Michel Dansel, Corbière has all along remained a *marginal*: whose 'unreadable' texts (to use Roland Barthes's[7] terminology) largely evaded, parodied, or innovated upon prevailing conventions, and thus persistently shocked, baffled, and frustrated the standard expectations of readers. Perhaps G.M. Turnell was right when he commented in *The Criterion* in April 1936: '[Corbière's] neglect in his own country was complete. . . He has never been for any writer what Rimbaud was for Claudel or Laforgue for the young Alain-Fournier'.[8] Recent French criticism, P.O.

Walzer regrets in his preface to Michel Dansel's *Language et Modernité chez Tristan Corbière*,[9] has failed to resurrect him. He remains the eternal outsider in French poetry.

It seems that Eliot—submerged as he was in Jules Laforgue at the time—had not 'discovered' Corbière in his Harvard and Paris years. For this, I think, we may safely put the blame on Arthur Symons, who had chosen to ignore him in his *The Symbolist Movement in Literature*. And there is no evidence that Eliot's friend and tutor in Paris, Alain-Fournier, had introduced him to the contumacious poet. In his correspondence with Jacques Rivière,[10] Fournier did not mention Corbière even once, though he referred to Laforgue at least 90 times.

It took Eliot almost half a decade to realize that it was Corbière the 'uncataloguable' (Laforgue's description of Corbière in *Mélanges Posthumes*),[11] who was the real precursor of Laforgue (hereafter, Eliot would always bracket them together), and that he too could serve his special kind of need to launch an offensive on the general floppiness of contemporary English poetry. But before we move on to the details of Eliot's interaction with Corbière's texts, let us try and locate the possible co-ordinates of their first encounter.

Curiously, although Symons's book had made no reference to Corbière, he was still indirectly responsible for their eventual intersection of paths. Writing about his debt to Symons, Eliot reminisced in 1930 in *The Criterion*: '. . . but for having read his book, I should not, in the year 1908, have heard of Laforgue or Rimbaud; I should probably not have begun to read Verlaine; and *but for reading Verlaine; I should not have heard of Corbière*' [emphasis mine]).[12] So we may legitimately assume from Eliot's statement that it was Paul Verlaine (his 1884 anthology *Les Poètes Maudits* opened with Corbière) who acted as the intermediary. Eliot scholars have failed to notice this important role played by Verlaine.

There could be two other reasons for Eliot's sudden interest in Tristan Corbière. Firstly, the rather unusual homage paid to Corbière by his mentor Laforgue in *Mélanges Posthumes*,[13] which I shall discuss shortly. Although most English and American commentators of Eliot seem to be curiously oblivious of Laforgue's close links with Corbière, contemporary French critics of Laforgue found him 'trempé, imbu, sursaturé de Corbière ('steeped, soaked, supersaturated with Corbière).[14] The second reason for Eliot's interest was possibly the publication of Charles le Goffic's definitive edition of Corbière's *Les Amours Jaunes* in 1912, still regarded as the finest. Ezra Pound, too, discovered Corbière in 1913, possibly in the same edition, and called him 'the greatest poet of the period'.[15] As usual, Eliot and Pound shared the excitement of their new discovery, and suddenly began to consider Corbière very important. Pound thought that he had finally found 'another poet to put on the same little rack with Villon and Heine,'[16] and in his introduction to a selection of French poetry in *The Little Review* in February 1918, regarded Corbière, Laforgue, and Rimbaud as the high watermark of symbolist poetry. He even came to believe that Corbière was 'perhaps the most poignant poet since Villon, in very much Villon's manner.'[17] An infatuated admirer of Laforgue, he began to see the distinctive qualities of Corbière: 'Laforgue conveys his intent by comment, Corbière by ejaculation, as if the words were wrenched and knocked out of him by fatality.'[18]

Interestingly, Eliot, too would soon regard him as one of the 'most important successors of Baudelaire.'[19] By 11 July 1919, T.S. Eliot, then thirty, was privately admitting in a letter to Mary Hutchison that Laforgue was *'really inferior to Corbière at his best'*.[20] Given Eliot's passionate admiration for Laforgue at that time, it would be unwise to take the statement lightly. This admiration did reach a high pitch, which is evident from Eliot's unpublished French sonnet on Corbière, now included in *Inventions of the March Hare*.[21]

What Eliot unearthed in Corbière was stunning, especially the uncanny similarity with Laforgue (Eliot listed the parallels in the eighth Clark Lecture and the third Turnbull Lecture[22]). Like the latter, who died at 27, Corbière's life, too was snuffed out at the tender age of less than 30. Both battled with consumption: Laforgue had pleurisy, and Corbière was handicapped by the deadliest kind of rheumatism and tuberculosis. Ugly, thin, and sickly, he was nicknamed 'Ankou' (Eliot was aware of all this, which is clear from his French sonnet on Corbière) by his neighbours: 'the spectre of death'![23] Both came to live in Paris for only a few uncertain years, wrote some of their finest poems on the metropolis and yet lived like complete strangers. Most importantly, both fought against the handicap of their despairing illness by laughing at it, and mocked their fate. Corbière provided T.S. Eliot with what he was frantically looking for in those years: fresh means of shrugging off the trauma of modern experience, 'face à la malédiction et à éphémère' ('in the fact of curse and ephemerality').[24] This defiantly unrhetorical poet would help Eliot further in 'cleaning up the verbal situation'[25] in English poetry (Eliot's own words about Valéry). It would be interesting to note that Stephen Spender, too, found Eliot 'totally unrhetorical'.[26]

It is essential to understand the Laforgue-Corbière relationship for a closer understanding of Eliot's mind. One must admit for the sake of history, that Laforgue was—perhaps with greater artistry, though later on Eliot himself would contradict this by declaring that 'Corbière was a finer poet'[27]—rehearsing Corbière's role, possibly with greater intellect, in French poetry. Laforgue's *Mélanges Posthumes* shows that he was actually conscious of this; he was accused of plagiarism as early as in 1885,[28] and suffered throughout his life from guilt complex. Both were dandies because of their desperation to be different—excellent illustrations of the Baudelairian hero ('dandysme à la Baudelaire', in Gourmont's words).[29] In fact, Corbière's self-sketch with a hat and a walking stick bears an uncanny resemblance with Laforgue's one of a dandy[30] and wonderfully tallies with Conrad Aiken's description of Eliot on his return from France in 1911.[31] This self-sketch (reproduced in Jean Rousselot's *Tristan Corbière*)[32] can easily pass for an illustration of Eliot's Prufrock.

The disconcerting similarity between Laforgue and Corbière—an inevitable bête-noire of French literary critics—was possibly first flashed to Eliot by none other than Remy de Gourmont in *Le Livre des Masques* (1896):

Tristan Corbière est, comme Laforgue, *un peu son disciple*, l'un de ces talents inclassables et indéniables qui sont dans l'histoire des littératures, d'étranges et précieuses exceptions—singulières même dans une galerie de singularités.

(Like Laforgue, *a bit his disciple*, Corbière is one of those indubitable but unclassified talents, a strange and precious singularity—a singularity even in a gallery of singularities.)[33]

And discreetly by Laforgue, too, in *Mélanges Posthumes*, which Eliot presumably thumbed very often along with the other works of Laforgue. (*Mélanges Posthumes* was in the third volume of Laforgue's *Oeuvres Complètes*, published by Mercure de France in Paris, 1903, which Eliot bought in 1908). It could not have escaped his notice that Laforgue acknowledged 'un grain de cousinage d'humeur avec l'adorable et l'irréparable fou Corbière' ('a grain of cousinage of mood with the adorable and irreparably crazy Corbière').[34] Much like Verlaine, Laforgue was quick to recognize his originality:

Ce n'est pas l'originalité de quelqu'un revenu des romantiques et des parnassiens successivement, mais du primesaut à la diable . . . Ce fut l'art de Corbière. Pas de couchants, pas de poésie de la mer, pas de ciels, pas de spleens pantoumes . . . c'est un insaisassable et boucané corsaire hardi à la course.

(This is not the originality of someone breaking free from the Romantics and the Parnassians, in that order, but real devil-care originality . . . its art has nothing to do with the poets of sunsets, of the sky, of the sea, of spleen. He is a pirate on the prowl.)[35]

What is it that struck Verlaine, Laforgue, and Eliot as so extraordinary in Corbière? Perhaps a clue could be found in the following description of

Verlaine's first introduction to *Les Amours Jaunes*, recounted by Charles Morice:

Cette nuit de l'hiver...that winter night of 1883 during which we read in turn, Trézenik and I, the precious volume, from the first to the past page, to the master of *Sagesse* . . .

Unforgettable hours! . . . Verlaine laughed continuously and in the most moving, the most poignant passages, his laughter interrupted us: *laughter that held tears.*[36]

In his preface of 25 February 1884 to *Les Poètes Maudits*,[37] Verlaine saw Corbière as pre-eminently a man of scorn.

> Son vers vit, rit, pleure très peu, se moque bien, et blague encore mieux.
>
> (His verse is alive, it laughs, weeps very little, mocks well and teases still better.)

It is this strident scorn and laugher of a 'savage poet' and his 'girouette folle' ('crazy somersaults': self-description in 'Le Poète Contumace'[38]) which isolated him from his contemporaries, and made him a *poète maudit*. It is significant that Verlaine had decided to begin his anthology with Corbière; he was conscious that Corbière with his 'brutalité charmante' ('charming brutality')[39] might be ushering in a new age. He was right, which is evident from Laforgue's arrival within fifteen years of Corbière's death and the latter's own admission of his kinship with Corbière.[40] And, significantly, despite the general apathy to his works, at least three pioneers of twentieth century poetry recognized him as a forerunner: one is the revolutionary modern poet Tristan Tzara,[41] the other is the surrealist André Breton, who paid tribute to Corbière by including him in his *Anthologie de l'humour noir*.[42] The third person to rediscover Corbière, and benefit from his works, is T. S. Eliot.

The best way to analyse Eliot's somewhat belated curiosity for Corbière would be to look at the latter through Laforgue's eyes; for Eliot's feeling of kinship and his brotherly admiration for Laforgue were strikingly similar to the latter's own for Corbière. This should be obvious enough (Laforgue was probably more dishonest about this) from the way Laforgue reenacted the same destabilizing modalities, clutching at self-irony and self-ridicule as a possible means of survival in a more and more uncongenial world. Indeed, Eliot arguably imbibed much the same elements from Laforgue as Laforgue himself had done from Corbière a little more than two decades ago.

Laforgue recognized that 'there isn't another verse-artist who has so completely freed himself from poetic language . . . The effect is of a whiplash, the drypoint burin; he is frisky, making puns and words with rude romantic abruptness—*he wants to remain outside definition*, not to be catalogued, to be neither loved, nor hated—in short, he wanted to be . . . beyond every custom on this side or the other side of the Pyrenées'.[43] A man of extraordinarily keen sensibilities, but physically weak like Corbière, Laforgue needed this sense of liberation. He learnt from Corbière's natural gift of parody and talent for caricatures; and one can well imagine that the day after he bought a copy of *Les Amours Jaunes* from Vanier in 1884,[44] Laforgue was in all probability a transformed, rejuvenated man, just like Eliot after his discovery of Laforgue at Harvard.

He (and subsequently, through him his disciple Eliot) learnt from Corbière's 'crazy somersault' how a 'jeune philosophe en dérive' could still write poetry by pushing his levity to the furthest point, which has the effect of 'intensifying the seriousness of a poem in an almost unbelievable degree'.[45] As we know, this is exactly what Eliot himself would try to do in the early and the middle periods of his career.

Corbière's ruthless humour was a defensive one; his artlessness ('L' Art ne me connaît pas,/Je ne connais pas l'Art': 'Art does not know me,/I do not know Art') the basis of his art. Of course when he wanted to, this 'artiste sans art, à l'envers' ('artless, overturned artist') could bring off lines as spectacularly refined as any in Mallarmé:

Ces gras graillons grouillants qu'un torrent d'or inonde?

(These seething gobs of fat in golden grease?)[46]

As René Martineau argues, the words perfection and imperfection are irrelevant in the case of Corbière.[47] If Corbière the verse-maker is often incorrect and wayward (Laforgue complains: 'pas un vers à détacher poétiquement'—'not a verse to be separated as poetically beautiful'),[48] it is because he *wanted* to be so. In his own words, 'ses vers faux furent ses seuls vrais' ('His false verses were his only truth').[49] They were his raison-d'être, his expiation.

Both Laforgue and his disciple Eliot comfortably fit in his scheme, where the poet—because of his own inadequacies—is no longer an entity. 'Acteur, il ne sut pas son rôle' ('Actor, he didn't know his role'), whose 'naturel était sa pose' ('his natural behaviour was his pose').

At this point it may be worthwhile to quote from one of Corbière's many poems which can, ironically, help us to know and understand Laforgue and early Eliot.

Epitaphe

Il se tua d'ardeur, ou mourut de paresse
S'il vit, c'est par l'oubli; voici ce qu'il se laisse—
—Son seul regret fut de n'être pas sa maîtresse.
. . . Coureur d'idéal—sans idée;
Rime riche,—et jamais rimée;
Sans avoir été,—revenu;
Se retrouvant partout perdu.
Poète, en dépit de ses vers;
Ariste sans art,—à l'envers,
Philosophe,—à tort à travers.
Un drôle sérieux,—pas drôle.
Acteur, il ne sut pas son rôle;
Peintre, il jouait de la musette;
Et musicien: de la palette.
Une tête!—mais pas de tête:
Trop fou pour savoir être bête;
Prenant pour un trait le mot *très*.
—Ses vers faux furent ses seuls vrais.
Oiseau rare—et de pacotille;
Très mâle . . . et quelquefois très *fille*;
Capable de tout,—bon à rien;
Gâchant bien le mal, mal le bien.
Prodigue comme était l'enfant
Du Testament,—sans testament.
Brave, et souvent, par peur du plat,
Mettant ses deux pieds dans le plat.
Coloriste enragé,—mais blême;
Incompris . . .—surtout de lui-même;
Il pleura, chanta juste faux;
—Et fut un défaut sans défauts.
Ne fut *quelqu'un* ni quelque chose
Son naturel êtait la *pose*.
Pas poseur,—posant pour *l'unique*;
Trop naïf, étant trop cynique;
Ne croyant à rien, croyant tout.
—Son goût était dans le dégoût.
Trop cru,—parce qu'il fut trop cuit,
Ressemblant à rien moins qu' à lui,
Il s'amusa de son ennui,

Jusqu' à s'en reveiller la nuit.
Flâneur au large,—à la dérive,
Epave qui jamais n'arrive . . .
Trop *Soi* pour se pouvoir souffrir.
L'esprit à sec et la tête îvre,
Fini, mais ne sachant finir,
Il mourut en s'attendant vivre
Et vécut, s'attendant mourir.
Ci-gît,—coeur sans coeur, mal planté,
Trop réussi,—comme *raté*.

(He killed himself with zeal, or died of laziness.
It was thoughtless of him to live; he leaves but this:
—His only regret was not to have been his own mistress.
. . . He ran after the deal,—with no idea;
A rich rhyme, you wouldn't hear;
Returning,—without having been there
Finding himself again lost everywhere.
Poet, in spite of his verse;
Artless artist,—inverse,
Philosopher,—random, perverse.
A funny guy—not droll.
An actor, he didn't know his role.
A painter, he played the cornet
And a musician: with the palette.
A head!—but he had no head;
Too mad to know how to be dull-witted.
For strokes of styles, used *very's*
—His false were his only true verse.—
A rare bird—and a load of rubbish
Very male . . . and sometimes very *whorish*;
Capable of anything,—good for nothing;
Bungling bad well and badly good things;
Prodigal like the son in the Testament
—Ultimately without a will. A gallant temperament,
And often, from fear of the unstimulating.
Putting his foot in it, unsimulating.
Dim, but a rabid artist in colour.
Misunderstood . . .—by himself in particular;
His song was truly false, with tears fraught;
And he was faultlessly in default.

Was neither *someone*, nor something
A *pose* was his natural leaning.
No poser, he posed as *unique*
Too naive, being too much believing all, but cynic
With gusto trusting in nothing.
He chose the disgusting.
Too ripe,—because he was too raw
Resembling nothing less
Than himself, boredom was a delight, and more
His ennui amused him all night
Even waking him up at night.
Derelict, drifter,—in short,
A wreck that never reaches port . . .
Too much himself to be able to relish,
Dried wits and drunken head
Done, didn't know how to finish,
With an expectation of life he died
And lived, expecting to die.
Here lies,—a heartless heart misplaced, a man
Too successful—as an *also-ran*.[50]

I quoted such a long poem only to show that this is the quintessential Laforgue or Eliot in his formative years. Under the guise of his ruthless attack, by sarcasm, irony, and caricature, on what seemed to him the sentimental rhapsodizings of Romantic poetry, he was indeed expressing his intensely personal reactions in non-stereotyped, new, dynamic images and taut, staccato rhythms of unusual vitality.

Eliot observed in his eighth Clark Lecture[51] that Laforgue was 'at once a sentimentalist over the *jeune fille* at the piano with her geraniums, and the behaviourist inspecting her reflexes'. And Corbière was a behaviourist *par excellence*, studying himself with almost complete detachment, and expressing himself in a language of thought-feeling probably unmatched in French literature since Villon. His own piano was, as it were, unaccorded; and the sound emanating was, to quote Huysmans, 'a cry of sharp pain like the breaking of a cello string'.[52] It brought back into French poetry, 'qualities which had been alien to its spirit since François Villon's day.'[53]

Writing about Eliot's poems, E.M. Forster had once remarked that they belong to the succession of Ben Jonson, Marvell, and Donne: they are a protest again the personal raptures of the Lake school.[54] No wonder then that Eliot was drawn like a magnet towards the poignant, informal, ironic naivete of Corbière, his 'self-mockery scurrilous and savage' (to quote

Edmund Wilson),[55] his essentially oral anti-poetry, which helped him to 'break free of the classical corset'[56] and fight his battles with the syntax. Almost as much as Laforgue, Corbière was an exciting discovery for him because of his startling and subversive use of colloquialism and pungent lucidity, which exploded the stale Georgian stockades. 'Cut out the poetry, that's what I've been trying to do all my life', Eliot had confessed to T.S. Matthews.[57] One good reason for Eliot's interest in Corbière was obviously the latter's apoetic preference for the spoken word incorporated into the rhythm of verse, which diminishes the distance between *parole parlée* (spoken speech) and *parole écrite* (written speech). This was done by Corbière with vehemence. Eliot's own preoccupation with common speech is well-known. Long under the compelling influence of Laforgue, Eliot suddenly discovered indent, shrill texts of Corbière: 'Picaro and vagabond, brusque, succinct, forcing his verse along with a whip . . . without an aesthetic, with nothing at all of poetry or versification, scarcely anything literary about them . . .'.[58] He was, in Verlaine's words, 'le dédaigneux par excellence' ('the disdainer par excellence')[59] of all prevalent codes: in poetry and in life.

Apart from this fundamental stylistic aspect of the Corbière-Eliot relationship, there could be another equally important one. I presume that Eliot's 'aboulie and emotional derangement'[60] had set in by that time. He was already thrown into the orbit of a woman of uncertain nerves. What was probably little more than a literary exercise—possibly too clever and coquettish at times—now became a horrifying reality. And ill of a sudden, Corbière became very important, for Eliot discovered in him the kind of serious irony he was unable to find among the seventeenth century poets. 'The metaphysical poets', he reiterated in the course of his discussion on Corbière, 'were witty, but not ironic—not ironic in so serious a way as this. *Real irony is an expression of suffering*, and the greatest ironist was the one who suffered the most—Swift'.[61] Interestingly, Corbière's friend Pol Kalig, too, called him 'un tendre comprimé ('a repressed soft heart').[62]

I would like to draw attention to the reference to a jaundiced love apparent in the title of Corbière's book: *Les Amours Jaunes* ('Yellow Loves'). Tristan Tzara, who emphasized this point in his famous preface, suggested that the Breton poet used 'aimer jaune' like the French idiom 'rire jaune', probably proclaiming himself a cuckold.[63] Eliot, himself in a complete mess soon after his marriage, probably looked forward to Corbière's irony to transmute his nightmare. The Laforguian mask, which sometimes betrayed his anguish, did not always come to his aid; the hard-crusted Corbière seemed more useful at certain periods. His language of relentless aggression expressed a self-destructive and yet peculiarly liberating introspection that suited Eliot, because for him the courage to struggle along 'constitutes life for a poet to transmute his personal and private agonies into something rich and strange, something universal and impersonal'.[64]

In the spring of 1871, Corbière had made the acquaintance of Count Rodolphe de Battine and his mistress, an Italian actress Armida-Josefina Cuchiani, with whom Corbière fell in love. She is the 'Marcelle' of his poetry. In 1872, he chased Armida and Count Battine to Paris and settled in Montmartre for the last four years of his life. Though Marcelle did not entirely deprive him, Tristan remained the eternally frustrated lover, 'être faussé et mal aimé' ('falsified and ill-loved'):

> Allons! La vie est une fille
> Qui m'a pris à son plaisir.
>
> (Here goes! Life is a whore who's taken me
> For her sensuality.)[65]
>
> Eternel feminin de l'éternel Jocrisse! . . .
> Fais claquer sur nos dos le fouet de ton caprice.
>
> (Eternal Feminine to the eternal Noddy! . . .
> Crack on our backs the whip of your caprice.)[66]

or

> Lui cracher à la bouche
> Cet *amour*!, il l'a merité.
>
> (To spit in the mouth
> This *love*!—He deserved it.)[67]

Eliot may have been surprised to notice the resemblance between his life and that of Corbière, 'un roman pauvre entr'ouvert': 'a bad novel—half-opened'.[68]

> Amour mort, tombé de la boutonnière.
> —A moi, plaie ouverte et fleur printanière.
> Camelia vivant, de sang panaché!
>
> (Dead love, fallen from my lapel.
> —For me, the vernal flower, and a round as well!
> Living Camelia,—with blood variegated!)[69]
>
> La mort dans tes bras me berce
>
> (Death in your arms cradles me.)[70]

To Corbière, a woman is 'lascive, féroce, sainte et bête' ('lascivious, ferocious, holy and stupid',[71] Eliot's day to day relationship with Vivienne, we know, evoked the same picture of a jaundiced love.

But primarily important for Eliot was Corbière's sensibility, which he thought was exactly like what he had learnt from his study of Elizabethan drama, the poetry of Donne, Gourmont's critical theories, and Dante. Tristan Corbière, as much as Jules Laforgue, seemed absolutely the right specimen for research in his own laboratory; there was the same kind of 'cooperation between acute sensation and acute thought'.[72] So fascinated was he with Corbière that he could say: 'Corbière at his best can find an image a parallel, which in its way, is as fine as Dante or Shakespeare'.[73] Eliot's theory of 'sensuous appreciation of thought' and 'thinking in images' may have had their origin in Gourmont's analysis of the 'organic relation between an idea, an image and a sensation'.[74] But no less important is his debt to the synthesis of the subjective and the objective in Baudelaire, Laforgue, and Corbière, their intensely personal nature of impersonality, and their physiological poetics.

To the young enthusiast in quest of a new horizon in language, Corbière seemed to corroborate Gourmont's views that 'Le style est un produit physiologique et l'un des plus constants, quoique dans la dépendance des diverses functions vitales' ('The style is a physiological product and one of the most constant despite the dependence on various vital functions')[75] and 'la sensibilité comprend la raison elle-même, qui n'est que la sensibilité crystalliseé' ('Sensibility includes reason itself which is nothing but crystallized sensibility').[76] Whether the 'thought-feeling' of Corbière was close to the 'metaphysical' (or the Dantean) metaphysics is immaterial; the fact remains that Eliot thought it was.

Reading the poetry of Corbière a century after his death, one cannot help wondering at the injustice done to him by Eliot critics. The *dédoublement* an irony of the dissenting, artless artist, and the topsy-turvy philosopher, who 'died hoping to be alive/And lived hoping to die' were echoed in Eliot's poetry for a longer period of time than one would imagine. If Laforgue had given him 'nourishment' in his youth and 'directed [his] first steps',[77] Corbière helped him to stop and ponder over those first steps. His admission to E.J.H. Greene that he took up Corbière seriously again between 1915 and 1920 is crucial. It was exactly the period when, in the words of Grover Smith, 'Eliot, having lost his original facility, was obliged to learn his art again'.[78] Eliot was, obviously enough, still under the Laforguian spell and was desperately trying to branch out: the possible cross with Corbière at this particular point of time has, therefore, a special interest for any reader of Eliot's poetry. Eliot had brought out his first two volumes of poetry during this period, and a third was on the anvil.

We have noticed the basic similarity of the predicament of alienation in Corbière and Eliot. Bonamy Dobrée called Eliot a 'contumacious' poet, 'who finds himself ill at ease in life, unable to accept current valuations, urged to mock, to flout, to outrage, he is hurt by life—he will harden, but cannot rot into cynicism'.[79] Dobrée does not go far to discover the roots of this contumaciousness. For example, the monotony of life in 'Prufrock' or 'Rhapsody'—rightly attributed to Laforgue—is also the core of Corbière's poetry:

> Repasser à la ritournelle,
> Se depasser et trépasser!
>
> (To pass through the ritual,
> To surpass oneself and kick the bucket!)[80]

This is no less Laforguian than Laforgue's poems, although probably Corbière was harder on himself than Eliot's mentor. And there is the same sense of being a non-entity, who is hurt by life:

> Je suis là . . . mais comme une rature.
>
> (I am there, but like a thing rubbed out.)[81]

This was enough, one would imagine, to set Eliot on the prowl. His 'an aimless smile that hovers on the air' could be a transposition of Corbière's 'L'inerte sourire/Qu'il porte là comme un faux pli' (The inert smile he displays like a false crease')[82] or even

> Et moi, le tire, en me rongeant,
> Un sourire idiot—d'un air intelligent.
>
> (And I, while in torment,
> Put on an imbecile smile—with an air of discernment.)[83]

Writing about Eliot's 'dull tom-tom', Stephen Spender says, 'The tom-tom, incidentally, is an early example of the savage and the jungle which Eliot hears ever more insistently under the mask of the so-called civilization'.[84] It would perhaps be relevant here to add that Eliot was—with great assurance—quietly pilfering from Corbière's 'Rapsodie du sourd':

> Va donc, balancier soûl affolé dans ma tête!
> Bats en branle *ce bon tam-tam* . . .
>
> (Go them, pendulum, distracted in my head, boozed!
> Beat with a swing *this fine tom-tom* . . .)[85]

The 'paper rose' ('Her hand twists a paper rose') could be a straight translation of 'fleur en papier'.[86] The famous street lamp in 'Rhapsody on a Windy Night' may have been suggested by 'la lampe d'habitude jetait par instants sur nous un éclair tremblotant, tout le reste me semblait de l'autre monde' ('Off and on, the binnacle lamp threw a trembling beam over us, everything else seemed of the other world').[87] Eliot's Baudelairian revulsion and fascination for women—expressed in 'female smells' or 'hearty female stench' in 'Rhapsody' may have their origin in 'ce poison, *l'odeur de femme*, m'emplissait les narines' ('This *poison, female smells,* filled up my nostrils'). We remember the great disgust with which Eliot refers to the 'rank, feline smell' of Grishkin.[88]

The Sweeney poems have an outward resemblance with those of Théophile Gautier, whom Eliot and Pound would consciously try to emulate towards the end of the second decade of the twentieth century; but in effect the savage, ferocious cartoons are possibly the fruit of Corbière's influence. The use of irony in the quatrains of 'A Cooking Egg' and 'Whispers of Immortality' is hauntingly close to Corbière's quatrains:

—Lord Byron, gentleman-vampire,
Hystérique du ténébreux;
Anglais sec, cassé par son rire,
Son noble rire de lépreux.

—Hugo: l'Homme apocalyptique,
L'Homme-ceci-tûera-cela,
Meurt, gardenational épique;
Il n'en reste qu'un—celui-là!—

(—Lord Byron, gentleman-ghoul,
Hysteric of the somber;
A Briton, dry and shaken
By his noble leprous laughter.

—Hugo: apocalypse man,
The Man of this-will-end-that
Dies, an epic national guard;
There is only one Hugo—he's that.)[89]

Eliot's familiarity with the poem is clear from his allusion to it in the Turnbull Lectures.[90] The stringent irony in this description—strangely Eliotic, in retrospect—suits the poet himself more than Byron or Hugo. Besides, 'son noble rire de lépreux' ('his noble laugh of a leper') is possibly the origin of the Laforguian (and Eliotic) shrug. Though René Taupin and Edward Greene[91] have taken great pains to demonstrate the external similarity of 'The Hippopotamus' with Gautier's poem of the same title, one feels that Eliot's poem is *in essence* closer to that of Corbière. I shall quote a quatrain from Eliot to demonstrate how the banality of an idea is conveyed by the rhyme or the use of an exalted name which deflates the balloon of romanticism. This is possibly best illustrated in:

> I shall not want Honour in Heaven
> > For I shall meet Sir Philip Sydney
> And have talk with Coriolanus
> > And other heroes of that kidney.
> I shall not want Capital in Heaven
> > For I shall meet Sir Alfred Mond.
> We two shall lie together, lapt
> > In a five per cent Exchequer Bond.[92]

The big descents from the serious to the mundane are part of the little jabs of Corbière:

> On frappe . . . oh! c'est quelqu'un . . .
> > Hélas! Oui, c'est un rat.
>
> (There is a knock...oh! It must be somebody . . .
> > But alas! Yes, it's a rat.)[93]

which, in retrospect, appear distinctly Eliotic!

René Taupin who was probably the first to study the French influence on Eliot, has mentioned the 'realism of extraordinary density' to be found in a poem like 'Dans le Restaurant' that the latter had supposedly absorbed from Baudelaire, Pound, and Corbière. He referred to 'Mr. Apollinax' and 'Gerontion', where every object is presentation of a real object, 'dépouillé de toute buée, et de toute poussière d'émotion et de sentimentalisme' ('stripped of all mist, of all dust of emotion and sentimentality').[94] Modern poetry, Taupin observed, does not have a poet with a rockier voice, nor a verse which is more scathing. He found echoes of Corbière's 'Frère et soeur jumeux' and 'Un riche en Bretagne' in 'Rhapsody' and 'Gerontion'.

Even though in *The Waste Land*, Eliot's vision was Dantesque and Baudelairian, and structurally the poem owes something to Valery Larbaud, Corbière's savage audacity—which in great moments of disarticulation would inspire him to rhyme a word with a vowel—bursts upon the surface through the veil of the grail legend, like the rat which crept through the vegetation:

> O O O O that Shakespearian Rag
> It is so elegant
> So intelligent.[95]

Surely, this enhances the feeling of chaos in Eliot's poem, reminding us of Corbière's:

Ay Panneau O O O O
Tu n'as pas besoin d'ombrelle
Tu peux tenir ton chapeau.

(Ay signpost OOOO
You don't need a parasol
You gonna keep the hat.)[96]

or

Aie, aie, aie, aie, aie
Aie, . . . qu'il est laid.

(Aie, aie, aie, aie, aie
Aie, . . . how ugly he is.)[97]

Corbière's experience had modified Eliot's sensibility, and he now used—with greater assurance—his deadly tools, his crazy somersaults, to subvert the the structural expectations of the readers.

Like Laforgue and Eliot, Corbière, too, frequently used quotes from other writers in the epigraph and burlesqued them with compelling effect in his poetry. He often made oblique references to Romeo, *Paul et Virginie* and Robinson Crusoe ('Le Poète Contumace'), which as we know, was also part of Eliot's own method. Both used scraps of popular songs and overturned others' lines (for example, he deliberately misquoted Macbeth[98]) with a confident, carefree abandon.

The cross with Corbière's sensibility and method is again reflected in certain passages of *The Hollow Men*, where Eliot uses a fairly straightforward style, very different from the cinematographic juxtaposition of *The Waste Land*. A reader of Corbière may be uncannily surprised at the verbal parallels (Eliot reminded us that in Corbière, the emphasis is on the *word* and the *phrase*[99]) and notice how an observation is transformed into a state of mind. Is it the kind of 'concentrated conceit' that Eliot compared with those of Dante in the Clark Lectures?

Ma parole est l'écho vide
Qui ne dit rien—et c'est tout

(My speech is an empty echo
Which is meaningless—and that's all.)[100]

Our dried voices, when
We whisper together

Are quiet and meaningless.[101]

Le vide chante dans ma tête
(Emptiness sings in my head)[102]

Le marteau bat ma tête en bois
(The hammer beats my wooden head)[103]

Corbière was unique among the French symbolists to use italics extensively: very often parts of sentences and even whole sections (for example, 24 stanzas of 'La Rapsode foraine', which Eliot regarded as his 'greatest poem'[104]) were written in italics. What is highly interesting for us is that Eliot's own use of italics in *The Waste Land* and *The Hollow Men* has a striking resemblance with Corbière's. In 'La Rapsode foraine', which is about the assemblage of the crippled and the diseased at a religious festival in Brittany, Corbière calls the long section in italics 'Le cantique spirituel' ('the spiritual chant'),[105] and this is exactly what it is too in *The Hollow Men*. The blind man's song in Corbière's 'Cris d'aveugle' has very strong claims to be the precursor-text of Eliot's poem; it has the same tone and mood, and evokes the same pattern of feeling:

Deus misericors
Le marteau bat ma tête en bois
Le marteau qui fera la croix
Deus misericors
Deus misericors

(*Deus misericors*
Deus misericors
The hammer beats my wooden head
The hammer that will drive iron into the cross
Deus misericors
Deus misericors.)[106]

The repetitive prayer of the man of stone with remorseless eyes:

Pardon de prier fort
Seigneur, si c'est le sort

. . .

Pardon de crier fort
Seigneur, contre le sort

(Sorry for praying loudly
O Lord, if it is the destiny

. . .
Sorry for praying loudly
O Lord, against the destiny)[107]

anticipates Eliot's

For Thine is
Life is
For Thine is the
This is the way the world ends
This is the way the world ends
This is the way the world ends
Not with a bang but with a whimper.[108]

and even sections of *Ash-Wednesday*:

Because I do not hope to turn again
Because I do not hope
Because I do not hope to turn[109]

Here I would like to draw special attention to the French poems of Eliot. When he was in France in 1910–11, he, by his own admission, had flirted with the idea of settling down and scraping along in Paris and 'gradually write French'.[110] He did write in French during a barren period after 'Prufrock' in order to lift his block. 'I did these things as a sort of *tour de force* to see what I could do. That went on for some months. The best of them have been printed. I must say that Ezra Pound went through them, and Edmond Dulac, a Frenchman we knew in London, helped with them a bit.'[111] Four of these were published in *Poems 1920*.

E.J.H. Greene believes that Eliot's French poems are literary exercises in the manner of Corbière: he may have got the hint from Eliot's title "Mélange Adultère de Tout", which was indeed the opening line of Corbière's 'Epitaphe pour Tristan-Joachim-Edouard Corbière. Philosophe, Epavemort'. While the French poems do have similarities with Corbière's, few have noted that Eliot's poetry from the beginning was *always* a 'mélange adultère de tout' ('adulterous medley of everything'), which was also the basis and the *point de départ oi* Eliot's modernism, and possibly of the Corbière-Laforgue diversion from Symbolism.

Tristan Corbière seems to have helped Eliot in getting rid of the bald patch after 1916. Although Eliot's French poems are rather stilted and artificial, and hardly qualify as good poetry in French, there are unblended elements of almost all his recent readings, of Rimbaud,

Apollinaire, Gide, and especially Corbière. 'Le Directeur' (1917) resembles Corbière's 'Epitaphe' to the extent that it may be called an abridged version of Corbière's famous ironic self-portrait, where he publicly undresses: his acute self-mockery is an expression of acute pain. Eliot's 'Mélange Adultère', too, turns back ironically on himself, like Corbière's 'coureur d'idéal—sans idée' ('One who runs after an ideal, without a clue about it'), who stumbles on his centotaph in Mozambique.

Another short 17-line version of Corbière's 'Epitaphe', to be found in the second Vanier edition of *Les Amours Jaunes*,[112] which Eliot may have read, and which is more alike in size and texture, could well be the real parent-text. Moreover, Eliot's 'En Amérique, professeur/En Angleterre, journaliste'[113] seems to be a poor carbon copy of Corbière's 'Un riche en Bretagne': 'C'est le bon riche, c'est un vieux pauvre en Bretagne/. . . c'est un philosophe-errant dans la campagne' ('He is a good rich, an old poor in Brittany/ . . . a wandering philosopher in the countryside').[114]

'Le Directeur' too shows a Corbièrian mannerism of staccato rhymes ('Le Directeur/Conservateur/Du Spectateur', etc.[115]), but is too slight a poem, and lacks the bite of Corbière. On the other hand, Eliot's 'Dans le Restaurant' has brilliant examples of merciless pun à la Corbière:

> Bavard, baveux, à la croupe arrondie
> Je te prie, au moins, ne bave pas dans la soupe.[116]
>
> (Garrulous, slimy, with a rounded ass
> I request you at least not to splutter in the soup.)

The poem seems to have strong resonances of Corbière's 'Le Bossu Bitor', especially of the conversation with the waiter. The jerky snatches of conversation in the poem are much like those of Eliot's *garçon délabré*, and Bitor's lecherousness and misery anticipate those of the waiter. The final passage of drowning in Corbière's poem is transmogrified in Eliot's poem: in the former, the drowned, hunchbacked sailor had once known love; in the latter, the dissipated waiter was once handsome. The structural analogy is revealing. As for Eliot's 'Lune de Miel', the wretched honeymoon with hundreds of bedbugs ('centaines de punaises'[117]) and the strong smell of a bitch ('une forte odeur de chienne'[118]) bring back memories of Corbièrian bitterness in a travel-poem like 'Veder Napoli Poi Mori', where a customs officer is compared with 'verminous kings'.[119]

Tristan Corbière had learnt to hate Romanticism from Baudelaire and his father Edouard Corbière. He lived among simple men, and yet was endowed with a complex modern sensibility. His deformity and physical suffering isolated him from those he desired to be with: in frustration and anger, he wished to be a prostitute's dog who could lick up unpaid love ('Je voudrais être alors chien de fille publique/Lécher un peu d'amour qui ne soit pas payé').[120] At the bottom, he thirsted for the sea, which, for him, stood for natural vigour and health. Eliot, who addressed Corbière as a 'sailor' in his French sonnet,[121] would not have failed to notice Remy de Gourmont's reference to his father's 'violent amour pour les choses de mer' ('violent love for things of the sea'),[122] which had influenced a man of his talent and acute nervous tension: the sea was possibly a kind of sexual release. 'La mer n'est plus qu'une fille à soldats' ('The sea is no more than a soldier's whore'). The sea, not altogether unsoiled by man, can still absorb his ugliness. It becomes a symbol, which, as G.M. Turnell argues, 'is an antidote to the disintegration of man'.[123] While Eliot mourns the 'lost sea-voices' and 'lost sea-smell', he does bring back memories of the broken cello strings of the imaginary seafarer in the shabby quarters of nineteenth century Montmartre.

Although Eliot may have initially learnt to exploit the water-image from Laforgue, I suggest that Corbière's hunger for the sea ('Le sort est dans l'eau': 'The destiny is in the water'[124]) added a new dimension to it. The image of drowning in the last lines of 'The Love Song of J. Alfred Prufrock' and that of death in water in *The Waste Land* and 'Dans le Restaurant' were probably seized upon and welded into his poetry from such suggestive stray lines as Corbière's 'nous étions mangés par la mer' ('we were being eaten up by the sea').[125] In Eliot's case, the vitality of water gradually became associated with his spiritual pursuit.

I do not agree with G.M. Turnell, who, a little impetuously, concludes that Corbière's poetry was 'an affirmation of life',[126] that 'it was a plea for the integrity of man'.[127] The kind of man that he was, a rank outsider in society, a true *poéte maudit*, Corbière could not care less about 'affirmation' and 'integrity' (Laforgue, for that matter, believed that he lacked these). Yet his was a deeply subversive influence and his tools proved to be lethal in the hands of T.S. Eliot in disrupting the genteel Georgian discourse of the time. Thanks to Eliot, Corbière, the 'wry, agitated joker' (Gustave Kahn's epithet)[128], unwittingly became the inspiration behind a crucial turning point in the history of English poetry.

One of Corbière's major contributions to twentieth century poetry was his journey towards the unwritten sentence: 'vers une phrase désécrite' (title of a chapter in Christian Angelet's *La poétique de Tristan Corbière*),[129] his labouriously unskilled qualities (Remy de Gourmont's words in *Le Livre des Masques*),[130] his strong passion for automatism, his contemptuous disregard for punctuation, his phonetic writing. No wonder that foremost surrealists like Tristan Tzara and André Breton have acknowledged their debt to him.[131] Philippe Soupault encouraged MacIntyre[132] to translate Corbière—one of his 'most authentic ancestors'.[133] To quote Michel Dansel:

En effect, sa langue revêt à nos yeux, presque cent ans après la mort du poète, une modernité à toute épreuve. Car le langage poétique de son temps couvant une mutation qui devait aboutir, après diverses révolutions, à la désarticularion d'une technique traditionnelle, à un éclatement du verbe. La poésie de Tristan Corbière fit donc l'office de contre-poison posthume.

(In fact, his language takes on, almost a hundred years after his death, a modernity which has stood all tests. Because in the poetic language of his time, a mutation was brewing which had to end, after diverse revolutions, in the disarticulation of traditional technique, in the explosion of the verb. The poetry of Tristan Corbière served, therefore, as a posthumous counter-poison.)[134]

His typographic style influenced Apollinaire's cryptograms, the surrealists, and many minor scribblers (like Birot, Marinetti, and Raymond Roussel) learnt from him as did Céline, Prévert, and Raymond Queneau. The absence of all punctuation in the burlesque epigraph of 'Epitaphe' and 'Cris d'aveugle' suggests Corbière's exasperation with technical devices. His non-conformist poetic style showed that one could say almost anything: 'volonté de communicabilité totale' ('desire of total communication').[135] There was a constant refusal to use the old counters. Tristan Tzara asserts that this 'volonté d'expression' ('desire of expression') which reaches a point of exasperation, is far from being disorderly; on the contrary it is a 'déroulement cohérent de la pensée poetique' ('coherent unfurling of the poetic thought').[136] A reader of *The Waste Land* would not fail to notice Eliot's love of the cryptogrammatic, clearly a heritage of Laforgue and Corbière. At the same time, there could perhaps be no second opinion about Eliot's desperate search for the coherence of poetic thought that Tzara speaks of. In Eliot, the disparate elements always tend to coagulate to form a coherent whole.

Ironically, this 'isolated eccentric'[137] from France, who taught Eliot the language of disarticulation (which remained the central characteristic of Eliot's poetry till well into the twenties) also helped him with one of his most harmonious constructions ever: 'In my beginning is my end'. There is every reason to believe that this is transposition of the elaborate play on 'fin' (end) and 'commencement' (beginning) in Corbière's epigraph to his poem 'Epitaphe':

Sauf les amoureux commençants ou finis qui peuvent commencer par la fin il y a tant de choses qui finissent par le commencement que le commencement commence à finir par être la fin en sera que les amoureux et autres finiront par commencer à recommencer par ce commencement qui aura fini par n'être que la fin retournée ce qui commencera par être égal à l'éternité qui n'a ni fin ni commencement et finira par être aussi finalement égal à la rotation de la terre où l'on aura fini par ne distinguer plus où commence la fin d'où finit le commencement ce qui est toute fin de tout commencement égal à tout commencement de toute fin ce qui est le commencement final de l'infini défini par l'indéflni—Egale une épitaphe égale une préface et réciproquement.

(Except for lovers beginning or finished who want to begin with the end there are so many things that end with the beginning that the beginning begins to end by being the end the end of which will be that lovers and others will end by beginning to begin again with this beginning which will have ended by being only the end reverted which will begin by being equal to eternity which has neither end nor beginning and will end by being also finally equal to the rotation of the earth when you'll have ended by no more distinguishing when the end begins from when the beginning ends which is every end of every beginning equal to every final beginning of the infinite defined by the infinite—This equals an epitaph which equals a preface and conversely).[138]

In fact, Pierre Leyris's French translation of 'East Coker' (first and last lines) and 'Little Gidding' (V) shows the analogy more clearly; for Leyris uses the same words (*fin* and *commencement*) as Corbière.[139]

Eliot would state in the eighth Clark Lecture: 'In the work of Corbière, there is less evidence of philosophic reading; he has less direct feeling of the "the absolute" [than Laforgue]'.[140] Yet Corbière's desperate fatalism reflected in these words form a major philosophic premise of Eliot in *Four Quartets*. This of course shows how Eliot's anxiety of influence operated at varying and indeterminable levels of awareness. (If, as J.J. Sweeney suggests,[141] Eliot heard of Mary Stuart's motto 'En ma fin est mon commencement' from Maurice Baring's *In my End is my Beginning* [1931], and even John Masefield's play *End and Beginning* [1933], his encounter with Corbière still remains vital). Who else but Eliot, always aware of the plural character of a text, could transmogrify it by introducing a philosophic backbone in such a way? Reading the memorial tablet with the two phrases 'In my beginning is my end' and 'In my end is my beginning' at the Church of St. Michael's in East Coker, Eliot's ancestral village, how many would know that the lines may belong to Tristan Corbière?

Most of Eliot's models (Dante, Baudelaire, Laforgue, Larbaud), it would seem, moved from scepticism to belief. Was Corbière a believer? He was, thought Verlaine, but in Satan.[142] Interestingly, Corbière's biographer A. Sonnenfield believed that his *Les Amours Jaunes* was a 'document *spirituel* de premier ordre' ('*spiritual* document of the first order').[143] Corbière, he believed, admitted the transcendent, without losing the perspective of the world and his own life. Religiosity in Corbière, according to Burch,[144] is best expressed in *Armòr* ('Saint-Tupetu de Tu-Pe-Tu', 'La Rapsode foraine', 'Cris d'aveugle'). We have already noticed the thematic and linguistic analogy between 'Cris d'aveugle' ('The Blind Man's Cry') and *The Hollow Men*: there is the same cry of despair, the same broken utterance of a prayer. As for Corbière's 'La Rapsode foraine', Eliot singled it out in the eighth Clark and in the Turnbull Lectures as a 'remarkable poem'.[145] There are elements of spiritual love in poems like 'Litanie' and 'Chapelet'. Burch argues that Corbière was not a new Job; his poetry was an expression of protest against his own suffering. Although 'sans guère de pratique catholique' ('without any Catholic practice'),[146] since his childhood Corbière was called upon to reflect on one of the central questions of Christianity: the problem of physical suffering and human misery. Sonnenfield's contentions may be merely an interpretation, for Corbière never made any direct reference to Christianity, nor did he receive the last Sacrament.[147] Yet this could help us in the long run in explaining the far-reaching impact of Corbière on Eliot's mind. Like Dante, Baudelaire, and Laforgue, he too seems to have signalled to Eliot an end and a beginning: the end of a life of worldly anguish and the beginning of that of a redeemed sinner.

NOTES

1. *Edouard Joachim Corbière* (1845–75), known as *Tristan Corbière*, published only one book of poems, *Les Amours Jaunes* (1873). (This book is included in a list of Eliot's books made by Vivienne Eliot in her diary, now in the New Bodleian Library at Oxford). It evoked no response in France till Paul Verlaine included him in his anthology *Les Poètes Maudits* (1884), alongside Mallarmé and Rimbaud. Jules Laforgue, who was accused of plagiarising Corbière, highlighted his distinct qualities in an article later included in *Mélanges Posthumes* (1903).

2. T.S. Eliot, 'Lettre d'Angleterre', *La Nouvelle Revue Française*, November 1923, p. 619.

3. There are rare exceptions like Edmund Wilson; see Edmund Wilson, *Axel's Castle* [1931], London: Fontana, 1967, pp. 81–2. Herbert Howarth and Leonard Unger do not even mention the name of Corbière.
   For new useful insights, see T.S. Eliot, *Inventions of the March Hare*, ed. Christopher Ricks, London: Faber and Faber, 1996.

4. Tristan Corbière, 'Un Jeune qui s'en va', *Les Amours Jaunes* (hereafter referred to as *LAJ*), 1873; Paris: Gallimard, 1988, p. 54.

5. C.F. MacIntyre, 'Introduction', in Tristan Corbière, *Selections from Les Amours Jaunes*, tr. C.F. MacIntyre, Berkeley: University of California Press, 1954, p. 10.

6. Corbière, 'Un Jeune qui s'en va', p. 53.

7. According to Barthes, it is a text 'that imposes a state of loss, that discomforts (perhaps to the point of a certain boredom), unsettles the reader's historical, cultural, psychological assumptions, the consistency of his tastes, values, memories, brings to crisis his relation with language'. See Roland Barthes, *Le Plaisir du texte*, Paris: Ed. du Seuil, 1973, pp. 25–6.

8. G.M. Turnell, 'Introduction to the Study of Corbière', *The Criterion*, April 1936. p. 396.

9. Michel Dansel, *Langage et Modernité chez Tristan Corbière*, Paris: Lib. Nizet, 1974, p. 15.

10. See the index of proper names in Alain-Fournier and Jacques Rivière, *Correspondances*, 2 vols., Paris: Gallimard, 1991.

11. Jules Laforgue, *Mélanges Posthumes*, 1903; Geneva: Slatkine Rpts., 1979, p. 125.

12. T.S. Eliot, Review, '*Baudelaire and the Symbolists*, by Peter Quennell', *The Criterion*, January 1930, p. 357.

13. Laforgue, *Mélanges Posthumes*, pp. 119–28.

14. L.G. Mostrailles (pseudonym of Leo Trézenik) in *Lutéce*, August 1885, quoted in Jean-Lous Debauve, *Laforgue en son temps: Langages et documents*, Neuchâtel: A la Baconnière, 1972, p. 199.

15. Ezra Pound, 'French poets', *The Little Review*, February 1918; quoted in Tristan Corbière, *The Centenary Corbière*, tr. Val Warner, Cheadle, Chesire: Carcanet New Press, 1975, p. li.

16. Ezra Pound, 'The Approach to Paris', quoted in Cyrena Pondrom, *The Road from Paris*, Cambridge: Cambridge University Press, 1974, p. 192.

17. Ezra Pound, *Literary Essays*, London: Faber and Faber, 1954, p. 282.

18. Ezra Pound, *Investigations*, quoted in René Wellek, *A History of Modem Criticism*, vol. V, London: Jonathon Cape, 1985–6, p. 165.

19. Eliot, Review, '*Baudelaire and the Symbolists*, by Peter Quennell', p. 358.

20. T.S. Eliot, *Letters of T.S. Eliot*, ed. Valerie Eliot, vol. I, London: Faber and Faber, 1988, p. 318.

21. Eliot, *Inventions of the March Hare*, p. 88.

22. T.S. Eliot, *The Varieties of Metaphysical Poetry* (hereafter referred to as *VMP*), ed. Ronald Schuchard, London: Faber and Faber, 1993, pp. 217, 285–6.

23. See notes by Jean-Louis Lalanne, in Corbière, *Les Amours Jaunes*, p. 278.

24. Dansel, *Langage et Modernité chez Tristan Corbière*, p. 130.

25. Eliot's own words about Paul Valéry; see the introduction (by T.S. Eliot) to Paul Valéry, *The Art of Poetry*, New Work: Bollingen Foundation, 1958, p. xxi.

26. Stephen Spender, *Eliot*, Glasgow: Fontana, 1986, p. 10.

27. T.S. Eliot, 'Clark Lecture VIII', in *VMP*, ed. Ronald Schuchard, London: Faber and Faber, 1993 p. 217.

28. Debauve, *Laforgue en son temps*, pp. 251–2. In Gustave Kahn, *Symbolistes et Décadents*, Paris, 1902, p. 28, Kahn revealed that he had indeed introduced Laforgue to Corbière's poetry in 1880. An exasperated Laforgue wrote to Léo Trézenik: 'Tout le monde me jette Corbière à la tête' ('Everybody throws Corbière on my head'). See François Ruchon, *Jules Laforgue, sa vie, san oeuvre*, Geneva: Albert Ciana, 1924, p. 73.

29. Remy de Gourmont, *Le Livre des Masques*, Paris: Mercure de France, 1896, p. 154.
30. The sketch on the cover of Jules Laforgue, *Poesies Complètes*, Paris: Le Livre de Poche, 1970.
31. Richard March and Tambimuttu, eds., *T.S. Eliot: A Symposium*, London: Frank and Cass, 1965, p. 20.
32. Jean Rousselot, *Tristan Corbière*, Paris: Ed. Seghers, 1951, p. 64.
33. Gourmont, *Le Livre des Masques*, p. 155.
34. Michael Collie, *Jules Laforgue*, London: University Press, 1977, p. 42.
35. Laforgue, *Mélanges Posthumes*, pp. 126–7.
36. Charles Morice, *Tristan Corbière*, Paris: Messein, 1912, p. 22; quoted in Corbière, *Centenary Corbière*, tr. Val Warner, p. xi.
37. Paul Verlaine, ed., *Les Poètes Maudits*, 1884; Cognac: Le temps qu'il fait, 1990, p. 20.
38. Corbière, *LAJ*, p. 69.
39. Verlaine, ed., *Les Poètes Maudits*, p. 24.
40. Collie, *Jules Laforgue*, p. 42.
41. Rousselot, *Tristan Corbière*, p. 69.
42. André Breton, ed., *Anthologie de l'humour noir*, Paris: Ed. du Sagittaire, 1950, pp. 163–8.
43. Laforgue, *Mélanges Posthumes*, pp. 121, 126.
44. Collie, *Jules Laforgue*, p. 43.
45. Turnell, 'Introduction to the Study of Corbière', p. 396.
46. Tristan Corbière, 'Paris Diurne', *LAJ*, Paris: Gallimard, 1988, p. 243.
47. René Martineau, *Tristan Corbière*, Paris: Le Divan, 1925, p. 50.
48. Laforgue, *Mélanges Posthumes*, p. 123.
49. Tristan Corbière, 'Epitaphe', *LAJ*, Paris: Gallimard, 1988, p. 29.
50. Ibid., p. 30.
51. Eliot, *VMP*, p. 216.
52. Wilson, *Axel's Castle*, p. 81.
53. Ibid.
54. E.M. Forster, in Leonard Unger, ed., *T.S. Eliot: A Selected Critique*, New York: Rinehart & Co., 1948, p. 15.
55. Wilson, *Axel's Castle*, p. 81.
56. Michel Dansel's words about Corbière; see Dansel, *Langage et Modernité chez Tristan Corbière*, p. 60.
57. T.S. Matthews, *Great Tom: Notes Towards the Definition of T.S. Eliot*, London: Wiedenfeld and Nicholson, 1974, p. 159.
58. Laforgue, *Mélanges Posthumes*, pp. 119–120.
59. Verlaine, ed., *Les Poètes Maudits*, p. 19.
60. Eliot to Richard Aldington, 26 October 1921, quoted in the introduction to T.S. Eliot, *The Waste Land: A Facsimile and Transcript*, London: Faber and Faber, 1971, p. xxii.
61. Eliot, 'Clark Lecture VIII', p. 219.

62. Personal communication by René Marineau, quoted in Micha Grin, *Tristan Corbière, poète maudit*, Paris: Evian, 1972, p. 55.

63. See the preface by Tristan Tzara to Tristan Corbière, *Les Amours Jaunes*, Paris: Club François du Livre, 1950; quoted in Rousselot, *Tristan Corbière*, p. 61.

64. T.S. Eliot, *Selected Essays*, London: Faber and Faber, 1951, p. 137.

65. Tristan Corbière, 'Paria', *LAJ*, Paris: Gallimard, 1988, p. 129.

66. Tristan Corbière, 'Féminin singulier', *LAJ*, Paris: Gallimard, 1988, p. 34.

67. Tristan Corbière, 'Femme', *LAJ*, Paris: Gallimard, 1988, p. 60.

68. Ibid., p. 59.

69. Tristan Corbière, 'Duel aux camelias', *LAJ*, Paris: Gallimard, 1988, p. 61.

70. Corbière, 'Un Jeune qui s'en va', p. 55.

71. Tristan Corbière, 'A l'Eternel Madame', *LAJ*, Paris: Gallimard, 1988, p. 33.

72. Eliot, 'Clark Lecture VIII', pp. 220–1.

73. Ibid., p. 218.

74. Remy de Gourmont, *La Culture des idées*, Paris: Mercure de France, 1900, p. 66.

75. Remy de Gourmont, *Le Problème du style*, Paris: Mercure de France, 1902, p. 19.

76. Ibid., p. 107.

77. T.S. Eliot, *To Criticize the Critic*, London: Faber and Faber, 1978, p. 126.

78. Grover Smith, *T.S. Eliot's Poetry and Plays: A Study in Sources and Meaning*, Chicago: University of Chicago Press, 1961, p. 39.

79. Bonamy Dobrée, *The Lamp and the Lute*, New York: Barnes and Noble, 1964, p. 101.

80. Tristan Corbière, 'Paris', *LAJ*, Paris: Gallimard, 1988, p. 23.

81. Tristan Corbière, 'Le Poète Contumace', *LAJ*, Paris: Gallimard, 1988, p. 67.

82. Corbière, 'Femme', p. 60.

83. Tristan Corbière, 'Rapsodie du sourd', *LAJ*, Paris: Gallimard, 1988, p. 100.

84. Spender, *Eliot*, p. 44.

85. Corbière, 'Rapsodie du sourd', p. 101.

86. Corbière, 'Paris', p. 26.

87. Tristan Corbière, 'L'Americaine', *LAJ*, Paris: Gallimard, 1988, p. 266.

88. T.S. Eliot, 'Whispers of Immortality', *The Complete Poems and Plays of T.S. Eliot* (hereafter referred to as *CPP*), London: Faber and Faber, 1990, p. 53.

89. Corbière, 'Un Jeune qui s'en va', p. 54.

90. Eliot, *VMP*, p. 286.

91. E.J.H. Greene, *T.S. Eliot et la France*, Paris: Boivin, 1951, pp. 97–8.

92. T.S. Eliot, 'A Cooking Egg', *CPP*, London: Faber and Faber, 1990, p. 44.

93. Corbière, 'Le Poète Contumace', p. 69.

94. René Taupin, *L'Influence du symbolisme français sur la poésie américaine, 1910 à 1920* [1929], Geneva: Slatkine Rpts., 1975, p. 235.

95. T.S. Eliot, 'The Waste Land', *CPP*, London: Faber and Faber, 1990, p. 130.

96. Tristan Corbière, 'Les pannoides', *LAJ*, Paris: Gallimard, 1988, p. 226.

97. Tristan Corbière, 'Sous une photographie de Corbière', *LAJ*, Paris: Gallimard, 1988, p. 215.

98. Tristan Corbière, 'Litanie du sommeil', *LAJ*, Paris: Gallimard, 1988, p. 103.

99. Eliot, 'Clark Lecture VIII', p. 217.

100. Tristan Corbière, 'Paria', *LAJ*, Paris: Gallimard, 1988, p. 128.

101. T.S. Eliot, 'The Hollow Men', *CPP*, London: Faber and Faber, 1990, p. 83.

102. Corbière, 'Un Jeune qui s'en va', p. 52.

103. Tristan Corbière, 'Cris d'aveugle', *LAJ*, Paris: Gallimard, 1988, p. 148.

104. Eliot, 'Clark Lecture VIII', p. 218.

105. Corbière, *LAJ*, p. 139.

106. Corbière, 'Cris d'aveugle', p. 148.

107. Ibid., p. 150.

108. Eliot, 'The Hollow Men', p. 86.

109. Eliot, *CPP*, p. 89.

110. Interview given by T.S. Eliot in *Paris Review* (Spring/Summer 1959), partly reprinted in B.C. Southam, ed., *T.S. Eliot: 'Prufrock', 'Gerontion', 'Ash-Wednesday' and other Shorter Poems*, London: Macmillan, 1993, p. 50.

111. Ibid.

112. Corbière, *LAJ*, p. 282n.

113. Eliot, *CPP*, p. 47.

114. Corbière, *LAJ*, p. 134.

115. Eliot, *CPP*, p. 46.

116. Ibid., p. 51.

117. Eliot, *CPP*, p. 48.

118. Ibid.

119. Corbière, *LAJ*, p. 116.

120. Tristan Corbière, 'Sous un portrait de Corbière', *LAJ*, Paris: Gallimard, 1988, p. 237.

121. Eliot, *Inventions of the March Hare*, ed. Christopher Ricks, p. 88.

122. Gourmont, *Le Livre des Masques*, p. 158.

123. Turnell, 'Introduction to the Study of Corbière', p. 403.

124. Tristan Corbière, 'Le Naufrageur', *LAJ*, Paris: Gallimard, 1988, p. 190.

125. Corbière, 'L'Americaine', p. 266.

126. Turnell, 'Introduction to the Study of Corbière', p. 397.

127. Ibid., p. 401.

128. Kahn's comment on Corbière during the Laforgue-Corbière controversy in *Lutèce*, August 1885, quoted in David Arkell, *Looking for Laforgue: An Informal Biography*, Manchester: Carcanet, 1979, p. 168.

129. Christian Angelet, *La Poétique de Tristan Corbière*, Bruxelles: Palais des Académies, 1961, p. 103.

130. Gourmont, *Le Livre des Masques*, p. 155.

131. See Rousselot, *Tristan Corbière*, pp. 69, 84–5.

132. See the preface by MacIntyre to Tristan Corbière, *Selections from 'Les Amours Jaunes'*, tr. C.F. MacIntyre, Berkeley: University of California Press, 1954, p. vii.

133. Rousselot, *Tristan Corbière*, p. 82.

134. Dansel, *Langage et Modernité chez Tristan Corbière*, p. 137.

135. Rousselot, *Tristan Corbière*, p. 79.

136. Ibid., p. 85.

137. Albert Sonnenfield, *L'oeuvre poétique de Tristan Corbière*, Paris: PUF, 1960, p. 121.

138. 'Sagesse des Nations' in Corbière, 'Epitaphe', p. 28.

139. T.S. Eliot, *Poésie*, tr. Pierre Leyris, Paris: Ed. du Seuil, 1969, pp. 185, 225.

140. Eliot, *VMP*, p. 217.

141. Grover Smith, 'Tourneur and Little Gidding; Corbière and East Coker', *Modern Language Notes*, June 1950, pp. 420–1.

142. Verlaine, ed., *Les Poètes Maudits*, p. 11.

143. A. Sonnenfield, 'Tristan Corbière, poète chretien?', *Les Cahiers de l'lroise*, January–March 1960, pp. 1–9.

144. Francis Burch, *Tristan Corbière: l'originalité des Amours Jaunes et leur Influence sur T.S. Eliot*, Paris: Lib. Nizet, 1970, p. 123.

145. Eliot, *VMP*, p. 286.

146. Verlaine, ed., *Les Poètes Maudits*, p. 11.

147. Corbière, *Centenary Corbière*, tr. Val Warner, p. xxiii.

4

Valery Larbaud and Eliot
The Pattern of Feelings

IF BAUDELAIRE SHOWED ELIOT how to express the sterile and the intractably unpoetic, if Corbière and Laforgue provided him with the ammunition of irony to explode an outworn poetic code, and helped him to forge his own idiom, there was another Frenchman whose textual resonance in Eliot's poetry made it so distinctively sophisticated and original: Valery Larbaud[1] (1881–1957). A study of his works seems to me essential for disentangling the complex web of multiple sources in Eliot's poetry.

In his crucial romantic year in Paris in 1910–11 when Eliot was still under the sustained magic spell of Laforgue, Larbaud quietly came to occupy, or so I guess, a special place in Eliot's heart. He was a genuine poet and one of the earliest Modernists who exerted, in the words of Octavio Paz, 'a secret but decisive influence on modern poetry'.[2] According to Richard Aldington, Larbaud's *Les Poésies de A.O. Barnabooth* is 'inimitable' and should be regarded as 'the begetter of many of the recent books of cosmopolitan psychology'.[3] Larbaud was a man of extensive learning and cultural interests, who believed that he had exhausted 'tout ce qu'il y a de neuf dans la littérature française' ('everything new in French poetry')[4] and wanted to do something totally new: 'quelque chose de plus neuf encore, et du moins quelque chose de tout différent que nous connaissons' ('something even newer, and at least something totally different from what we are familiar with').[5] He had narrowly missed the Goncourt Prize for his novel *Fermina Marquez*, which was serialized (March-June 1910) in *La Nouvelle Revue Française* (*NRF*) during Eliot's year in Paris. By that time, Larbaud had already become a Messiah of sorts, and his *Barnabooth* drew

*I must acknowledge here my gratitude to Mlle Monique Kuntz, Librarian of Bibliothèque Valery Larbaud, Vichy (1989–90), for her kind help with documents during my visit to Vichy, France, in May–June 1989. My speculations were confirmed when I stumbled on T.S. Eliot's inscriptions in books dedicated by him to Larbaud.

the respect of most young writers in the literary circles. 'Barnabooth?' Andre Gide wrote to him in 1911, 'I think you cannot imagine how eagerly I await more of his self-expressions'.[6] The poet Jacques Rivière exchanged no less than one hundred and forty-eight letters with Larbaud;[7] Pound has referred to the prestige and significance of Larbaud and his *Barnabooth* in *Lettres de Paris*.[8] A polyglot, the most avowedly cosmopolitan of the new French writers, a genuine spokesman of Cultural Relativism, the most prolific and perhaps the finest translator in French of continental literature[9] till date, he introduced to the French, with scrupulous seriousness, the works of Walt Whitman, Landor, Samuel Butler, Ramón de la Serrm, Joseph Conrad, and James Joyce, among others. André Gide and Paul Claudel, too, translated at times, but no one in the *NRF* quite matched Larbaud's spectacular success as a translator. And, surely, Eliot would have met the discerning poet-critic in the pages of the *NRF*, where Larbaud wrote regularly the *Lettres anglaises*. What must have been no less important for Eliot, Larbaud was also a great admirer and a close friend of Charles-Louis Philippe, who exerted a conspicuous influence on Eliot's poetry (Eliot would use lines from Philippe's novels *Bubu de Montparnasse* and *Marie-Donadieu* in 'Preludes', and openly acknowledge his debt to him in an introduction to Laurence Vail's English translation of *Bubu* in 1932).[10] He wrote a memorable obituary of Philippe in 1909; André Gide's booklet on Philippe, too, was dedicated to Larbaud.[11] All this may have whetted Eliot's curiosity about the latter. Two years later, his French tutor Alain-Fournier would write to Jacques Rivière that the 'most talented man at the *NRF* was Valery Larbaud'.[12]

Curiously, Larbaud and Eliot shared—apart from that unflinching commitment to Europeanism—a somewhat uncommon attachment to Jules Laforgue and Tristan Corbière as well. In an article in Spanish in *Nación* (1923), Larbaud declared that Laforgue was 'one of the great masters', who 'in spite of his short life and silence of the critics, was one of the great influences of his time' and *'helped the transition to modernity'*. Pierrot-Hamlet, he thought, was more like 'an admired elder brother' (Eliot used exactly the same words about Laforgue[13]), who was a 'revelation', 'who knew everything, who sang everything, a new commentator of the Book of Knowledge', one who 'elevated the turmoils of the soul to the level of art'.[14]

Eliot was also likely to be aware that it was Larbaud who had 'unearthed' Saint-John Perse,[15] the *only* poet Eliot would translate in his entire literary career (*Anabasis*, 1930). He must have known that Perse always held Larbaud in the highest esteem, both as poet and critic. 'Larbaud . . . even the two syllables thrilled the mind', wrote Saint-John Perse in his homage in 1957; he was sure that he had never encountered anyone who had a better sense of 'honneur littéraire' ('literary honour').[16]

Another startling indication of the strange affinity of minds of Eliot and Larbaud may be found in the fact that the latter was an ardent admirer of John Donne,[17] the man and the poet, with his 'joli vaccin contre toute formule acádemique' ('nice vaccine against all academic formulae').[18] Together with Edmund Gosse and André Gide, Larbaud had formed a John Donne Club in 1912, which also included Saint-John Perse.[19] It is little known whether Eliot was aware of this fact (since Larbaud, Gide, and Perse later became Eliot's correspondents, the possibility cannot be ruled out), but this shows how similar the approaches of these two literary activists were to metaphysical poetry at a particular point of time. The conspicuous circle of relationships[20] between Donne, Laforgue, Corbière, Larbaud, Saint-John Perse, and Eliot possibly shows that the present study is far from hypothetical.

By the time Eliot came to know him in 1910–11, Larbaud had created a stir with his *Poèms par un riche amateur* by A.O. Barnabooth (1908): an elaborate pseudonym that reminds us of J. Alfred Prufrock. There is a similar generic or social suggestion in the name. It is surprising that none has noticed this curious analogy. Indeed, Larbaud's self-masking could well have seemed the right thing to Eliot for his Laforguian camouflage of actual emotions in 'Prufrock'.

Laforguian as it is in tone and spirit, 'Prufrock' also shares some of Barnabooth's qualities of a rich amateur who loses his identity in a crowd of faceless passers-by:

> Passants! gens qui me coudoyez, o flots immenses!
> Ne me sera-t-il donc jamais possible de me mêler à vous?
> Quand est-ce que je cesserai d'être
> Ce vagabond sans caste et sans métier?
>
> (Passers-by! People who rub shoulders with me, Oh! great streams!
> Will it never be possible for me to mingle with you?
> When shall I cease to be
> This vagabond without caste and profession?)[21]

This reminds us of Harry's words: 'alone/In an overcrowded desert'.[22] Both Larbaud and Eliot singled out intellectual understanding as a means of organizing one's life-world. There is the same degree of awareness, observation, and detachment, which, according to D. Fokkema, are 'at the centre of the Modernist semantic universe'.[23] If, as Fokkema observes, 'extreme wealth and a colonial background make Larbaud into a *detached* observer',[24] the end result in the text of Eliot (with his slightly different background) is disconcertingly similar. 'The significance of these poems', said Larbaud, 'is not what one reads, but what transpires from them in spite of myself.'[25]

Interestingly, Barnabooth, who is an American by birth living in Europe like T.S. Eliot, and a *déclassé* (according to Spender, Eliot was 'an expatriate who looked to Europe for civilisation')[26]—a similarity which the hawk-eyed New Englander from Saint-Louis would not have failed to notice—finds himself alone and miserable:

> Mais qui viendra en aide à ma misere, à moi?
>
> (But who will come to my aid in my misery?)[27]

Like the bitter and ironic self-realization in Eliot's poem ('I have seen the moment of my greatness flicker'), Larbaud too speaks in the same vein:

> Comme un bon poète français que j'efforce d'être
> Comme tous les poètes français, ironique—et cocu.
>
> (Like a good French poet that I try to be
> Like all the French poets, ironic—and cuckolded.)[28]

What strikes us immediately is the cosmopolitanism and suave humour in Larbaud's poetry, which are the only means of sustenance in a more and more inhuman and disquieting world:

> O société des Hommes!
> Je m'habitue à mon amertume.
>
> (O society of Men!
> I am getting used to my bitterness.)[29]

This, as we know, is also the story of Eliot's poetry. Eliot was possibly attracted to Larbaud's cosmopolitanism because he too, like Larbaud, always treated all European literature as one ('the hope of perpetuating the culture of any country lies in communication with others'[30]), Europe as one big city, and mixed those diverse memories and desires with the unmistakable stamp of his own. Like Eliot in English poetry, Larbaud too was the first French poet who wished to make 'a fusion of the countries of an ancient continent'.[31] A thoroughly professional man of letters like Eliot, he was one of the first to exploit the resources of exoticism and, like Laforgue, studded his verse with foreign names, expressions, fragments of songs, and refrains. More often than not, Larbaud would break into English:

> Et mon age gardien
> When he looks into it

> He will find in it
> Just a tiny girl.[32]

or into Spanish or Italian,[33] strangely anticipating the style which has come to be known as typically Eliotic. It would almost seem, as René Lalou points out, that 'Larbaud caressed the soft foreign syllables with a voluptuous abandon'.[34] This was equally true of Eliot.

Like Eliot, Valery Larbaud was primarily a city-poet:

> O ma Muse, fille des grandes capitales
>
> (O my Muse, daughter of big capitals)[35]

or

> Des villes et encore des villes
> J'ai des souvenirs de villes comme on a des souvenirs d'amour.
>
> (Cities and still more cities
> I have memories of cities just as one has memories of love.)[36]

The extraordinary deftness with which he juggled the city-pictures to give a new dimension to Baudelaire's 'fourmillante cité' remains unmatched in modern French poetry. There is a whole section called 'Europe' in *Les Poésies de A.O. Barnabooth*, apart from the numerous clusters of city images in his journal and tales. What Georges Cattaui calls the 'outlandish charm' and the 'transatlantic tang'[37] in Eliot's poetry may have rubbed off from Larbaud. Along with the 'charm of the colours and odours of cities', refreshingly different from Charles-Louis Philippe's evocation of the city life, Larbaud often came up with startling descriptions of the 'architectural desert' ('le désert architectural'[38]), the chilled delirium of the hysterically dreadful, unreal city of Eliot himself. For Eliot, too, walking the streets of Paris and London, felt the desert in his system. As he roamed incessantly, trudging through the dark mazes of the city-desert, which is 'half in the real world, hall in haunted wilderness',[39] the faceless shapes and shadows overlap and fuse with those in other cities:

> Jerusalem Athens Alexandria
> Vienna London
> Unreal.[40]

If the vision is reminiscent of Baudelaire, and even of James Thomson, the expansive horizon of cities reminds us forcibly of Larbaud's complex kaleidoscopic projection of Stockholm, London, Athens, Vienna, Berlin, Barcelona, Budapest, and even Tasmania, Sebastopol, and Caxamarca.

This, then, brings us to the central point of our discussion. While the hold of Laforgue and Corbière was still tight enough, Eliot's world view or *weltanschauung*, towards the end of the tens and the beginning of the twenties, I would venture to say, became more and more palpably transcultural in the Larbaudian sense. As for Eliot, though he never openly acknowledged his awareness of Larbaud's works in public, he certainly did so in private. Copies of two of Eliot's books, with the poet's inscriptions, stand at the Valery Larbaud archives in Vichy, France (see Plates 4.1 and 4.2).[41]

Peter Ackroyd has recounted to us how, in the first days of *The Criterion*, Eliot was eager to form a 'phalanx of the best mind'[42] in Europe. For the opening number, he requested a contribution from Larbaud, because he wanted to 'get works by *the best writers in the continent*'[43] and added that he looked forward 'with keen pleasure towards reading a critique' of Larbaud.[44] Larbaud's brilliant study of James Joyce's *Ulysses* was subsequently published in the prestigious first issue of *The Criterion* in October 1922 (pp. 94–103); it was the only contribution that Eliot had solicited from France. The essay was translated into English by Eliot, his *first* translation, as he himself admitted in a letter to Larbaud on 5 October 1922.[45] A year later, the former would send him a copy of *The Waste Land* with the inscription: 'A Valery Larbaud, témoignage d'admiration et d'estime' ('To Valery Larbaud, token of admiration and esteem') and a copy of *Poems 1920* 'with the homage of the author'[46]—a rare accolade from someone as selective and discreet as T.S. Eliot. Finally, in another deliberate gesture, clearly a happy rebuke to the ignorance of the English literati, he showed his special reverend for Larbaud by annexing his essay on Saint-John Perse in his book of translation of *Anabasis* (1930).[47]

It must be sufficiently clear by now that Eliot was an admirer of Larbaud. For someone who believed that 'appreciation is akin to creation' and 'is related to the stirring to suggestion',[48] this should not be taken lightly. Both poets, as has been pointed out, shared the same predicament. If Eliot wrote about the horror and the boredom of the modern city life, Larbaud, too, at least in the first half of his book, wrote about 'une angoisse sans bonheur sans cesse alimentée' ('an anguish, without happiness, ceaselessly growing').[49]

Like Baudelaire's 'De Profundis Clamavi' (see chapter on Baudelaire), one of Larbaud's better-known poems 'Centomani'[50] has disturbing similarities with Eliot's *The Waste Land*, of which even the title was perhaps unceremoniously lifted from Larbaud's poem. While it is possible that Larbaud's 'pays stérile' ('sterile land') becomes 'waste land' in Eliot's hands, the two poems—so dissimilar in style—have evoked the same images of

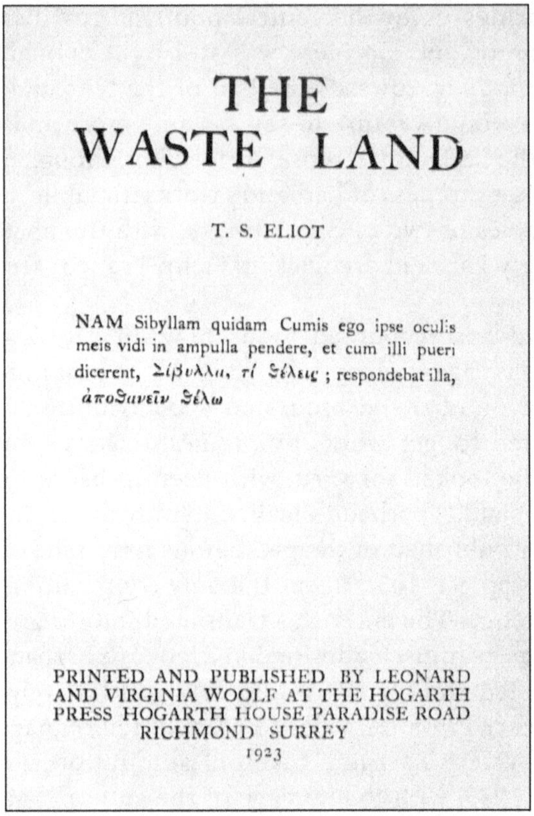

THE
WASTE LAND

T. S. ELIOT

NAM Sibyllam quidam Cumis ego ipse oculis
meis vidi in ampulla pendere, et cum illi pueri
dicerent, Σίβυλλα, τί θέλεις ; respondebat illa,
ἀποθανεῖν θέλω

PRINTED AND PUBLISHED BY LEONARD
AND VIRGINIA WOOLF AT THE HOGARTH
PRESS HOGARTH HOUSE PARADISE ROAD
RICHMOND SURREY
1923

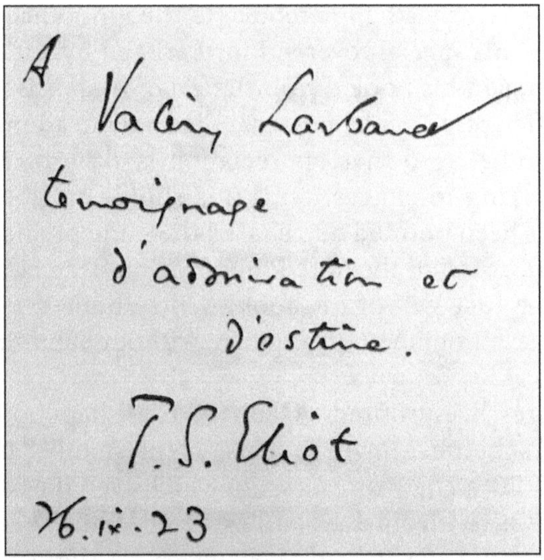

PLATE 4.1: Copy of Eliot's *The Waste Land* with his Inscription

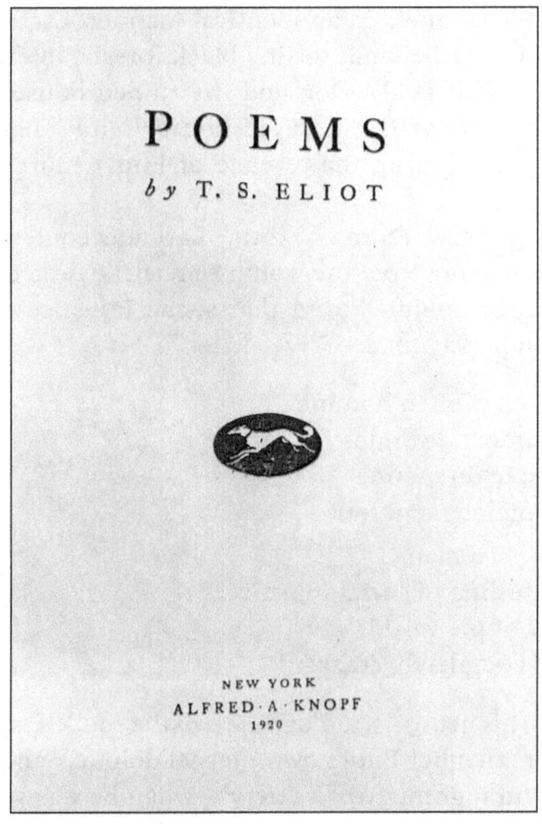

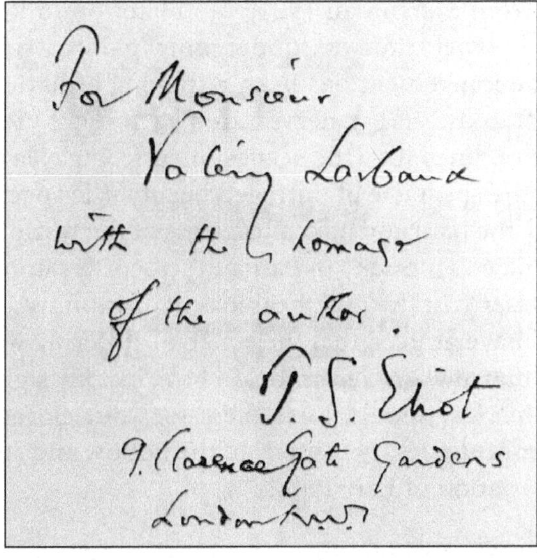

PLATE 4.2: Copy of Eliot's *Poems* with his Inscription

desolation and barrenness in an identical manner. Larbaud's poem, with its memories of a sterile land, rotting black forests, interminable deserts, stagnant pools of infernal water, and the ruined house in the pale grey meadow (cf. 'My house is a decayed house'[51] and 'helpless in a ruined house'[52]) seems to sum up the essence of Eliot's more celebrated chef-d'oeuvre.

In another poem 'L'Eterna Voluttà', Larbaud confesses that nothing distracts him any more from the 'volupté eternelle de la douleur' ('Eternal voluptuousness of dolour')[53] and that social injustice and misery have turned him completely mad:

> Vous voyez en moi un homme
> Que le sentiment de l'injustice sociale
> Et de la misère du monde
> A rendu complètement fou!
>
> (You see in me a man
> Whom the feeling of social injustice
> And misery of the world
> Has turned completely crazy!)[54]

He speaks of his neurosis, the 'darkness of the soul' ('l'esprit de ténèbres'). Of course, we remember Eliot's own 'eternal dolour'[55] and his own state of mind—his 'awful nightmare of anxiety'—when he was writing *The Waste Land*. 'I want rather a specialist in psychological troubles', he wrote to Julian Huxley from Margate in 1921,[56] and later on to Richard Aldington from Lausanne, where he was undergoing psychiatric treatment, that his 'emotional derangement has been a lifelong affliction'.[57] And, finally, with pathetic frankness: 'My nerves are bad tonight. Yes, bad, stay with me'.[58] In any case, lines like 'the scenes of suffering' ('la vue de toutes les souffrances'), 'the spectacle of outraged beauty' ('le spectacle de la beauté outragée'), and 'the pain and naked baseness of the world' ('la douleur et la bassesse toute nue du monde') in Larbaud's poem[59] epitomize marvellously 'what Tiresius *sees*'[60] in the junk heap of civilization.

Eliot would have noticed that their map of suffering was the same. 'The anguish of the marrow' in 'Gerontion' ('I have lost my sight, smell, hearing, taste and touch:/How should I use them for your closer contact?'[61]) and the 'quiet and meaningless' whisper[62] of the hollow and stuffed men would seem to be a variation of Larbaud's:

> Il y a quelque chose en moi
> Au fond de moi, au centre de moi

Quelque chose d'infiniment aride . . .

Un être fait de néant, si c'est possible,
Insensible à mes souffrances physiques,
Qui ne pleure pas quand je pleure,
Qui ne rit pas quand je ris,
Qui ne rougit pas quand je commets une action honteuse,
Qui me gémit pas quand mon coeur est blessé,
Qui se tient immobile et ne donne pas de conseils,
Mais semble dire éternellement:
'Je suis là, indifferent à tout'.

C'est peut-être le vide comme est le vide,
Mais si grand que le Bien et le Mai ensemble
Ne le remplissent pas.
La haine y meurt d'asphyxie,
Et la plus grand amour n'y pénètre jamais.

. . .

Prenez, prenez, vous n'avez rien.
Et où que j'aille, dans l'univers entier,
Je rencontre toujours,
Hors de moi comme en moi,
L'irremplissible Vide,
L'inconquérable Rien.

(There is something in me
Deep within me, at the centre
Something infinitely barren . . .

A being of nothingness, if that's possible,
Insensible to my physical suffering,
Which does not cry when I cry
Which does not laugh when I laugh
Which does not blush when I commit a shameful act,
Which does not groan when my heart is hurt,
Which remains still and gives no advice,
But seems to say for ever:
'I am there, indifferent to everything.'

It's perhaps the emptiness is empty,
But it's so vast that Good and Evil together
Cannot fill it,
Hatred dies of asphyxiation,

And the greatest of love can never enter there.

. . .

Take, take, you have nothing.
And wherever I go in the whole world,
I always meet
Outside and inside me
An unfillable Void,
The unconquerable Nothing.)[63]

Nowhere else, not even in Baudelaire, do we find such a clinical description of vacuity. The 'infinite aridity' of the soul, the death of the retina (cf. the blindness of Tiresius in *The Waste Land* and 'The eyes are not here' in *The Hollow Men*),[64] the insensibility to physical suffering, the inability to laugh and cry, love and react, and the overpowering emptiness and Nothingness, internal as well as external, in the above poem are appropriated and transmitted by Eliot into *The Waste Land* and *The Hollow Men.*

'Empty' and 'nothing' are, of course, key words in Eliot, especially in *The Waste Land.* The two recur at least ten times and convey the same degree of intensity as in Larbaud's

L'irremplissible Vide,
L'inconquérable Rien.

(The unfillable Void,
The unconquerable Nothing.)[65]

The 'preciosity and the banter' of Laforgue and the 'slapdash doggerel'[66] of Corbière obviously could not fully express Eliot's terrifying experience of the 'awful nightmare of anxiety' that was tearing him apart at the time. Unfortunately, the matter could no longer be bitten off with a smile. I suggest that it was possibly Valery Larbaud, who provided him with a scheme to poetically—that is, impersonally, in Eliot's thought—project the 'fragments shored against (his) ruins' and weave a pattern, which would transfigure the chaos. The great craftsman that he was, Eliot knew better than most others that 'the pattern we make of our feelings is the centre of value'.[67]

The kaleidoscopic presentation of the splintered images of horror, one would fathom, was suggested by Larbaud's A.O. Barnabooth:

Je passerai cette nuit avec mon passé,
Près de mon passé par un trou
Comme dans les diaromas des foires

(I shall spend this night with my past,
Near my past, through a hole,
Like in the kaleidoscopes in fairs.)

where he would

Je reverrais des gens que j'ai connus
Sans les aimer.

(I shall revisit these people I had known
Without loving them.)[68]

In Eliot, too, we find a similar attempt to impersonalize his intense experience by looking through 'a multiple variety/In a wilderness of mirrors'.[69] In Larbaud, the history of the experience is relived 'sans aimer' ('without love') and seen as if through a viewfinder.

And if, indeed, *The Waste Land* is a jigsaw puzzle, containing pieces of a total situation, the music and the harmony, albeit forced, that Eliot finds among the sterile rocks has a strange parallel in Larbaud's 'Europe' (IV):

Dans la nette aridité grise de ses gouffres minéraux . . .
Eclate soudain, comme si les pierres parlaient, une musique,
Dure, triste et bien scandée, et qui remplit
Le ciel encombrée de rochers avec sa fanfare grandissante.

(In the terrible, grey aridity of mineral gulfs . . .
Suddenly bursts forth a music of the stones
Hard, sad and very clear, which fills
The rock-cluttered sky with its growing fanfare.)[70]

Was it also Larbaud then who (along with Dante, Baudelaire, and Laforgue) suggested to Eliot the way out of the impasse? After all, Eliot did openly acknowledge in his essay on Baudelaire that 'the poetry of flight' owed 'a great deal to the poems of A.O. Barnabooth of Valery Larbaud'.[71] Was it he (and not any theologian) who in a flash helped him to understand the overall pattern and the design of the universal Order, to apprehend 'the point of intersection of the timeless/With time?' 'Only the form, the pattern/Can words or music reach/The stillness . . .'.[72] Even if his conviction came from inside, or from his reading of Baudelaire, Dante, and Claudel, Eliot's poetry seems to have been enriched by his reading of Valery Larbaud.

Interestingly, there have been attempts in the recent past by critics like Théophile Alanjouantine[73] to consider the lesser-known religious aspects of his personality. But Edmond Jaloux had written in the *NRF* long ago:

'L'homme appelé Barnabooth que fera-t-il en face de la réalité? Cherchera-t-il à réaliser *son idéal mystique*?' ('The man called Barnabooth, what will he do in the face of reality with *his mystic ideals*?' [emphasis mine])[74] As early as in 1913, Paul Claudel found this mystic ideal in Larbaud, 'le coeur profound d'un chrétien' ('the profound heart of a Christian').[75] Born a Protestant, the latter became a Catholic at 30, which a shows significant similarity with Eliot. In 1912, Valery Larbaud told André Gide about his 'passage à Rome' ('going over to Rome'),[76] who, in turn, conveyed the news to Claudel and Francis Jammes.[77] On 2 March 1912, Gide wrote to Larbaud from Florence: 'Ce matin dans une grande lettre, j'ai parlé de votre *conversion*' ('This morning I wrote a long letter to Claudel about your Conversion').[78] In one of his moments of religious enlightenment, Larbaud wrote about the city:

> Les boulevards de brume rose,
> Les ombres du soir vert et bleu,
> Tous ces gens, et toutes ces choses,
> Tout cela, c'est à vous, mon Dieu.
>
> Le sourd grondement de la ville
> Ne résonne, qu'en Votre honneur
> En nous, d'un coeur simple et docile,
> Nous Vous lovons sur la hauteur.
>
> La tâche du jour est finie:
> Nous rentrons fatigués chez nous.
> Mais le meilleur de notre vie,
> Seigneur: notre joie, est à Vous!
>
> (The rose-coloured fog in the boulevards,
> The shadows of the green and blue evening,
> All these people, all those things,
> All this is Yours, my Lord.
>
> The muffled rumbling of the city
> Resonates in Your honour,
> And we, with a simple and docile heart
> Coil up with You towards the top.
>
> The day's work is over:
> We return exhausted to our homes,
> But the best in our life,
> Lord: our joy, is Yours.)[79]

Elsewhere he wrote, 'Je suis agi par la Divine Variété visible' ('I am stirred by the visible Divine Variety')[80] and 'J'ai mis sous Votre protection mon amour' ('I have put my love in Your protection').[81] This reinforces our assumption that Eliot might have found in Larbaud's poetry—among others—a clue towards the solution of the terrifying puzzle of *The Waste Land*.

I hope I have shown enough to suggest that any comparison of Eliot with the latter is not tentative. Eliot's debt in the use of words and images is there for the asking. A master miniaturist, he picked up 'like a magpie, various shining fragments of ideas as they struck his eye, and stuck them about here and there in his verse'.[82] In the same way, Larbaud's 'crevasses de lointaines montagnes' ('cracks in far-way mountains')[83] could well have been translated as 'decayed hole among the mountains';[84] 'pays stérile' ('sterile land'), 'sans verdure' ('no greenery'),[85] etc., as 'waste land' and 'arid plain';[86] 'volupté éternelle de la douleur' ('the eternal voluptuousness of dolour')[87] as 'eternal dolour';[88] 'ce pays de pierre grise' ('this country of grey stones') and 'ce pays gris et noir' ('this grey and dark country'),[89] and 'ce talus de caillous' ('this embankment of stone-chips')[90] as 'the agony in stony places',[91] and 'stony rubbish';[92] 'le vent long et féroce, le vent pirate/ Sifflant dans les cordages et faisant claquer comme un fouet' and so on ('the long and ferocious wind, the long wind, the pirate wind/Whispering in the rigging and cracking like a whip')[93] possibly as 'the wind shakes a thousand whispers';[94] 'l'épaisseur de la boîte craniène' ('the thickness of the box of the skull')[95] as 'the hollow round of my Skull';[96] and so on. Francis Scarfe,[97] the only critic to have mentioned Larbaud *en passant* in connection with Eliot, has pointed out that 'Summer surprised us, coming over the Starnbergersee with a shower'[98] may have been lifted from Larbaud's

> . . . l'odeur du foin frais coupé, comme en Bavière,
> Un soir, après la pluie, sur le lac de Starnberg.
>
> (. . . Odour of fresh reaped hay as in Bavaria,
> One evening, after the rain, over the Starnbergersee lake.)[99]

Not only that, even some of the richly evocative urban details in Eliot's poetry, for example, 'the luncheon at the Canon Street hotel',[100] echoing Larbaud's 'Elsenore hotel with all modern facilities',[101] 'Grand-Hôtel Vuletich',[102] or 'Sonora Palace hotel',[103] may have been deliberately sifted and gleaned from the latter's poems.

The versification of the two poets, too, is, at some points, of the same kind, of the same fibre, the influence being of phrase and rhythm. It should be on record that *The Waste Land* does begin, as Scarfe suggests, in the typical Larbaudian style before being drowned in other voices. A comparison between the poems of Barnabooth with Pierre Leyris's translation of Eliot can indeed be most revealing . . . . The quality of great lyric, of 'anguished music' ('l'angoissante musique')[104] in Larbaud's words, characterize the works of both poets. Admirers of Laforgue as they were, both seemed to have a 'special taste' for the banal, which these two amazing artisans sought to recreate in their works by their 'grande poésie des choses banales' ('great poetry of the banal').[105] The following will confirm this:

> Chocolats, bonbons sucrés jusqu'à brûler, boissons glacées,—
> Cigares engourdisseurs; vous, endormeuses cigarettes . . .
> Tziganes, promenade en traîneau, pluie sur la mer,
> Folie de la nuit fièvreuse . . .
>
> (Chocolates, sugary sweets, cold drinks,
> Drowsy cigars; you, sleepy cigarettes . . .
> Tsiganes, sleigh ride, rain on the sea,
> Madness of feverish nights . . .)[106]

Compare Eliot's lines:

> The river bears no empty bottles, sandwich papers,
> Silk handkerchiefs, cardboard boxes, cigarette ends,
> Or other testimony of summer nights.[107]

But then, as always in Eliot, the words and images coalesce, impressions and expressions combine in peculiar and unexpected ways, and 'the language itself penetrates more and more deeply into the structure, the word becomes more and more loaded with meaning'.[108]

Unfortunately, with the passage of years, Larbaud has been relegated to the rank of a minor poet, even in France. To quote Eliot himself, 'No poetic reputation ever remains in the same place: it is a stock market in constant fluctuation'.[109] But Eliot's interaction with Larbaud, at one stage, remains one of the most fruitful in the former's career, and it has gone wholly unnoticed.

NOTES

1. *Valery Larbaud* (1881–1957): French poet, translator, and critic. He started with a volume of Parnassian verses called *Portiques* (1890) and gradually found his own idiom in *Poèmes par un riche amateur* (1908), which was accompanied by the biography of Barnabooth, replaced in 1913 with his

Journal intime. Apart from translating many foreign authors into French, he wrote several novels, notably *Fermina Marquez* (1911), *Amants, Heureux Amants* (1923), *Jaune, bleu, blanc* (1928), and *Aux couleurs de Rome* (1938). He also provided illuminating commentaries to the works of several key figures in twentieth century literature, including T.S. Eliot. His critical writings can be found in *Ce vice impuni, la lecture* (1941) and *Journal* (1954–55) and his theories of translation in *Sous l'invocation de Saint-Jérôme* (1946).

2. Octavio Paz, 'Croisements et bifurcations', *La Nouvelle Revue Française* (hereafter referred to as *NRF*), June 1989, p, 1.

3. Richard Aldington, 'Foreign Reviews', *The Criterion*, October 1923, p. 107.

4. Larbaud, conversation with Léon-Paul Fargue, quoted in Michel Décaudin, *La Crise des valuers symbolistes*, Geneva: Slatkine Rpts., 1981, p. 353.

5. Ibid.

6. Quoted in G. Jean Aubry, *Valery Larbaud*, Monaco: Edition du Rocher, 1949, p. 161.

7. This piece of information is given in Alain-Fournier and Jacques Rivière, *Correspondance*, vol. II, Paris: Gallimard, 1991, p. 615 n.

8. Ezra Pound, *Lettres de Paris*, Paris: Cahiers Ulysse, fin de siécle, 1988, p. 53.

9. As Frederick Lehner has pointed out, Larbaud overcame 'French nationalism' and 'bridged the gap between nations by his translations and linked one foreign people to another' (Stanley J. Kunitz, ed., *Twentieth Century Authors: A Biographical Dictionary of Modern Literature*, New York: H.W. Wilson, 1985, Supplement I, p. 550. Larbaud, who knew English, Spanish, Greek, Latin, Italian, Portuguese, and perhaps also German and Russian (*Confluences*, Paris, Valery Larbaud Number, December–January 1945, pp. 267, 292–3), translated Coleridge's *Ancient Mariner*, Whitman's *Selected Poems* (with Laforgue and Gide), almost all the books of Samuel Butler including his diaries, Joyce's *Ulysses* (with Auguste Morel), G.K. Chesterton's *Bernard Shaw*, Ramón Gómez de la Serna, Gabriel Miró, Ricardo Güiraldes, Alfonso Reyes (from Spanish), José-Maria Eça de Queiroz (from Portuguese), Emilio Cecchi, Ricardo Bacchelli, Ettore Settanni, Linoello Fiumi, Gianna Manzini, Bruno Barilli (from Italian) among others; and wrote prefaces to the French translations of Shakespeare's sonnets, Joyce's *Dubliners*, William Faulkner's *As I Lay Dying* and the poems of Whitman and Gomez de la Serna. Larbaud kept the readers well-informed about the latest developments in Spanish, English, and American literature, about the works of, for example, J.M. Synge, Bernard Shaw, H.G. Wells, Francis Thompson, Joseph Conrad, T.S. Eliot, and Richard Aldington. Sometimes he would love to pause and reflect on the contributions of Wyatt, Marvell, Fielding, and Carlyle! (Source of information: Chronology of Larbaud's life by Jacqueline Famerie, in Valery Larbaud, *Oeuvres*, Paris: Bibliothèque de la Pléiade, 1977, pp. 1125–43).

10. For Eliot's use of Charles-Louis Philippe's (1871–1909) projection of the suffering of ordinary men in a city of exhaustion, degradation, poverty, and pessimism like Paris, see Grover Smith, 'Charles-Louis Philippe and T.S.

Eliot', *American Literature*, November 1950, pp. 254–9. Smith points out that Eliot's combination of images in

> Smells of chestnuts in the streets
> And female smells in shuttered rooms . . .

was, in fact, a variation of Philippe's in *Marie Donadieu*:

> . . . des odeurs de filles publiques melées à des odeurs de nourriture.
> (. . . Smells of public girls mixed with smells of food.)

According to him, Eliot drew on Philippe's material in 'Preludes' (III) and 'Rhapsody on a Windy Night', an influence acknowledged by the poet in a letter to Smith on 11 May 1949.

Eliot also acknowledged his debt to Philippe in his preface to Laurence Vail, tr., *Bubu de Montparnasse*, Paris: Crossby Continental Editions, 1932. Eliot may have looked up the works of Larbaud—a well-known patron of Philippe—because of his interest in the latter.

11. Source of information: Larbaud, *Oeuvres*, p. 1126, and Aubry, *Valery Larbaud*, p. 158.
12. Fournier to Rivière, 25 March 1913, in Alain-Fournier and Jacques Rivière, *Correspondance*, vol. II, Paris: Gallimard, 1991, p. 487.
13. T.S. Eliot, *To Criticize the Critic*, London: Faber and Faber, 1978, p. 126.
14. All quotations from Larbaud, 'A propósito de la publicatión de un libro inédito de Julio Laforgue', *La Nación*, 15 April 1923, n.p., translated into English by Prof Arup Rudra, Department of English, Jadavpur University, Kolkata.
15. See the index to Valery Larbaud and A.A.M. Stols, *Correspondance*, vol. II, Paris: ed. des Cendres, 1986, p. 75.
16. Saint-John Perse's homage to Larbaud—'Larbaud ou l'honneur littéraire', which was published in the *NRF* in September 1957, is reprinted in Saint-John Perse, *Oeuvres Complètes*, Paris: Bibliothèque de la Pléiade, 1972, pp. 487–98. The given quotation is from p. 488.
17. Ibid.; Perse wrote in his homage:

    Je puis attester que Larbaud, s'éprenant de John Donne, s'intéressait autant à l'homme qu'à l'écrivain . . .

    (I can certify that Larbaud, deeply in love with John Donne, was as much interested in the man as in the writer . . .)

    Perse, *Oeuvres Complètes*, p. 493.
18. Perse, letter to G. Jean Aubry, 17 June 1949, in Perse, *Oeuvres Complètes*, p. 1035.
19. Perse, *Oeuvres Complètes*, p. 799.
20. Eliot placed the French symbolists in the 'metaphysical' tradition of Donne in the Clark Lectures. Larbaud (see note 14), Perse, and Eliot loved Laforgue, who, on the other hand, is widely regarded as a follower of Corbière. Larbaud and his admirer Perse were greatly interested in John Donne.
21. Valery Larbaud, 'Le Devoir avant tout', *Les Poésies de A.O. Barnabooth* (hereafter referred to as *Les Poésies*) [1908], Paris: Gallimard, 1966, p. 112.

22. T.S. Eliot, 'The Family Reunion', *The Complete Poems and Plays of T.S. Eliot* (hereafter referred to as *CPP*), London: Faber and Faber, 1990, p. 294.

23. Douwe Fokkema, *Issues in General and Comparative Literature*, Calcutta: Papyrus, 1987, p. 103.

24. Ibid.

25. Valery Larbaud, *A.O. Barnabooth: ses oeuvres complètes*, Paris: NRF, 1913, p. 70; quoted by Fokkema, *Issues in General and Comparative Literature*, pp. 100–1.

26. Stephen Spender, *Eliot*, London: Fontana, 1986, p. 19.

27. Larbaud, 'Le Devoir avant tout', p. 112.

28. Valery Larbaud, 'I.M. Anastasie Retzuch', *Les Poésies*, Paris: Gallimard, 1966, p. 113.

29. Valery Larbaud, 'Dialogue', *Les Poésies*, Paris: Gallimard, 1966, p. 117.

30. T.S. Eliot, *On Poetry and Poets* (hereafter referred to as *OPP*), London: Faber and Faber, 1969, p. 23.

31. Robert Mallet, 'Préface', in Valery Larbaud, *Les Poésies*, Paris: Gallimard, 1966, p. 16.

32. Valery Larbaud, 'Milan', *Les Poésies*, Paris: Gallimard, 1966, p. 101.

33. Valery Larbaud, 'Valence-Du-Cid', *Les Poésies*, Paris: Gallimard, 1966, p. 100.

34. René Lalou, *Histoire de la littérature contemporaine*, Paris: Presse Universitaire, 1947, p. 542.

35. Valery Larbaud, 'Europe', III, *Les Poésies*, Paris: Gallimard, 1966, p. 77.

36. Larbaud, 'Europe', IX, *Les Poésies*, p. 86.

37. Georges Cattaui, *T.S. Eliot*, tr. Claire Pace and Jean Stewart, London: Merlin Press, 1966, p. vii.

38. Valery Larbaud, 'Trafalgar Square la nuit', *Les Poésies*, Paris: Gallimard, 1966, p. 68.

39. Edmund Wilson, 'The Poetry of Drouth', *The Dial*, December 1922, reprinted in Michael Grant, ed., *T.S. Eliot: The Critical Heritage*, vol. I, London: Routledge and Kegan Paul, 1982, p. 140.

40. T.S. Eliot, 'The Waste Land', V, *CPP*, London: Faber and Faber, 1990, p. 73.

41. I discovered this during my visit to Larbaud's personal library in the archives of Bibliothèque Municipale Valery Larbaud in Vichy, France in May–June 1989. Photocopies reproduced here.

42. Peter Ackroyd, *T.S. Eliot*, London: Hamish Hamilton, 1984, p. 221.

43. Eliot to Valery Larbaud, 12 March 1922, in T.S. Eliot, *Letters of T.S. Eliot*, ed. Valerie Eliot, vol. I, London: Faber and Faber, 1988, p. 508.

44. Eliot to Valery Larbaud, 20 March 1922, in Eliot, *Letters of T.S. Eliot*, ed. Valerie Eliot, vol. I, pp. 516–17.

45. Eliot, *Letters of T.S. Eliot*, ed. Valerie Eliot, vol. I, p. 578.

46. The first inscription is dated '26.IX.1923'. The second is undated.

47. This was actually the translation of Larbaud's introduction to a Russian translation of Perse's *Anabase,* which came out in the *NRF* in January 1926.

48. T.S. Eliot, 'Ben Jonson', *Selected Essays* (hereafter referred to as *SE*), London: Faber and Faber, 1951, p. 105.

49. Larbaud, 'Europe', V, *Les Poésies*, p. 82.

50. Larbaud, *Les Poésies*, pp. 27–8.
51. T.S. Eliot, 'Gerontion', *CPP*, London: Faber and Faber, 1990, p. 37.
52. T.S. Eliot, 'Chorus II, The Rock', *CPP*, London: Faber and Faber, 1990, p. 151.
53. Larbaud, *Les Poésies*, p. 36.
54. Ibid.
55. T.S. Eliot, 'Ash-Wednesday', IV, *CPP*, London: Faber and Faber, 1990, p. 94.
56. Quoted in Valerie Eliot's introduction to T.S. Eliot, *The Waste Land: A Facsimile and Transcript*, ed. Valerie Eliot, London: Faber and Faber, 1971, p. xxii.
57. Ibid.
58. Eliot, 'The Waste Land', II, *CPP*, p. 65.
59. Valery Larbaud, 'L'Eterna Voluttà', *Les Poésies*, Paris: Gallimard, 1966, pp. 36–7.
60. Eliot, 'The Waste Land', p. 78, notes.
61. Eliot, *CPP*, p. 38.
62. T.S. Eliot, 'The Hollow Men', *CPP*, London: Faber and Faber, 1990, p. 83.
63. Valery Larbaud, 'Le Don de soi-même', *Les Poésies*, Paris: Gallimard, 1966, pp. 57–8.
64. Eliot, *CPP*, p. 84.
65. Larbaud, 'Le Don de soi-même', pp. 57–8.
66. Edmund Wilson, *Axel's Castle*, 1931; London: Fontana, 1967, p. 81.
67. See the introduction by T.S. Eliot to Paul Valéry, *Le Serpent*, London: published for *The Criterion* by R. Cobden-Sanderson, 1924; quoted in Ronald Bush, *T.S. Eliot: A Study in Character and Style*, New York: Oxford University Press, 1985, p. 82.
68. Valery Larbaud, 'Nuit dans le Port', *Les Poésies*, Paris: Gallimard, 1966, p. 30.
69. Eliot, 'Gerontion', p. 38.
70. Larbaud, *Les Poésies*, p. 81.
71. Eliot, *SE*, p. 390.
72. T.S. Eliot, 'Burnt Norton, Four Quartets', *CPP*, London: Faber and Faber, 1990, p. 175.
73. Théophile Alanjouantine, *Valery Larbaud sous divers visages*, Paris: Gallimard, 1973.
74. Edmond Jaloux, 'Valery Larbaud', *NRF*, February 1924, p. 139.
75. Alanjouantine, *Valery Larbaud sous divers visages*, p. 43.
76. Ibid., p. 46.
77. Ibid.
78. Ibid.
79. Valery Larbaud, 'Hymne', *Les Poésies*, Paris: Gallimard, 1966, p. 96.
80. Valery Larbaud, 'Chant de la variété visible', *Les Poésies*, Paris: Gallimard, 1966, p. 109.
81. Larbaud, 'Milan', p. 101.
82. Eliot, *SE*, pp. 138–9. T.S. Eliot said this about John Donne, but it seems to be a self-projection.
83. Valery Larbaud, 'Centomani', *Les Poésies*, Paris: Gallimard, 1966, p. 27.
84. Eliot, 'The Waste Land', p. 73.
85. Larbaud, 'Centomani', p. 27.

86. Eliot, 'The Waste Land', p. 74.

87. Larbaud, 'L'Eterna Voluttà', p. 36.

88. Eliot, 'Ash-Wednesday', IV, *CPP*, p. 94.

89. Larbaud, 'Europe', IV, *Les Poésies*, p. 80.

90. Larbaud, 'Centomani', p. 27.

91. Eliot, 'The Waste Land', V, *CPP*, p. 72.

92. Eliot, 'The Waste Land', I, *CPP*, p. 61.

93. Valery Larbaud, 'Thalassa', *Les Poésies*, Paris: Gallimard, 1966, p. 54.

94. Eliot, 'Ash-Wednesday', IV, *CPP*, p. 95.

95. Valery Larbaud, 'Prologue', *Les Poésies*, Paris: Gallimard, 1966, p. 24.

96. Eliot, 'Ash-Wednesday', II, *CPP*, p. 91.

97. Francis Scarfe, 'Eliot and Nineteenth Century French Poetry', in *Eliot in Perspective*, ed. Graham Martin, London: Macmillan, 1970, p. 45.

98. Eliot, 'The Waste Land', I, *CPP*, p. 61.

99. Valery Larbaud, 'Nevermore', *Les Poésies*, Paris: Gallimard, 1966, p. 33.

100. Eliot, 'The Waste Land', p. 68.

101. Valery Larbaud, 'Carpe Diem', *Les Poésies*, Paris: Gallimard, 1966, p. 60.

102. Larbaud, 'Europe', IV, *Les Poésies*, p. 81.

103. Valery Larbaud, 'La Mort d'Atahuallpa', *Les Poésies*, Paris: Gallimard, 1966, p. 67.

104. Valery Larbaud, 'Ode', *Les Poésies*, Paris: Gallimard, 1966, p. 25.

105. Valery Larbaud, 'Alma Perdida', *Les Poésies*, Paris: Gallimard, 1966, p. 44.

106. Ibid.

107. Eliot, 'The Waste Land', III, *CPP*, p. 67.

108. Elizabeth Drew, *T.S. Eliot: The Design of his Poetry*, London: Eyre and Spottiswoode, 1950, quoted in Sheila Sullivan, ed., *Critics on T.S. Eliot*, 1973; New Delhi: Universal Book Stall, 1990, p. 2.

It may be interesting to know that Valery Larbaud, too, as I found out during my investigations, had genuine interest in Eliot's poetry. When John Rodker had accused him in *Les Ecrits Nouveaux*, December 1922, of indifference to Eliot in his article on contemporary English poetry, Larbaud retorted in *La Revue Européenne* (March 1923, pp. 81–4) that he regarded Eliot as an American poet, and went on to express his deep admiration for *The Waste Land*. To him, it was a marvel of the 'burlesque', where

> . . . all sublime is appropriated, one passes from the burlesque to the sublime in the same verse without any jarring effect. . . . Everything shows the serenity of great poetry, of great music; almost every single verse is beautiful, full of sonority, prosodic vigour and music showing the word-sense of the composer. . . . But many readers—discouraged by the effort required to taste such poetry—might think that it is merely an extravagant exercise, an accumulation of incoherent oddities. A little bit of application, and everything should be comprehensible.

See Sullivan, ed., *Critics on T.S. Eliot*, p. 84. Did Larbaud respond so sensitively to Eliot's poetry because they were on the same wavelength?

109. T.S. Eliot, 'What is Minor Poetry?', *OPP*, London: Faber and Faber, 1969, p. 48.

5

Claudel and Eliot
In Search of the Still Point

THEIR POETRY LOOKED HAUNTINGLY similar, they sang the same hymn, theirs was the same pilgrimage of expiation: T.S. Eliot and Paul Claudel[1] (1868–1955). Yet no one dares to compare these two greats of twentieth century English and French poetry. Was it simply an example of polygenesis? Was there really an interaction?

This brings us to perhaps the most controversial part of my argument, which hopes to throw light on one of the central problems in Eliot's poetry: his major emotional and stylistic readjustments after *The Waste Land*, the shift towards a lapidary style, 'the conversion of the words to the Word,/ A journey towards the still point'. A new life sheds the old in life and poetry; the charged, dramatic diction is replaced by one of 'deferred immediacy'.[2] How did Eliot evolve from one kind of poetry to another, his elliptic, discontinuous syntax giving way to a solemn litany-like intonation? While a moral and intellectual answer to this problem is not difficult to find,[3] few seem to have found an aesthetic explanation for this change of style.

For a man who believed that it was the task of a poet to always look for 'new literary influences',[4] who could be the new influence? While Eliot's poetry became pronouncedly religious, culminating in his conversion to Anglo-Catholicism in 1927, there is a sense of relief among his critics that he was finally able to eliminate vast tracts of foreign influences from his works,[5] that he was probably willing to 'return to the English poetic tradition'.[6] Most commentators of Eliot's poetry, including the experts of

*My first acquaintance with Claudel's works was electrifying: it reminded me inevitably of T.S. Eliot's later poetry. This 'discovery' was corroborated by the fact that Eliot bought and read Claudel (Peter Ackroyd, *T.S. Eliot*, London: Hamish Hamilton, 1984, p. 42) during his crucial year in Paris in 1910–11. Later on, I found a confirmation of my opinion in Herbert Howarth's illuminating passage on Claudel in his *Notes on Some Figures Behind T.S. Eliot* (1965). Subsequently, I found Eliot's homage to Claudel after his death, which convinced me that I was on the right track.

French literature E.J.H. Greene and Francis Scarfe,[7] have gently subscribed to this view.

But, as I hinted at the beginning of this chapter, this was probably not the whole story. Did the French influence really wear off? Interestingly, Eliot, always the best critic of his own poetry, made clear in the third Turnbull Lecture in 1933 at the Johns Hopkins University that his debt to French poetry had 'if anything increased over the years'.[8] He wrote elsewhere: 'It is merely that what has best responded to my need in middle and later age is different from the nourishment I needed in my youth'.[9] It seems, logically, that he was hinting at another cross with another author.

This would mean that even in the final phase of his career, Eliot denied that he had his complete meaning alone. Yet again we confront what Jonathon Culler calls 'the complex vraisemblance of specific intertextualities',[10] where one work takes another as its basis or point of departure and must be assessed in relation to it. I shall suggest in this chapter that although he still remained faithful to the memory of Laforgue, and Dante continued to inspire him, Eliot from the mid-twenties onwards, slowly drifted into the circuit of one of the great masters of contemporary French poetry, Paul Claudel, who had remained embedded in his subconscious for one and a half decades.

The uncanny similarity of their poetry have struck critics as diverse as Herbert Howarth[11] and Francis Scarfe ('Claudel left a mark', wrote Scarfe, 'on some of the *Rock* choruses and perhaps on the versification of *Murder in the Cathedral* and *The Family Reunion*')[12] but, unfortunately, they did not elaborate. The most obvious logic for this new association could be their devout Catholicism amidst a carnival of scepticism. To quote Wallace Fowlie, 'In our time, Catholic theology has hardly inspired a more vehement, more impersonal and more articulate literary output than Claudel's'.[13] The same could be said, with some qualifications, about Eliot too. Claudel was at the pinnacle of glory in Eliot's youth, and was the kind of religious poet the latter himself was destined to be one day. If Claudel has restored the lyrical ode, the hymn, and the prayer, the thoroughly remodelled, orchestrated language of Eliot in the late twenties and thirties reminds us unfailingly of him. The similarity of these two Catholic poets lies not only in their subject-matter and style, but also in the historical fact that both these major poets were stage-struck and made conscious attempts to recreate the verse-drama in a modern setting. Willy-nilly, Claudel was one poet already too important and influential for Eliot to ignore for a long period of time. In my opinion, Claudel could well have helped an indecisive Eliot to reconcile the opposites and transcend the paradoxes in order to reach 'the still point'. Eliot may have also learnt from

Claudel the magical, incantatory style of his last phase, with those long-flowing lines, very near to rhythmic prose: 'the formal word precise, but not pedantic/The complete consort dancing together'.[14]

It is possible that critics have never paid much attention to Claudelian resonance because of Eliot's own disparaging remarks about Claudel in *The Sacred Wood*.[15] Eliot may have been temporarily biased by the adverse opinions of Ezra Pound and Julien Benda.[16] Moreover, critical jibes in Eliot are not always to be taken seriously. We shall remember his surprising admission to Stephen Spender in May 1935: 'You don't really criticize an author to whom you have not surrendered yourself'.[17] We should also bear in mind his crucial remark in his 1937 essay on Byron about writers who had initially left him 'cold'—'obstinate-cases of authors of high rank whom we continue to find antipathetic'.[18] But, according to Eliot, there is a third and final phase in the development of taste and critical judgement of a poet when:

We begin to enquire into the reasons for our failure to enjoy what has been found delightful by men . . . as well-qualified or better-qualified, for appreciation than ourselves. In trying to understand why one has failed to appreciate rightly a particular author, one is seeking for light, not only about the author, but about oneself. . . . It is an effort to understand that work, and to understand oneself in relation to it.[19]

Nothing explains better, in my view, Eliot's chequered relationship with Claudel.

Biographers of Eliot[20] agree that Eliot was introduced to this unofficial poet-laureate of France by his French tutor Alain-Fournier. Eliot himself has admitted that he bought books by Paul Claudel in his romantic year in Paris in 1910–11, on the *first day* of publication.[21] Subsequently, during his six lectures at Oxford in 1916, Eliot recommended to the students no less than three books of Claudel: *Art Poétique, L'Annonce faite à Marie* (*The Tidings brought to Mary*), and *Connaissance de l'Est* (*The East I know*).[22] In the fifth lecture, entitled 'The Return of the Catholic Church', on the tendency of the French intellectuals to return to orthodox Christianity, he specifically referred to Claudel as 'a writer of *great force* and *great influence*, [who] often falls into rhetoric and verbiage' [my italics]. He was described as a 'nationalist', whose 'Christianity is that of medieval philosophy', whose national and Christian sentiments were 'the mainspring of his poems and his poetic dramas'.[23]

It probably took Eliot more than a decade to really know what he was talking about, till he worked out the implications of Claudel in the post-*Waste Land* phase. Thirty-six years later, in a preface to Joseph Chiari's *Contemporary French Poetry*, Eliot wrote in 1952:

In 1910, when I had my first introduction to literary Paris, Claudel was already a great poet in the eyes of a younger generation—my own generation. He had published *Connaissance de l'Est*, *Art Poétique*, and those plays which appeared in one volume under the title of *L'Arbre*: and I am not sure that these three books do not constitute his strongest claim to immortality.[24]

Eliot's preface to a book on Claudel, *The Poetic Drama of Paul Claudel* (1954),[25] also by Joseph Chiari, confirms his admiration. Finally, Eliot corroborates our hypothesis that Claudel had indeed made an impact on him in his obituary note on Paul Claudel:

It was forty-five years ago that Alain-Fournier put in my hands *L'Arbre* and *Connaissance de l'Est*. The impression that these two books, the prose essays and the five plays made upon my mind at that time is still very dear in my memory. I think he never surpassed the work of this early period: on the other hand, I do not believe that he wrote subsequently anything unworthy of the standard he had set for himself: to have been able to maintain such a standard throughout so long a lifetime is itself some evidence of greatness.[26]

Interestingly, Eliot denied any influence of Claudel on his theatre, but being 'in this way, disinterested', regarded him as the greatest poetic dramatist of the century.[27]

I shall suggest that instead of being 'influenced' in an obvious sense, Eliot's later poetry was enlivened by his memory of Claudel.

Let us examine, at first, the circumstances which could have led Eliot to Claudel.

Biographers and critics of Eliot have always believed that his visit to France in 1910–11 was crucial, and, therefore, the fact of his acquaintance with Claudel in his Paris year must be taken seriously. He was indoctrinated about both Laforgue and Claudel by Alain-Fournier, who played such an important part in the making of Eliot's poetry. While going through the correspondence between Fournier and his brother-in-law Jacques Rivière (written before and during Eliot's stay in Paris), I found as many as 258 references to Claudel.[28] 'As-tu l'intention de t'éterniser avec le petit Laforgue? Je te blesse, mais Claudel est si grand, si grand!' ('Do you intend to stay for ever with your little Laforgue? I hurt you, but Claudel is so great, so great!),[29] wrote Rivière to Fournier on 5 April 1906 and he planned to spend his holidays with Laforgue and Claudel.[30] If these two appear today too incongruous a pair to appreciate and emulate, one has only to read the correspondence cited above: it seems to foreshadow Eliot's poetic fate.[31]

There is no doubt that the two friends desperately tried to transmit their awesome admiration for Claudel to the young francophile from

Harvard. Thus, it is not at all surprising that Eliot would buy a new book of Claudel 'on the day it came out'[32]—a fact uneasily glossed over by Eliot critics, possibly because of their unfamiliarity with Claudel.

I would like to suggest that Fournier's unusual interest in the religious poetry of Charles Péguy and subsequently their friendship[33] bore the germ of Eliot's later interest in Claudel. Indeed, Fournier's infatuation for Laforgue and Péguy-Claudel (his letters testify to this) contains the seed of Eliot's whole poetic life. (Claudel himself was an admirer of Laforgue and read *Moralités Légendaires* in *La Vogue* as early as 1886).[34] I would also like to draw attention to an important letter of Jean Verdenal (Eliot's friend and fellow-lodger in Paris to whom he dedicated his *Prufrock and Other Observations*), written in July 1911, urging Eliot to read, among others, Paul Claudel:

> Il convient surtout de dire pour chacun en quelle measure il peut influencer notre vie intérieure vers la connaissance du bien suprême.

> (But the main thing is to say, in the case of each, how far he can influence our inner life towards the knowledge of the supreme good.)[35]

As early as in 1911, then, Verdenal and Eliot thought of the 'inner life' and the 'knowledge of the supreme good'.

It is also quite likely that Eliot learnt about Claudel from *La Nouvelle Revue Française* (*NRF*), and Paul Claudel was always very important to the *NRF* group.[36] Claudel's part in lending prestige to this periodical was considerable, especially just before and after the First World War. The publication of the first act of *L'Otage* in the December issue of the *NRF* (Eliot had just landed in France) was a memorable event and the new year saw yet another major contribution from Claudel, the revised version of *La Jeune Fille Violaine*, now renamed *L'Annonce faite à Marie*, which Eliot would recommend to his audience in his Oxford lectures in 1916. This acquaintance with Claudel, as Eliot himself admitted, was significantly one of the *first* direct encounters with literary France. *Cinq Grandes Odes*, considered to be Claudel's poetic masterpiece, also came out in 1910, the year of Eliot's arrival in Paris. Claudel's works were regularly discussed in the *NRF*, notably *Cantate à trois voix*, which was reviewed at great length by Henri Ghéon in June 1913. Herbert Howarth[37] informs us that a copy of the issue, with T.S. Eliot's signature on the cover, now stands at the Widener Library.

Every road led to Claudel. It is interesting to note that even F.S. Flint wrote about Paul Claudel in *Poetry* in 1915, making a special reference to *Art Poétique:*

In the *Art Poétique*...the whole work is constantly upheld by the intensity of his visual imagination constantly creating new metaphors that have the power of primitive sensation.[38]

Eliot, for all practical purposes, must have read Flint's homage to Claudel.

Therefore, there was no way Eliot could avoid the latter. If, for confirmation, he had looked up Remy de Gourmont, his Aristotle, the latter too had nothing but admiration for Claudel: '(Il) m'a enviré d'une violente sensation d'art et de poésie'. ('I was intoxicated by his violent feeling for art and poetry'.)[39] Now, all this may or may not have shaken him at that stage, but the seeds remained in the subconscious and germinated. The poetical works of Baudelaire, Laforgue, and Dante had shown Eliot the direction of beatitude he was desperately searching for by the end of the twenties. But no one quite embodied in poetry the blissful new life as Claudel had done, like the seventeenth century Anglican divine Lancelot Andrewes in the sermons.

One reason, however, for Eliot's initial failure to respond to Claudel could be that he was too overwhelmed with Laforgue at the time, measuring out his life with coffee-spoons. Within a few years, however, he was to know 'the drought, the dark night of the soul', which he was to consider in his 1931 essay on Pascal as 'an essential stage in the progress of the Christian mystic'.[40] Yet, as Lyndall Gordon has argued in two successive books, *Eliot's Early Years* (1977) and *Eliot's New Life* (1988), Eliot's private poetry was already basically quasi-religious in nature,[41] stemming from the partial belief of a mind in a peculiar and unusual state of spiritual sickness'.[42] In one of his Oxford Extension Lectures in 1916, 'The Reaction against Romanticism', he alludes to T.E. Hulme's theory: 'The classical point of view has been defined as essentially a belief in Original Sin—the necessity for austere discipline.'[43]

Like Claudel, therefore, Eliot was probably always haunted by religiosity, despite the non-religious posture of his early poetry. Eliot's nurse Annie Dunne, to whom he was greatly attracted, was a devout Catholic and took him to the Catholic Church. 'The memory lingered with him', writes Ackroyd.[44] Lyndall Gordon would have us believe that already in 1914, Eliot was circling, in moments of agitation, on the edge of Conversion.[45] Her supposition is based on a group of intensely religious poems Eliot never published: 'After the Turning', 'I am the Resurrection', 'So through the evening', 'The Burnt Dancer', and 'The Love Song of St. Sebastian'. 'Eliot's tortuous path should lead to a Christian terminus was obvious even in the Paris poems', writes Gordon.[46] Almost everything he wrote divulged a passionate spiritual craving for Order. The monastic impulse provided relief to his dusty soul, as it happened in the case of his French friend and editor of the *NRF*, Jacques Rivière. Jean Verdenal, who would die at the age of twenty-five, also showed a growing spiritual awareness (see his letter to Eliot in July 1911 quoted earlier).

When Eliot's first success at sustained contemplation came towards the end of *The Waste Land*, Claudel was still nowhere in the picture. But as time went by, Claudel's light of Christianity may have beckoned him in his hours of depravity, as the Laforguian Nirvana or the hymns of the *Upanishads*, 'the Peace that passeth understanding', seemed no longer a feasible alternative. Eliot may have reminded of Claudel's example by Jacques Maritain:

Notre problème, aujourd'hui, est de penser ainsi le monde moderne: non pas seulement penser l'éternel hors du monde, ce qui est le premier précepte de la pensée contemplative mais aussi par un second précepte semblable au premier, penser le monde et le moment présent dans l'éternel et par l'éternel.

(Our problem, today, is to think thus of the modem world: not only to think of the eternal as outside this world, which is the first precept of contemplative thought, but also according to a second precept similar to the first, to think of the world and the present as the eternal and by the eternal.)[47]

Maritain argues that, to achieve this intellectual liberty, a dependence on the divine Truth is indispensable. He offered only one possible means of meaningful survival:

Quelle est cette nuit où nous sommes? Est-ce la nuit bienheureuse qui, resplendissante comme le jour, nous illumine dans les délices de l'esprit, et joint les choses humaines aux divines? Ou bien la nuit de misère?

(What is this dark night where we are? Is it the benevolent night, resplendent like the day, that illuminates our mind, and joins the human to the divine? Or is it a night of misery?)[48]

Interestingly, Eliot's favourite thinker of the twenties, Maritain, used Claudel's lines (*Connaissance de l'Est*, chapter 4) as an epigraph in the chapter 4 of his book *Antimoderne:*

Qui ne croit plus en Dieu, il ne croit plus en l'être, et qui hait l'être, il hait sa propre éxistence./Seigneur, je vous ai trouvé.

(He who does not believe in God any longer, he does not believe in the being any longer, and he who hates the being, hates his own existence./Lord, I have found you.)[49]

If Eliot's early reservations about Claudel[50] changed into admiration in the mid-twenties (his confession in *Le Figaro littéraire* cited earlier shows that he always admired Claudel), Maritain could be one person who pointed out to him that, of all his contemporaries, Claudel and Eliot were very much in the same boat. 'Where there is no vital connection, the man may be a brilliant virtuoso, but is probably nothing more', Eliot wrote in 1928.[51] As the new attitude towards Claudel indicates, the vital connection was now clear to him. Eliot's own new convictions were corroborated in an article by Valery Larbaud in the *NRF*;[52] the latter asserted that it was by now obvious that Claudel would outlast others. Lastly, Emily Hale herself decided to stage a play of Claudel in Christmas, 1933.[53]

It is surprising that no one has taken serious note of the fundamental similarity of *Cinq Grandes Odes*, Claudel's *tour de force*, and Eliot's *Four Quartets*. The former had written to André Gide:

Ce sont de grands monologues lyriques où je reprends poétiquement certains thèmes de mon livre de philosophie; ce que peindront mes odes, c 'est la foi d 'un homme que le silence des espaces n 'effraie plus.

(These are long lyrical monologues where I take up poetically certain themes of my books of philosophy; what characterizes these odes is the joy of a man no longer daunted by the silence of the spaces.)[54]

The odes form an artistic whole, the sum and substance of his *Art Poétique*, to which Eliot referred in his foreword to Joseph Chiari's book and in the obituary to Claudel in *Le Figaro littéraire*, and which he recommended to the students during his 1916 Oxford Extension Lectures. The odes are also diary of a soul. If we agree that Eliot's quartets, as a whole, comprise a single poem, then the developments of Eliot and Claudel seem to be somewhat identical, more so because both the works are expressed in a similar incantatory, rhythmic language of rich, sonorous verse.

Poetry, to Claudel, is one continuous text, which sees in its totality of the world a vaster system. The odes are a 'momentous attempt to assemble reality, to repeat and imitate the eternal'.[55] To quote Claudel, 'Nous ne sommes plus avec le temps/Nous sommes avec la source du temps.' ('We are no longer with time/We are with the source of time.')[56] On the other hand, the whole of Eliot's life is a pilgrimage to the 'source of the longest river'. From *Ash-Wednesday*, there is in Eliot a superhuman Claudel-like endeavour to envisage 'l'immense octave de la creation' ('the immense Octave of the creation').[57]

The immensity of the enterprise is strikingly Dantesque, and both poets were till the last trying to achieve in their respective languages what Dante had done. Claudel started reading Dante at 20, and according to French experts like Paul-André Lesort, Dante's influence on him became clear towards the end of the first decade of the twentieth century.[58] In 'L'Ode des Muses', there are two verses on Dante.[59] Eliot's views on Dante are well known; it may be worthwhile for the English-speaking readers to know Claudel's:

L'oeuvre et la leçon de Dante sont particulièrement utiles à mediter dans le temps où nous vivons.

(The works and the lesson of Dante are particularly useful to meditate in the present time).[60]

. . . le but . . . pour Dante n'était pas avant tout de nous enseigner, mais de nous conduire, de nous prendre avec lui, de nous faire voir et toucher, et, tout en rassurant l'intelligence en ne l'entourant que de figures connues et d'objets familiers. Tel était son dessein, non pas de missionnaire, mais de poète, et il s'en acquitte d'une manière si vive, si convaincante, et dans un langage si beau, que peu à peu, et malgré nos doutes et nos résistances nous cedons à ce pied du compagnon qui nous entraîne, et nous aussi nous nous mettons en marche corporellement, nous rhythmons notre pas sur le sien, nous voyons ce qu'il nous décrit, et son prodigieus voyage devient pour nous réel . . .

(. . . Dante's intention was not to teach us, but to guide us, to take us with him, to make us see and touch, while reassuring our intelligence with known figures and familiary objects. His design was not that of a missionary, but of a poet, and he carried it out in such a lively and convincing manner, and in such a beautiful language that gradually, despite our doubts and resistances, we submit to this companion who trains us, and we physically walk together, rhyming our footstep with his, seeing what he describes and his prodigious journey becomes so real for us . . .)[61]

Eliot would say the same things about Dante.

In *Art Poétique*, Claudel presented his metaphysical arguments already implicit in the prose-poems of *Connaissance de l'Est* in support of his concept of the universe. His basic postulates are that in the universe each order of the creation alludes to all the others and find its *raison d'être* only in its relationship to the whole, and that the whole is homogeneous and continuous in time. Eliot, too, seems to echo similar thoughts in the *Quartets*.

In Claudel's universe, as well as in Eliot's, man's vocation is to discover the meaning of the great drama of which he is a part, to submit to the order established by his Master. For both, therefore, poetry becomes a tormented *drame intérieur* to reconcile the mind and the world. Man, as Claudel wrote to Jacques Rivière, is made for God, whether or not he derives from this condition good or evil, although Claudel hastens to add, 'Only good can come of it',[62] which reminds us of Eliot's 'Our Peace is in His Will'.[63] But although Eliot tried to 'explain to himself his intenser human feelings in terms of the divine goal',[64] to come to such a resolution was by no means easy. Both Claudel and Eliot had to experience great metaphysical anxiety, frustration, and need for love before they could realize their true vocation.

For Claudel, says Wallace Fowlie, 'the Catholic lives in a world of harsh reality, where life becomes a continuous effort, where life is constantly at stake'.[65] In his moment of knowledge, Eliot too cannot extricate himself from darkness:

> O dark dark dark. They all go into the dark,
> The vacant interstellar spaces, the vacant into the vacant . . .[66]

As 'the mental emptiness deepens', he tells himself:

> . . . be still, and let the dark come upon you
> Which shall be the darkness of God.[67]

So

> The darkness shall be the light, and the stillness the dancing.[68]

Thus, when Eliot forcibly makes statements like 'all things exist/Only in Thy light'[69] or 'the darkness declares the glory of light',[70] he comes very close to the Claudelian position:

> Mes yeux sont pleins de nuit . . .
> . . . Si je marche, où que j'arrive! il n'y à rien.
> (My eyes are full of night . . .
> . . . I walk, and wherever I arrive! there is nothing!)[71]

where defeat inevitably opens the door to bliss. It was the same 'pilgrimage of expiation' for both poets.

If Eliot's own early and middle-period poetry revealed a Pascalian terror ('essential moments in the progress of the intellectual soul', according to Eliot[72]), Claudel too—himself steeped in Pascal—recalled 'experiencing a feeling of terror, almost of horror' even on the exultant day of his communion in Notre-Dame in 1886 ('Ma Conversion', published for the first time in 1913 in the October 10 issue of *Revue des jeunes*.[73] It is likely that Eliot—who, according to Gordon, wrote intensely religious poems at the time—read this article). This finally led to the 'la joie d'un homme que le silence des espaces n'effraie plus' ('the joy of a man who is no longer scared of the silence of the spaces')[74].

What I intend to show here is simple: that Eliot, who came in contact with the religious thought of the French school of Maurras, Maritain, and

Claudel, shared an important characteristic of their spirituality. It is a down-to-earth school of spirituality. Referring to the French mind, René Bady thinks, 'La religion, en élevant vers le ciel, n'arrache pas le Français, né chretien, à la terre' ('Religion, while elevating towards Heaven, does not uproot the Frenchman, born Christian, from the earth').[75] It is a curious mixture of the sublime and the wretchedly real: to quote Claudel, 'une horrible, une superbe, une absurde, une éblouissante, une poignante réalité' ('a horrible, superb, absurd, dazzling, poignant reality').[76] We shall remember that when in *Le père Humilié*, Pensée confides to Orion, 'Nous ne voulons pas de la souffrance' ('We do not want to suffer'), the latter reminds him, 'Vous ne voulez donc pas de la joie' ('Then you do not want joy').[77]

Maritain, who seems to have reoriented much of Eliot's intellectual development in the mid-twenties, prescribed the same earthy outlook in the last lines of *Religion et Culture*. For him 'la pénsee catholique' ('Catholic thought') springs from 'la plus diligente compréhension des angoisses du temps' ('the most diligent comprehension of the anguish of the time')[78] and the need to reconcile the world with truth. 'You with your ass' muzzle, discover the huge divine laughter', writes Claudel.[79]

A poignant consciousness of the anguish of the time is also the hallmark of Eliot's spirituality. There is often in Eliot 'the backward half-look/Over the shoulder, towards the primitive terror'. He too speaks of 'darkness, deprivation and destitution', of 'the night fires going out, and the lack of shelters/And the cities hostile and towns unfriendly', where 'people change, and smile: but the agony abides'.[80] In *Murder in the Cathedral*, the chorus recognizes the purring leopard, the patting ape, and the waiting hyena as necessary units in an intelligible whole, implying, even by negation, the glory of God. And it is amidst this anguish that he was looking for *the still point*, the stillness between the two waves of the sea.

In a curious way, Claudel, too, looked for the same still point:

O grammarien de mes vers! Ne cherche point le chemin, *cherche le centre*! mesure, comprends l'espace compris entre ces deux solitaires!

(O grammarian within my verses! Do not seek the road, *seek the centre*! measure, encompass the space which lies between these two solitaries!)[81]

For Eliot, this still point is what gives meaning to our experience:

> A condition of complete simplicity
> (Costing not less than everything)
> And all shall be well and
> All manner of thing shall be well

When the tongues of flame are in-folded
Into the crowned knot of fire
And the fire and the rose are one.[82]

Claudel's 'centre' and Eliot's 'still point' seem to be synonymous. Surprisingly, or perhaps not really so, Claudel's fourth ode sets an identical mission:

Sois un seul esprit! Sois une seule intention!
Ce n'est pas l'auge et la truelle qui rassemble et qui construit
C'est *le feu pur et simple qui fait de plusieurs choses une seule.*

(Be one spirit! One sole intention!
It is not the hod and the trowel that assemble and construct
But *the fire, pure and simple, that makes several things into one.*)[83]

This is the still point of Eliot's *oeuvre*, 'where the dance is', the supreme illumination, the point of intersection of the timeless with time—the purification of motives in all our endeavour, the freedom. In Lyndall Gordon's words, applicable to both Claudel and Eliot, 'The dull repetition of meaningless existence fades into the circle, a singleness of being, self-contained, complete'.[84] No doubt, both these poets remind us of the fire of love in St. John of the Cross.[85] If in Eliot, it is a 'complete consort dancing together',[86] 'it is like a whole orchestra playing' in Claudel.[87]

As for the corresponding image of the rose in 'Burnt Norton', Eliot had only peered through the door into a rose garden:

Disturbing the dust on a bowl of rose-leaves
I do not know.[88]

But the final quartet brings him perceptibly near 'the moment of the rose and the yew-tree',[89] as he realizes that at the ultimate point of stillness, 'the crowned knot of fire', 'the fire and the rose are one'.[90] Exquisite as it is, the symbol of the perfect life of the rose garden recurs in a strangely identical manner in Claudel too, when he speaks of 'the hidden *garden* within':[91]

O rose!
Rose, je ne verrai plus votre visage en cette vie!
Et me voici tout seul au bord du torrent, la face contre terre,
Comme un pénitent au pied de la montagne de Dieu . . .

(O rose!
Rose, I shall not see your face again in this life!
And suddenly, here I am on the bank of the stream, face to the ground,

Like a patient at the feet of the mountain of God . . .)[92]
This is confirmed by the *Dictionnaire de littérature française et francophone* (Larousse):

The memory of the 'rose' is often present in the great odes, 'La Cantate à trois voix' and many other poems in *Corona benignitatis anni Deu* and *Feuille de Saints*, in particular 'Ténèbres' and 'Obsessions'.[93]

As for the garden image, we shall recall that Claudel had transformed into his own religious symbolism the symbolist practice of Baudelaire, Rimbaud, and Mallarmé: the tree becomes a symbol of renewal and continuity in Claudel's *L'Arbre*, which Eliot read in 1910–11.

Two great poets of our troubled time were searching for the stillness of divine Truth and Light, after resolving their inner contradictions (perhaps not fully in Eliot) in the same manner: 'So darkness shall be light and stillness the dancing';[94] in Claudel's words, 'La mesure sainte, libre, toute-puissante, créatrice!' ('Holy and free, all powerful and creative!')[95]

Eliot's submission to God has the unmistakable humility of Claudel's:

Ne me permettez point
De me soustraire à votre volonté, à la terre qui est votre volonté!

(Do not allow me
To withdraw myself from your will, from the earth which is your will!)[96]

Let us compare this with Eliot's

Teach us to sit still
Even among these rocks,
Our peace is in His will

. . .
Suffer me not to be separated
And let me cry come unto Thee.[97]

The moment of illumination and knowledge is the point of intersection of the timeless with time. In Claudel's words, 'en nous, à la fin/Eclate le commencement'. ('In us, at the end/Blazes the beginning').[98]

Tout être, comme il est un
Ouvrage de l'Eternité, C'est ainsi qu'll en est l'expression.
Elle est présente et toutes choses présentes se passent en elle.

(Every being, as the work
Of Eternity is also its expression.
Eternity is here, and the things of the moment happen within it.)[99]

In Claudel's idea of time, there is both repetition and renewal. Time is circular and generative. To quote Joy Nachod Humes:

This extraordinary dynamic of the idea of time leads to a contemplation of the present, which is always new. Physical forces and human will cooperate in the making of what Claudel calls *le mosaïque instant*: The present moment differs from all the other moments in that it does not express the same past, nor does it imply the same future ...

In the *Traité de la connaissance*, Claudel explores the whole question of the relation of the temporal to the eternal world, and man's situation in regard to both. 'Nous ne naissons pas seuls. Naître, pour tout, c'est connaître'. ('We are not born alone. To be born, for everything, is to know'.)[100] T. S. Eliot's

> Time past and time future
> What might have been and what has been
> Point to one end, which is always present.[101]

seems to wonderfully sum up Claudel's position, his tendency to reconcile movement and stasis, finite and infinite.

Therefore, in my opinion, it is no coincidence that Dominique Millet-Gérard subtitles her book on Claudel *Anima et Sagesse: Pour une esthétique comparée de l'éxègese claudelienne* (1990)[102] 'une terminaison et un commencement' ('An end and a beginning'). She seems to be unaware of Eliot's famous line, for the above quotation is ostensibly from Jankelevitch;[103] but it highlights the intra-poetic symbiosis of Claudel and Eliot, strangely ignored by Eliot critics.

These two great Christian poets in a non-Christian age attempted to decipher the text of the universe in the same way. But what takes away the breath of any reader of Eliot's later poetry is the scrupulous and painstaking exploitation of the immense possibility of the Claudelian verset. 'The strength and flexibility of the metre in *Four Quartets*', which Helen Gardner considers to be Eliot's 'greatest poetic achievement',[104] appears to have been a heritage of Claudel. If, according to Gardner, Eliot subordinates 'speech-rhythm to metrical pattern, while leaving the speech-rhythm all the time alive and springy within the pattern',[105] Claudel had done the same thing since the time of the *Art Poétique*. So had Claudel's disciple Saint-John Perse, whose *Anabase* Eliot translated into English in 1930.

The uniqueness of Claudel's style in French poetry which separates him from the other successors of nineteenth century symbolism, is the natural broad sweep and the minute observation, in retrospect strangely Eliotic, and the startling combination of the deeply personal and the impersonal.

'His technique of enumeration and repetition, hit metaphoric surcharged, his desire to put down the whole in its harmony', says an expert on Claudel, 'have an almost hypnotic effect on the reader'.[106] The great rassembleur that he was, Claudel 'gathers the forces of language, assembles, loosens them, now violent, now calm again, so that the listener is buffeted by the repetitions as the blasts of wind by their steady rhythm'. Trying to 'mine' the wealth of language, Claudel uses an enormous arsenal of vocabulary probably no other French poet has summoned to his command. Claudel's own explanation about his language is illuminating:

Il n'existe plus seulement, *il fonctionne*. Il n'est plus le résultat de l'élaboration Poétique, il en est aussi l'organe vivant, le battement régulier de la pompe qui puise dans l'inconnu le sentiment de l'idée.

(It not only exists, *it functions*. It is no longer the result of poetic elaboration, it is also its living organ, the regular beating of the pump which draws from the unknown the sentiment of the idea.)[107]

In Claudel, the varied rhythms of separate lines are supposed to reproduce the breathing of the poet. The metaphoric density and the rhythmic repetitiveness of the open lines in Claudel's poetry and drama, especially in the odes, remind us invariably of the magic spell of the orchestrated language of Eliot, his solemn litany-like intonation, from *Ash-Wednesday* onwards, especially in *Four Quartets*. When Claudel wrote, 'Let there be nothing slavish about my verses! Let them be like the sea-eagle that stoops on a great fish...',[108] he seemed to speak for Eliot too.

There is, in Eliot's Christian poetry, a growing Claudel-like sense of expansiveness in time and space, which can only be compared with the intrinsic richness of great music. The repetitions give a distinctly incantatory quality to his fairly straightforward utterances. This happens again and again in the Ariel poems, *Ash-Wednesday*, the choruses in *The Rock*, *Murder in the Cathedral*, and the *Quartets*, giving off the incense of biblical chants.

Critics have often drawn attention to the stylized rhythms of incantation and its repetitive charm in the *Four Quartets*. Ronald Bush[109] speaks of an enormous amount of psychic energy in *The Waste Land* working to displace images into an aural pattern, which is truer in case of the quartets. And Lyndall Gordon observes that the quartets are indeed unified not merely by:

... the formal repetitions of their five-part structure, but by a profounder strategy of repetition. It is the strategy of Emerson's essays, where each sentence is self-contained but repeats, in different terms, the same idea. It is also the tactic of the sermon: each unit, whether homely or poetic, is designed to awaken the audience, on different levels, to the same revelation. Eliot, like Emerson or Whitman, is writing a form of scripture. His poetry seeks the word, not mere words, but the word swaddled with darkness.[110]

Gordon, who can think of such disparate names as Emerson or Whitman, forgets the diction of Paul Claudel, which has all the elements of a sermon. Even as early as in 1919, Eliot was interested in the sermon as 'a form of literary art',[111] and one of the reasons for his fascination for Lancelot Andrewes was his finely built sermons. Yet Claudel's was the most living model of the kind of poetry he wished to write.

A good example of the incantatory and scriptural aspect of Claudelian verset, where 'the emotion controls its metre which expands or contracts in accord with the intensity of the emotion',[112] would be Eliot's lines in 'The Dry Salvages':[113]

> Between midnight and dawn, when the past is all deception.
> The future futureless, before the morning watch
> When time stops and time is never ending;
> And the ground swell, that is and was from the beginning,
> Clangs
> The bell.

or 'Marina':[114]

> What seas what shores what grey rocks and what islands
> What water lapping the bow
> And scent of pine and the wood thrush singing through the fog
> What images return
> O my daughter.

A random excerpt from Claudel will match this:

> De nouveau la dilatation de la houle!
> Ni
> Le marin, ni
> Le poisson qu'unt autre poisson à manger
> Entraîne, mais la chose même el tout le tonneau et la veine vive,
> Et l'eau même, et l'élément même, je joue, je resplendis!
> Je partage la liberté de la mer omniprésente!
> L'eau
> Toujours s'en vient retrouver l'eau
> Composant une goutte unique.
> (Once more the swell of the sea!

Not
The sea-wind, nor
The fish which hauls another fish in
To be eaten, but the thing itself and the whole barrelful, and the lively
    luck of it,
And the water itself and the element itself, I revel,
I am resplendent in these! I share the freedom of the omnipotent
    Ocean!
Water
Always finding mere water
To make up one great single drop).[115]

If creation is an ensemble of signs and figures to be deciphered, the water-symbol would recur as the dominating motif in Claudel and Eliot. In this book, I have earlier attempted to trace out how Eliot derived different meanings from the use of the water-imagery in Baudelaire, Laforgue, and Corbière, but, I think, it assumes great significance of another kind *after* his Conversion in 1927. Claudel's argument in his second ode gives us a lucid and seemingly valid interpretation of the construct.

No doubt, the Dantean example played an important part in the expansion of the imagery. The famous line in Dante's 'Paradiso' III,[116] which finds itself in both Claudel and Eliot: And in His will is our Peace' ('E'n la sua volontate è nostra pace') opened up a new horizon when it went on to say: 'It is that sea to which all things move'.

In *Four Quartets*, one could hear the voice of the hidden waterfall 'at the source of the longest river'.[117] This reminds us of Claudel's 'I would draw to me, summon through all my roots, the Ganges, the Mississippi'.[118] If the meaning of life for Eliot is reflected in a 'watery mirror', in Claudel we find: 'And I create the waters that nourishing all things, hold a *mirror* to all things'.[119] For Claudel, as well as for Eliot,

Ainsi l'eau continue l'esprit, et le supporte et l'alimente
Et entre
Toutes vos créatures jusqu'à vous il y a un lien liquide.

(Water is thus the extension of the spirit, it supports it and feeds it.
And between
All your creatures and you is a liquid bond.)[120]

The liquid bond ('L'eau m'a séduit./Tout ce qui vit, depuis la plante jusqu'à l'homme/Intérieurement par l'eau': 'Water has seduced me./Every living thing beginning from the plant to man lives inwardly on water')[121] is probably the most evident in Eliot's poetry, where it becomes the raison d'**être** of his world, the 'soul's sap'[122]: 'The river is *within us*, the sea is all about us'.[123] Claudel, too, had said: 'You who breathed life into the wet clay, and made man,/You command the *water within me*, you breathe into my nostrils the same spirit of creation and form'.[124]

Indeed, it would almost seem that the lines are interchangeable, Claudel could easily have written what Eliot would in two or three decades. If Claudel's 'lower waters' could be 'corruptible',[125] Eliot's are 'sullen, untamed, intractable'. And yet, if Eliot's vision of stillness is 'between the two waves of the sea', if water is finally the symbol of absolution he aspires to, Claudel too, had chanted a few years earlier: 'Toute mon âme hors de moi jaillit comme un grand jet d'eau claire' ('My whole soul leaps out of me like a great jet of clear water');[126] 'J'ai voulu l'âme, la savoir, cette eau, qui ne connaît point la mort' ('I wanted the soul, and to know that water ignorant of death').[127] Both, as I have noted before, were in search of the deathless still point, 'at the source of the longest river'. If Claudel's poetry becomes 'the diary of a soul', Eliot, too, was aiming to write his 'spiritual autobiography' in *Four Quartets*. For both, the universal vision is fundamentally Catholic and effortlessly acquires the musical qualities of a sermon. Eliot would wholeheartedly agree with Claudel when the latter wrote in 1928: 'La religion non seulement nous apporte le chant, elle nous apporte aussi la parole' ('Religion not only brings to us the chant, it furnishes also the word').[128]

There is the same commitment to the Word in the great odes and the quartets. Lyndall Gordon observes:

Ordinary words 'slip, slide, perish/Decay with imprecision, will not stay in place', but against the perpetual decay of languages in the course of time, Eliot has as his model 'The Word in the desert', language that has the permanence of scripture, as though graven on tablets of law. In Christian terms, the Word is in the deity.[129]

Its holiness is proven in the face of temptation. Eliot sets up the highest challenge that language can present: to make senseless words approach the perfect Word. This is strongly reminiscent of Claudel's 'Le verbe intelligible et la parole exprimée et la voix qui est l'esprit et l'eau' ('The intelligible word, and the speech that is truly expressed and the voice that is spirit and water').[130]

The impact of Claudel's poetry is, therefore, probably more seminal than one would imagine. To a reader who is even faintly familiar with Claudel, the appearance of Eliot's late poetry with the great flexibility and springiness of those long-drawn lines, should bring back memories of the French poet. (Herbert Howarth, the only Eliot critic who seems to be familiar with Claudel, has highlighted the 'pictorial resemblance' of their poetry.)[131] A visual comparison of Claudel's texts with Henri Fluchère's French translation of *Murder in the Cathedral*[132] or Pierre Leyris's of *Four Quartets*[133] can be most illuminating.

For both poets, it would seem, the end is the beginning of a much longer poem. While the title of *Four Quartets* suggests its musical structure, Peter Ackroyd records how, during the composition of these poems, Eliot spoke of a poem which might develop themes instrumentally and arrange transitions 'comparable to the different movements of symphony or a quartet'.[134] On the other hand, Claudel too wove the odes like true symphonies developing not in continuous sequence in the literary manner, but orchestrally with themes interlaced and varied. This also defines the method of the *Quartets*.

In a discussion on Blake, Eliot had once written that 'honesty' is the 'peculiarity of all great poetry' and that a poet should write 'from the centre of his crystal'.[135] The peculiar honesty of Claudel's chants converges with Eliot's own in the last phase, where the latter appears less clever than ever before (poetry, to him, it seems, is no longer a 'mug's game').[136] Both seem to speak out their spiritual monologues from the centre of their crystals. As David Perkins[137] rightly points out, if *The Waste Land* is an impersonal poem, *Four Quartets* is a personal speech. I suggest that this may have been the result of the impact of Paul Claudel.

To ignore the deep resonances of Claudel's works in Eliot's later poetry would be to overlook a vital aspect of his art. To be sure, it was not a conscious imitation like that of Laforgue in his Harvard days or Gautier in his quatrain poems, but one which remained deeply embedded in his subconscious and fecundated it like the child's memory of the sea anemone. It is a memory which appears to have inspired him to formulate his mature poetry and finally find his lost sea-voice.

Why then, was Eliot reluctant to openly express his gratitude? For reasons of ego or literary politics? Normally, he remained unusually frank and honest about his debts; but at the same time, we must bear in mind that apart from Dante and Baudelaire, others who had helped him were, more often than not, 'playmates nearer [his] size'.[138] Claudel was different, because he was one of the living greats and Eliot was always a little apprehensive about the greats. Sure enough, Eliot had to wrestle hard to avoid a cross with such an illustrious contemporary, but the memory lingered and spun its own magic web. To deny this might lead to a serious falsification of literary history.

NOTES

1. *Paul Claudel* (1868–1955): French poet and dramatist. Converted to Catholicism in 1886, he forged a versification known as *verset claudélien* out of the rhythmic prose-poems of Rimbaud and the New Testament. Major works include *Art Poétique* (1904), books of poems like *Cinq Grandes Odes* (1910) and *La Cantate à trois voix* (1913), and plays like *L'Annonce faite à Marie* (1912) and *Le Soulier de Satin* (1928–9). Ambassador of France in Tokyo, Washington, and Brussels, he was elected to the Académie Française in 1946.

2. Ronald Bush, *T.S. Eliot: A Study in Character and Style*, New York: Oxford University Press, 1985, p. ix.

3. This is well analysed in John D. Margolis, *T.S. Eliot's Intellectual Development 1922–1939*, Chicago: University of Chicago Press, 1972.

4. T.S. Eliot, *Ezra Pound: His Metric and Poetry*, New York: Knoff, 1917, p. 23. Also see T.S. Eliot, *To Criticize the Critic* (hereafter referred to as *TCC*), London: Faber and Faber, 1978, p. 177.

5. Francis Scarfe, 'Eliot and Nineteenth Century French Poetry', in *Eliot in Perspective: A Symposium*, ed. Graham Martin, London: Macmillan, 1970, p. 46.

6. David Perkins, *A History of Modern Poetry*, London: Harvard University Press, 1987, p. 26.

7. E.J.H. Greene, *T.S. Eliot et la France*, Paris: Boivin, 1951, p. 7; Scarfe, 'Eliot and Nineteenth Century French Poetry', p. 46.

8. See Bush, *T.S. Eliot*, p. 175.

9. Eliot, *TCC*, p. 23.

10. Jonathon Culler, *Structuralist Poetics*, London: Routledge, 1989, p. 140.

11. Herbert Howarth, *Notes on Some Figures Behind T.S. Eliot*, London: Chatto & Windus, 1965, pp. 162–7.

12. Scarfe, 'Eliot and Nineteenth Century French Poetry', p. 46.

13. Wallace Fowlie, *Paul Claudel*, London: Bowes & Bowes, 1957, p. 7.

14. T.S. Eliot, 'Little Gidding, Four Quartets', *The Complete Poems and Plays of T.S. Eliot* (hereafter referred to as *CPP*), London: Faber and Faber, 1990, p. 197.

15. T.S. Eliot, *The Sacred Wood* (hereafter referred to as *SW*), London: Methuen, 1982, pp. 66–7.

16. See Howarth, *Some Figures Behind T.S. Eliot*, p. 167.

17. Quoted from Frank Kermode's introduction to T.S. Eliot, *Selected Prose of T.S. Eliot*, ed. Frank Kermode, London: Faber and Faber, 1975, p. 13.

18. T.S. Eliot, *On Poetry and Poets* (hereafter referred to as *OPP*), London: Faber and Faber, 1969, p. 209.

19. Ibid.

20. Peter Ackroyd, *T.S. Eliot*, London: Hamish Hamilton, 1984, p. 42; Robert Sencourt, *T.S. Eliot: A Memoir*, ed. Donald Adamson, London: Grarnstone Press, 1971, p. 36.

21. 'What France Means to You', 'Réponse de T.S. Eliot', *La France Libre*, 15 June 1944, p. 94.

22. A.D. Moody, *Thomas Stearns Eliot: Poet*, Cambridge: Cambridge University Press, 1979, p. 42.

23. Ibid.

24. See the introduction by T.S. Eliot to Joseph Chiari, *Contemporary French Poetry*, Manchester: Manchester University Press, 1952, p. xii.

25. Joseph Chiari, *The Poetic Drama of Paul Claudel*, London: Harvill Press, 1954.

26. Special number on Claudel, *Le Figaro littéraire*, 5 March 1955.

27. Ibid.

28. Alain-Fournier et Jacques Rivière, *Correspondance*, 2 vols., Paris: Gallimard, 1991.

29. Fournier and Rivière, *Correspondance*, vol. I, p. 351.

30. Ibid., p. 357.

31. Claudel was trying to convert Rivière, the non-believer, since 1907. Much to this satisfaction, he finally took communion in 1913. Eliot, who knew Rivière personally and had subscribed to the *NRF* (Ackroyd, *T.S. Eliot*, p. 46), would not have missed his friend Jacques Rivière's article 'De la foi' ('Of Faith') dedicated to Paul Claudel in the November issue of 1912. Rivière wrote:

    Celui qui doute n'a rien à faire, n'a pas à bouger, son doute n'est pas quelque chose qu'il ait besoin pour suivre, d'atteindre et de conquérir; il est la première forme que prend sa pensée, la plus proche, la plus paresseuse . . .
    Mais croire est une toute autre besogne—la foi est un mouvement de l'âme, une sorte qu'en fait hors de ses murs.

    (The man who is sceptic has nothing to do, nothing to stir, his doubt is not something which he needs in order to follow, to reach, to conquer; it is the first form that his thought takes, the nearest, the laziest . . .
    But belief is a different kind of necessity—faith is a movement of the soul, which takes one outside the walls.)

    La Nouvelle Revue Française (hereafter referred to as *NRF*), November 1912, pp. 782–3.

32. Sencourt, *T.S. Eliot*, p. 36.

33. Their friendship is imprinted in the pages of Charles Péguy and Alain-Fournier, *Correspondance: Paysage d'une amitié*, Paris: Fayard, 1990.

34. I found this information in Jean-Louis Debauve, *Laforgue en son temps: Langages et documents*, Neuchâtel: A la Baconnière, 1972, p. 186.

35. T.S. Eliot, *Letters of T.S. Eliot*, ed. Valerie Eliot, vol. I, London: Faber and Faber, 1988, p. 21.

36. There is a whole book on Claudel's intimacy with the *NRF*. See Sylvia Caides Vaginaos, *Paul Claudel et La Nouvelle Revue Française, 1909–1918*, Geneva: Librairie Droz S.A., 1979.

37. Howarth, *Some Figures Behind T.S. Eliot*, p. 165.

38. F.S. Flint, 'Paul Claudel', *Poetry*, July 1915; quoted in René Taupin, *L'Influence du symbolisme français sur la poésie américaine* [1929], Geneva: Slatkine Rpts., 1979, p. 104.

39. Remy de Gourmont, *Le Livre des Masques*, Paris: Mercure de France, 1896, p. 176.

40. T.S. Eliot, *Essays Ancient and Modern* (hereafter referred to as *EAM*), London: Faber and Faber, 1947, p. 152.

41. Lyndall Gordon, *Eliot's Early Years*, Oxford: Oxford University Press, 1977, p. 27.

42. Ibid., p. 71.

43. Ibid.

44. Ackroyd, *T.S. Eliot*, p. 21.

45. Gordon, *Eliot's Early Years*, p. 58.

46. Ibid., p. 42.

47. Jacques Maritain, *Religion et Culture*, Paris: Desclée de Brouwer, 1930, p. 82.

48. Jacques Maritain, *Antimoderne*, Paris: Revue des jeunes, 1922, p. 195.

49. Ibid., p. 159.

50. As recorded in Eliot, *SW*, pp. 66–7.

51. T.S. Eliot, 'The Idealism of Julien Benda', *New Republic*, 12 December 1928, p. 107.

52. *NRF*, January 1926, pp. 65–6.

53. Lyndall Gordon, *Eliot's New Life*, Oxford: Oxford University Press, 1988, p. 42.

54. André Gide et Paul Claudel, *Correspondance 1899–1926*, Paris: Gallimard, 1949, p. 91.

55. Joy Nachod Humes, *Two Against Time: A Study of the Very Present Worlds of Paul Claudel and Charles Péguy*, Chapel Hill: University of North Carolina Press, 1978, pp. 58–9.

56. Paul Claudel, 'Un poète regarde la croix', *Oeuvre Poétique* (hereafter referred to as *OP*), 1967; Paris: Bibliothèque de la Pléiade, 1985, p. 536.

57. Paul Claudel, 'L'esprit de l'eau', *OP*, Paris: Bibliothèque de la Pléiade, 1985, p. 240.

58. Paul-André Lesort in an interview in Georges Cattaui and Jacques Madaule, eds., *Entretiens sur Paul Claudel*, Paris: Moutin, 1961, p. 21.

59. Information in the interview with Gilbert Godoffre, ibid., p. 21.

60. Paul Claudel, *Réflexions sur la poésie*, Paris: Gallimard, 1979, p. 156.

61. Ibid., pp. 157–8.

62. Paul Claudel and Jacques Rivière, *Correspondance 1907–1914*, Paris: Plon, 1926, p. 256.

63. T.S. Eliot, 'Ash-Wednesday', VI, *CPP*, London: Faber and Faber, 1990, p. 98.

64. Eliot's letter to William Force Stead, quoted in Helen Gardner, *The Composition of Four Quartets*, London: Faber and Faber, 1978, p. 29.

65. Fowlie, *Paul Claudel*, p. 20.

66. Eliot, 'East Coker, Four Quartets', *CPP*, p. 180.

67. Ibid.

68. Ibid.

69. T.S. Eliot, 'Murder in the Cathedral', *CPP*, London: Faber and Faber, 1990, p. 281.

70. Ibid.

71. Paul Claudel, 'Premiers vers', *OP*, Paris: Bibliothèque de la Pléiade, 1985, p. 9.
72. Eliot, *EAM*, p. 152.
73. Quoted in Richard Berchan, *The Inner Stage: An Essay on the Conflict of Vocations in the Early Works of Paul Claudel*, Michigan: Michigan University Press, 1966, pp. 7–8.
74. See note 54.
75. René Bady, *Littérature et Spiritualité*, Lyon: Presse Universitaire de Lyon, 1978, p. 298.
76. Ibid., p. 252.
77. Paul Claudel, *Théâtre Complet*, vol. II, Paris: Bibliothèque de la Pléiade, 1949, p. 508.
78. Maritain, *Religion et Culture*, p. 90.
79. Paul Claudel, 'La Muse qui est la grâce', *OP*, Paris: Bibliothèque de la Pléiade, 1985, p. 268.
80. T.S. Eliot, 'The Dry Salvages', *CPP*, London: Faber and Faber, 1990, p. 187.
81. Paul Claudel, 'Les Muses, Cinq Grandes Odes', *OP*, Paris: Bibliothèque de la Pléiade, 1985, p. 227.
82. Eliot, 'Little Gidding', p. 198, last few lines.
83. Claudel, 'La Muse qui est la grâce', p. 275.
84. Gordon, *Eliot's New Life*, p. 141.
85. Bernard Bergonzi, ed., *T.S. Eliot, Four Quartets: A Casebook*, London: Macmillan, 1993, p. 5.
86. Eliot, 'Little Gidding', p. 197.
87. Paul Claudel, 'L'esprit et l'eau', *OP*, Paris: Bibliothèque de la Pléiade, 1985, p. 242.
88. T.S. Eliot, 'Burnt Norton, Four Quartets', *CPP*, London: Faber and Faber, 1990, p. 171.
89. Eliot, 'Little Gidding', p. 197.
90. Ibid., p. 198.
91. Claudel, 'Les Muses', p. 229.
92. Claudel, 'L'esprit et l'eau', pp. 245–6.
93. *Dictionnaire de littérature française et francophone*, vol. I, Paris: Larousse, 1987, p. 347.
94. Eliot, 'East Coker', III, *CPP*, p. 180.
95. Claudel, *OP*, p. 247.
96. Claudel, 'La Muse qui est la grâce', p. 271.
97. Eliot, 'Ash-Wednesday', p. 98.
98. Claudel, 'L'esprit et l'eau', p. 241.
99. Ibid.
100. Humes, *Two Against Time*, p. 63.
101. Eliot, 'Burnt Norton', p. 172.
102. Dominique Millet-Gérard, *Anima et Sagesse: Pour une esthétique comparée de l'exégèse claudelienne*, Paris: P. Lethieulleux, 1990.
103. Ibid., p. 781.
104. Helen Gardner, *The Art of T.S. Eliot*, London: Faber and Faber, 1968, p. 15.

105. Ibid., p. 6.

106. Humes, *Two against Time*, p. 75.

107. Paul Claudel, *Positions et Propositions*, Paris: Gallimard, 1928, p. 18.

108. Claudel, *OP*, p. 224.

109. Bush, *T.S. Eliot*, p. 75.

110. Gordon, *Eliot's New Life*, pp. 96–7.

111. T.S. Eliot, 'The Preacher as Artist', *Athenaeum*, 28 November 1919, p. 1252.

112. Fowlie, *Paul Claudel*, p. 28.

113. Eliot, *CPP*, p. 185.

114. Ibid., p. 109.

115. Claudel, 'L'esprit et l'eau', pp. 236–7.

116. Dante, 'Paradiso', III, line 85, in *The Divine Comedy*, 3, tr. Dorothy L. Sayers and Barbara Reynolds, Harmondsworth: Penguin, 1975, p. 75.

117. Eliot, 'Little Gidding', p. 191.

118. Claudel, 'L'esprit et l'eau', p. 237.

119. Ibid., p. 241.

120. Ibid.

121. Paul Claudel, *Théâtre Complet*, vol. I, Paris: Bibliothèque de la Pléiade, 1949, pp. 576–7.

122. Eliot, 'Little Gidding', p. 191.

123. Eliot, 'The Dry Salvages', p. 184.

124. Claudel, 'L'esprit et l'eau', p. 243.

125. Ibid., p. 236.

126. Claudel, 'L'esprit et l'eau', p. 246.

127. Ibid., p. 245.

128. Claudel, *Réflexions sur la poésie*, p. 182.

129. Gordon, *Eliot's New Life*, p. 99.

130. Claudel, 'L'esprit et l'eau', p. 247.

131. Howarth, *Some Figures behind T.S. Eliot*, p. 164.

132. Henri Fluchère, tr., *Meurtre dans la cathédrale*, Paris: Ed. du Seuil, 1946.

133. Pierre Leyris, tr., *Poésie*, Paris: Ed. du Seuil, 1969, pp. 156–222.

134. Ackroyd, *T.S. Eliot*, p. 269.

135. Eliot, *SW*, pp. 151, 54–5.

136. Eliot quoted in Ackroyd, *T.S. Eliot*, p. 215.

137. Perkins, *History of Modern Poetry*, p. 25.

138. Eliot, *TCC*, p. 127.

Conclusion

ONE OF THE MOST OUTSTANDING qualities of T.S. Eliot was his intense awareness of 'the common element in European Culture', its 'interrelated history of thought and feeling and behaviour', its 'interchange of arts and of ideas'.[1] The works of Dante, as well as those of Baudelaire, Laforgue, Corbière, Larbaud, and Claudel, were no doubt part of the complex heritage out of which his poetry was born. I quote him at length because his views on 'the unity of European culture' are central to his poetic theory and practice:

We cannot understand any one European literature without knowing a good deal about others. When we examine the history of poetry in Europe, we find a tissue of influences woven to and fro. There have been good poets who knew no language but their own, but even they have been subject to influences taken in and disseminated by other writers among their own people. Now, the possibility of each literature renewing itself, proceeding to new creative activity, making new discoveries in the use of words, depends on two things. First, its ability to receive and assimilate influences from abroad. Second, its ability to go back and learn from its own sources. As for the first, when the several countries of Europe are cut off from each other, when poets no longer read any literature but that in their own language, poetry in every country must deteriorate.[2]

For the 'health of the culture of Europe',[3] Eliot prescribed that 'the different cultures should recognize their relationship to each other. So that each should be susceptible of influence from the others'.[4] He went on to say:

My last appeal is to the men of letters of Europe, who have a special responsibility for the preservation and transmission of our common culture.[5]

What matters is that we should recognize our relationship and mutual dependence upon each other.[6]

Surprisingly, even such significant statements from Eliot—marked by a clear moral stance and a theoretical position—have not propelled critics and scholars to examine his special debt to France, where he landed *before* he set foot on 'the small island on the north of the English Channel'.[7]

The present research project was an endeavour to comprehend the *horizontverschmelzung*—fusion of horizons—in the first decades of twentieth century English poetry, when, in the words of P. Van Tieghem, international relations multiplied and the influences got entangled with each other.[8]

The trajectory we have sketched here may be, in certain respects, incomplete, and leaves a few lacunae. But, arguably, these gaps should only establish the credibility of the proposition, for as André Morize described so well:

Influence by its very nature does not always declare itself by precise and well-defined signs; its study does not admit of the same exactness as, for instance, the investigation of sources. Frequently, it consists in following the capricious, unexpected meanderings of a stream whose waters are led hither and thither by the accidental contour of the ground and take their colour from various tributaries and the soil through which they flow at times even disappearing for a space to reappear further on.[9]

Territories overlap, and resonances blend and fuse with each other. The fact that the documents presented in the previous chapters still do not probably add up to form an Eliot only points to the unfathomable mystery of creative activity, something that cannot be wholly explained by the parent texts.

Moreover, 'influence' itself should no longer be defined in the narrow mechanical sense of 'borrowing'; we know, it also comprises the creative responses to various 'stimuli' and even 'negative influence'. Influence can be direct and indirect, it can not only mean 'analogy', 'affinity', and 'convergence', but perhaps also interpretation, reaction, resistance, and combat (It could have been 'combat' in the case of Claudel, before Eliot finally gave in). In 1900, speaking on Goethe, Gide made the famous statement:

L'influence ne crée rien, elle éveille.

(Influence does not create anything, it awakens.)[10]

Besides, a study of influences, as Eliot himself stated in a lecture given in French at Aix-en-Provence in 1948, may help us to assess the contribution of predecessor-poets to 'the extension of the civilized consciousness—the consciousness of language—as it has developed in the last hundred years'.[11]

We must also think of the paradigmatic nature of the encounter between the reader and the text. Eliot was a reader who was creative, and who was a product of history. And, subsequently, as a writer he had to dismantle the original structure of the parent text in order to reconstruct it for his own benefit, thus creating new structures.

Yet, I hope I have been able to establish why Eliot accorded so much importance to his French masters, and why he believed that without the tradition of French poetry starting from Baudelaire his own poetry would have been inconceivable.[12] The texts of Baudelaire, Laforgue, Corbière, Larbaud, and Claudel seem to absorb some essential characteristics of Eliot's ideas and modes of writing, and delineate a similar progression from scepticism to some sort of an affirmation: 'un symbolisme renforcé par la foi' ('a symbolism reinforced by faith').[13] In *Eliot's New Life*, Lyndall Gordon suspected such a development in Eliot's 'models'; although she did not specify who these models were, she seems to have referred to Dante and Baudelaire. My discovery of similar traits in Jules Laforgue could, therefore, have far-reaching implications.

Eliot clearly spotted in the works of the above poets, of already demonstrated efficacy, the ammunition to overhaul the poetic discourse in English. He took it as his *métier* to act as a mediator between English and European, notably French, poetic history. As Reilly says to Peter in *The Cocktail Party*:

You understand your *métier*, Mr. Quilpe—
Which is the most that any of us can ask for.[14]

Consequently, in the process of reconstructing Eliot's poetry in the light of his interaction with French poetic discourse (which of course does not negate other influences), I have tried to explode the myth that he had indeed ceased to borrow from others as he matured.

I have left out, as I have mentioned in the introduction, Eliot's cross with the French thinkers, notably Bergson, Maurras, and Maritain, but then that could be the subject of another study someone should take up some day. Saint-John Perse—to whom Eliot openly acknowledged his debt[15]—was not considered, because his highly flexible and richly orchestrated, rhythmic language is a widely-known Claudelian heritage: my evaluation of the resonances of Claudel's hymn and prayer in later Eliot seems to absorb the influence of Perse, the 1960 Nobel laureate from France. Eliot's translation (1930) of Perse's *Anabase* (1924) may have been instigated by Saint-John Perse's own translation of *The Hollow Men*, which was published in *Commerce* in 1922.[16]

It is true that some of these findings, which throw light on important turnings in Eliot's poetic career, seem to raise once more a few disturbing questions about creativity itself. Was Roland Barthes, after all, right when he said, 'Tout texte est un tissu de citations révolues?' ('Every text is a fabric of past citations?')[17] Or was Eliot's an exceptional case of literary kleptomania? Were his virtues forced upon him by his impudent crimes? Did he not say, 'Immature poets imitate, mature poets steal'? Or are these 'subconscious infiltrations', as a defenceless Eliot scholar, who read the typescript of this book, furiously claims? Where does one draw the line? Interestingly, Remy de Gourmont (see appendix A) himself made concessions for imitations and borrowings:

De grands poètes, Corneille, Molière, Racine, Victor Hugo n'ont pas assez dedaigné' l'emprunt, et même ils ne l'ont pas toujours assez dissimulé . . . pour les [plagiats] bien réussir, il faut un certain génie.

(Some great poets, Corneille, Molière, Racine, Victor Hugo have not sufficiently disdained borrowings, and even they have not always hidden it . . . to be successful in plagiarism, one should have a certain genius.)[18]

There is no doubt that Eliot had a special kind of genius to assimilate his borrowings into his oeuvre, and convert everything into fresh blood. But while appreciating the pattern in the carpet of Eliot's poetry, is it really necessary to disentangle the diverse material which went into the making of the carpet? Does an investigation into Eliot's creative process bring discredit to him? Writing about Pascal's debt to Montaigne, Eliot stated significantly:

. . . in the Pensées, at the very end of his life, we find passage after passage, and the slighter they are the more significant, almost 'lifted' out of Montaigne down to a figure of speech or a word . . . It would, however, be grossly unfair to Pascal, to Montaigne, and indeed to French literature, to leave the matter at that. It is no diminution of Pascal but only an aggrandizement of Montaigne.[19]

Surely, the same thing could be said about Eliot's own enriching relationship with French poetry.

At this point, I have no desire to theorize about the findings of the present book, which I wish to place before worthier scholars. But they do address some very pertinent questions. A century after Eliot's dramatic arrival, it would be wonderful to start a serious debate about the creative process of one man who almost single-handedly changed the poetic discourse of his time.

NOTES

1. T.S. Eliot, *Notes Towards the Definition of Culture* (hereafter referred to as *NTDC*), London: Faber and Faber, 1948, p. 119.
2. Ibid., pp. 112–13.
3. Ibid., p. 119.
4. Ibid.
5. Ibid., p. 123.
6. Ibid., p. 123-4.
7. See the 'Introduction' of this volume.
8. P. Van Tieghem, *Les Influences étrangères sur la littérature française*, Paris: PUF, 1967, p. 247.
9. André Morize, *Problems and Methods of Literary History*, Boston: Ginn and Co., 1922, p. 229.
10. Pierre Brunel et Yves Chevrel, *Précis de littérature comparée*, Paris: PUF, 1989, p. 17.
11. Eliot's lecture 'Edgar Poe et la France' delivered at Aix-en-Provence on receiving Hon. D ès Lettres in 1948. Typescript at John Hayward Bequest, Modern Archives, King's College, Cambridge, item HIK, p. 22.
12. Eliot, *NTDC*, p. 112.
13. Tribute to him in Eliot's letter to Jean Paulhan, *La Nouvelle Revue Française*, 7 December 1949.
14. T.S. Eliot, *The Complete Poems and Plays of T.S. Eliot*, London: Faber and Faber, 1990, p. 435.
15. Tribute to him in Eliot's letter to Jean Paulhan, *La Nouvelle Revue Française*, 7 December 1949.
16. Saint-John Perse's little-known French translation of *The Hollow Men*, part 1, was published in *Commerce* in November 1924. It was the French poet's only translation:

En hommage à T.S. Eliot:

Aumône aux hommes de peu de poids

Nous sommes les hommes sans substance,
Nous sommes les hommes faits de paille.
Pressés en foule fraternelle,
Têtes bourrées de paille, hélas!
Nos voix stériles, si tout bas
Nous nous murmurons en foule,
Sont voix plus douces et plus vaines
Que le souffle du vent parmi l'herbe stérile,
Que la course des rats sur les débris de verres
Dans nos caves stériles.
Ombres sans forme, nuances sans couleur,
Force sans mouvement et geste qui ne bouge . . .

Ceux qui s'en furent
Droit devant eux, vers l'autre Royaume de la Mort.
Songeant à nous, s'ils songent à rien, n'évoquent point des âmes
Violentes et perdues, mais seulement
Les hommes faits de paille.

Saint-John Perse, *Oeuvres Complètes*, Paris: Bibliothèque de la Pléiade, 1989, p. 465.

17. Pierre Brunel et Yves Chevrel, *Précis de littérature comparée*, Paris: PUF, 1989, p. 45.

18. Remy de Gourmont, *Le Problème du style*, Paris: Mercure de France, 1902, p. 306.

It would be very interesting to look up Eliot's comments on poetic creativity towards the end of the Turnbull Lectures. It mattered little, he thought, whether one is 'original' or 'derivative':

no honest man can be a hero to himself; for he must be aware how many causes in world history, outside of abilities and genius, have been responsible for greatness.

T.S. Eliot, *The Varieties of Metaphysical Poetry*, ed. Ronald Schuchard, London: Faber and Faber, 1993, p. 289.

19. T.S. Eliot, *Essays Ancient and Modern*, London: Faber and Faber, 1947, p. 150.

Appendix A
Remy de Gourmont

WE SHALL NOT APPRECIATE THE dynamics of intertextuality between T.S. Eliot and the French poets discussed in the previous chapters, if we fail to recognize the former's debt to Remy de Gourmont[1] (1858–1915), the great *apologist* for Symbolism. He basically gave Eliot *the stance* that the poet-reader must take in relation to the poetic text, helped him to formulate something like a theory and seems to have played a pivotal role in the development of his taste, at a turning point in history.

For Eliot and his friends, Gourmont's whole attitude to poetry and to the mechanism of creative intelligence embodied the modern spirit. To know him was tantamount to passing from one period of civilization to another, because he seemed to 'combine to a remarkable degree sensitiveness, erudition, sense of fact, sense of history and generalizing power'.[2] Gourmont was no doubt as important to Eliot as Laforgue was in his formative years as a poet-critic. In Eliot's words:

At that time, I was much stimulated and much helped by the critical writings of Remy de Gourmont. I acknowledge that influence and am grateful for it; and I by no means disown it by having passed on to another problem not touched upon in this book, that of the relation of poetry to the spiritual and social life of its time and of other times.[3]

Eliot, who believed that 'surprisingly few things can be said about poetry; and of these few, the most turn out to be either false or to say nothing of significance',[4] nevertheless, found acceptable, if controversial, formulas for crucial matters of poetry. This was possible largely because of the exemplary temperament, courage, and conviction of Gourmont.

Remy de Gourmont, who had to fight against the received idea that Symbolist poetry was obscure and decadent, sought to get rid of the

*I am indebted to the Bibliothèque Nationale de France for the original editions of Gourmont's books.

emotional dust by combining artistic sensitivity with scientific objectivity. Consequently, like Eliot, he transformed some of his personal impressions into iron laws.

A master polemicist, a 'real master of facts', and a 'master illusionist of facts',[5] according to his immediate needs, he adopted a peculiar aggressiveness, an air of almost disdainful superiority, which made him a high-brow iconoclast. In *La Culture des idées* (1900), Gourmont quoted Swift and advised the young writers to censure praise (for, in his opinion, destructive criticism was more useful for stealing the limelight) and belong to a coterie:

Quelle que soit votre force, vos armes et votre insolence, vous aurez besoin de faire partie d'un cénacle ou d'une coterie, comme on a besoin d'un cercle ou d'un café.

(Whatever may be your power, your arms and your insolence, you are required to belong to a group or a coterie, just as one requires a circle or a café).[6]

There is a good deal of pontifical solemnity in Gourmont's style (he said: 'It is always good to pretend'[7]), which was readily imbibed by Eliot. It would be interesting to remember that Middleton Murry, who praised Eliot's 'critical intelligence of a high order and sensibility of an unusual kind', at the same time, criticized his manner as 'often portentous and disdainful'.[8] What Gourmont, and subsequently Eliot, wanted was to 'sow the seeds of doubt' ('semer des domes') for 'doubt is liberating' ('le doute est libérateur').[9] Hence, 'the occasional note of arrogance, of vehemence, of cocksureness, of rudeness, the braggadocio of the mild-mannered man'.[10]

I wish to catalogue from Gourmont's books some of the epoch-making ideas which seem to have a direct bearing on Eliot's revolutionary role as poet and critic.

Gourmont's view on originality:

L'invention des thèmes n'a pas un grand intérêt en littérature . . . M. de Maupassant, qui inventa la plupart de ses thèmes, est un moindre conteur que Boccacce, qui n'inventa aucun des siens. L'invention des sujets est d'ailleurs limitée, encore que *flexible* à *l'infini* . . .

(Invention of themes does not have much importance in literature . . . M. de Maupassant, who invented most of his themes, is a lesser storyteller than Boccaccio, who invented nothing. Moreover, invention of subjects is limited in scope, and has *no great flexibility* . . .)[11]

According to Gourmont, 'Le génie est affaire d'apprentissage' ('Genius is a matter of apprenticeship'). This seems to anticipate Eliot's hasty declaration: 'The poem which is absolutely original is absolutely bad'.[12]

The following excerpts from Gourmont's essays should show how much he influenced Eliot's method of work.

On Imitation:

L'imitation des écrivains les uns par les autres, de ceux qui ne sont plus par ceux qui vont être, est *un fait nécessaire* . . .

Pour un adolescent—il y a des adolescences prolongées—admirer, c'est imiter. Les deux actes se rejoignent fatalement. La période imitatrice de la carrière est intéressante historiquement . . .

(Imitation of dead writers, by those who want to become writers, *is a necessity.*

For an adolescent—and there are prolonged adolescences—to admire is to imitate. The two acts join fatally. This period of imitation in a poet's career has a historic interest).[13]

On Plagiarism:

Il y a des plagiaires innocents. La mémoire . . . n'est pas autre chose qu'une bibliothèque de clichés sensoriels; les uns sont vifs, les autres alterés ou effacés . . . Le souvenir prend la forme de l'inspiration.

(There are innocent plagiarists. Memory . . . is nothing but a library of sensorial clichés; some are lovely, others mutilated or erased . . . Memory takes the form of inspiration . . .)[14]

Il est permis d'imiter, il est permis d'emprunter des documents, d'assimiler des idées. De grands poètes, Corneille, Molière, Racine, Victor Hugo, n'ont pas dedaigné l'emprunt et même ils ne l'ont pas toujours dissimulé. Balzac avant de trouver dans le réalisme sa voie, imita les romans anglais. Alexandre Dumas alla plus loin; ses premiers drames sont faits de pièces et de morceaux pris à droite et à gauche, cousus avec une suprême adresse.

(One is permitted to imitate, one is permitted to borrow documents, assimilate ideas . . . Great poets like Corneille, Molière, Racine, Victor Hugo have not disdained borrowing and have not even tried to conceal it. Before finding his true path in realism, Balzac imitated English novels. Alexandre Dumas went even further; his first plays were forged out of bits and fragments taken from here and there, but woven together with supreme skill).[15]

There could be factual fallibility in some of these arguments (F.W. Bateson complained of 'factual fallibility' in Eliot[16]), but the conviction and purposefulness of neither Eliot nor Gourmont is ever in doubt. Besides, this view could well have provided Eliot with the raison d'être for his ingenious method of freely using others' material in his creative and critical works.

On the use of common speech:

. . . les plus belles images, les plus vraies et les plus hardies, sont encloses dans nos mots de *tous les jours*.

(. . . the most beautiful images, the truest and the most daring are enclosed in our *everyday* words.)[17]

This is, of course, one of Eliot's basic premises. Few commentators of Eliot have pointed out to us that Gourmont was a great advocate of common speech in poetry.

On poetry which is difficult:

La clarté n'est pas une qualité essentielle de la poésie; il est même dangereux pour un poète d'être trop clair et de laisser trop bien voir le fond, généralement assez pauvre, de sa pensée.

(Clarity is not an essential quality of poetry. It is even dangerous for a poet to be too clear and let others discover the depth, generally quite poor, of his thought.)[18]

Eliot's own poetry would testify to this. This reminds us of his famous statement, which would have been in the manifesto of the modernists:

Poets in our civilisation must be difficult. The poet must be more and more indirect, in order to force, to dislocate if necessary, language into his meaning.[19]

On Style:

Le style est un produit physiologique et l'un des plus constants, quoique dans la dépendance des diverses fonctions vitales.

(The style is a physiological product and one of the most constant, although it depends on diverse vital functions.)[20]

Toute sensation actuelle ou emmagasinée dans les cellules nerveuses est propice à l'art.

(Every sensation current or stored up in the nerve cells is proper to art.)[21]

Eliot seems to have merely paraphrased him when he wrote: 'One must look into the cerebral cortex, the nervous system and the digestive tracts'.[22] And this view seems to be closely related with Eliot's theory of the sensuous apprehension of thought or of the recreation of thought into feeling.

On Sensibility:

La sensibilité comprend la raison elle-même, qui n'est que de la sensibilité crystallisée.

(Sensibility comprises reason itself, which is nothing but sensibility crystallised).[23]

A force de vivre, on acquiert la faculté de dissocier son intelligence de sa sensibilité: cela arrive ou tard, par l'acquisition d'une faculté nouvelle, indispensable quoique dangereuse, le scepticisme. Laforgue est mort avant d'avoir atteint cette étape.

(In the process of living, one acquires the faculty of dissociating intelligence from sensibility. This happens sooner or later by the acquisition of a new indispensable but dangerous faculty: scepticism. Laforgue died before reaching that stage.)[24]

This idea of dissociation, as Aldington has pointed out, is Gourmont's 'most important contribution to thought', and was 'a formulation of his delight in analysis'.[25] Eliot unceremoniously transferred to English literary history what Gourmont considered an inevitable part of the psychological growth of an individual: the dissociation of sensibility. In the words of Edward Lobb: 'Eliot had discussed the growth of the English language as though he were tracing the development of an individual's mind . . .'[26]

On Impersonality:

Il n'y a pas toujours de relation logique entre la vie et l'oeuvre d'un écrivain . . .

(There is not always a logical relation between the life and the work of a writer . . .)[27]

Le but de l'activité propre de l'homme est de nettoyer sa personalité, de la laver de toute souillure . . .

(The goal of a man's activity is to clean his personality and wash all dirt from it . . .)[28]

Etre impersonnel c'est être personnel, selon un mode particulier: voyez Flaubert. On dirait en jargon: l'objectif est une des formes du subjectif.

(To be impersonal is to be personal, according to a particular mode. Look at Flaubert. One would say in jargon: objectivity is another form of subjectivity.)[29]

Si personnel que soi l'Art symboliste, il doit par un coin toucher au non-personnel.

(However personal can Symbolist Art be, it must somewhere touch upon impersonality.)[30]

The apparent contradictions in Eliot's 'impersonal' theory of poetry and the simultaneous necessity of 'a personal point of view'[31] are comfortably resolved if one turns to Gourmont's synthesis of the subjective and the objective, the cerebral and the emotional, the thought and the feeling, and try to understand the equipoise he wanted in art. I hinted in the chapter on Laforgue that the continual self-sacrifice in the latter's poetic discourse could be chiefly responsible for such dialectical theorizing by Eliot; on the other hand, it is quite possible that Gourmont, too, was influenced by Laforgue. The latter was quite clearly Gourmont's favourite among the symbolists; he wrote more abundantly on him than on anyone else, a fact which Eliot commentators seem to be unaware of.

On Memory:

La mémoire est la piscine secrète où à notre insu, le subconscient jette son filet . . .

(Memory is the secret pool, where without our knowledge, the subconscious casts its net . . .)[32]

Gourmont also speaks of visual memory, which, as we know, is central to Eliot's poetic practice.

On Words:

J'aime les mots en eux-mêmes pour leur esthétique personnelle, dont la réalité est un des éléments; la sonorité en est un autre.

(I love words themselves for their own aesthetics; rareness is one of its qualities, sonority is another.)[33]

J'ai vu naître un mot; c'est voir naître une fleur.

(I have seen the birth of a word; it is like watching the blossoming of a flower.)[34]

On Classicism:

Malgré la profonde influence que le romantisme a exercé sur l'esprit française, il est resté classique . . .

(In spite of the profound influence of Romanticism on the French mind, he has remained a classicist . . .)[35]

Although Eliot stated in his preface to the 1928 edition of *The Sacred Wood* that Gourmont was 'not interested in the relation of poetry with the spiritual and social life' (see above), this seems to be no more than a half-trurh when one considers the latter's views on Catholicism and tradition in *La Culture des idées*, which remind us inevitably of Eliot's own:

Je crois que le catholicisme, en France, fait partie de la tradition littéraire. Le catholicisme est le christianisme paganisé. Religion est à la fois mystique et sensuelle, il peut satisfaire, il a satisfait uniquement, pendant longtemps, les deux tendances primordiales et contradictoires de l'humanité, qui sont de vivre à la fois dans le fini et dans l'infini, ou, en termes plus acceptables, dans la sensation et dans l'intelligence.

(I believe that Catholicism in France is a part of the literary tradition. Catholicism is paganised Christianity. Religion is mystic and sensual at the same time, it can satisfy, it has uniquely satisfied for a long time, two contradictory and primordial tendencies of humanity: to live in the finite and the infinite at the same time or to accept it in more acceptable terms to have simultaneously both feeling and intelligence.)[36]

Despite the fact that Gourmont was no great admirer of Christianity ('Christianity has given the world nothing but lies and poison'[37]), his rationalization of religion, tradition and culture, to my mind, brilliantly anticipates Eliot's own position.

It is, therefore, not a mere platitude when Eliot calls Remy de Gourmont 'the critical consciousness of a generation';[38] the latter seems to be possibly the only critic who could supply to him, at that particular point of time, 'the conscious formulas of a sensibility in the process of formation'.[39] As Aldington puts it, 'By refusing to leave any part of his mind uncultivated, by using his mind in its *totality*, Gourmont attempted a great thing . . . He tried to unite in the flow of one personality the various streams of French intellectual and artistic life.'[40]

Eliot seems to have understood quite early in his career the relevance of some of Gourmont's observations, and tried to exploit many of these in his own endeavour to purify the dialect of the tribe, with a high seriousness typical of him. Without Gourmont, he would probably have found it all the more difficult to clarify to himself and his readers his aims as artist and critic.

NOTES

1. *Remy de Gourmont* (1859–1915): French essayist, poet, novelist. One of the finest critics associated with the Symbolist movement in France, he founded in 1889, *Le Mercure de France*, the well-known Symbolist review, edited and modernized old texts, held a post at the Bibliothèque Nationale (1884–91). Gourmont began with impressionistic sketches of the Symbolists in *Le Livre des Masques* (1896), but wrote more serious criticism in *Promenades littéraires* (1904–27). He had a keen analytic mind and asserted the need to get away from an unquestioning acceptance of ideas. Important works include *La Culture des idées* (1900), *Le Problème du style* (1902), *Promenades philosophiques* (1905–9), and *Physique de l'amour* (1903).
2. T.S. Eliot, *The Sacred Wood* (hereafter referred to as *SW*), London: Methuen, 1982, p. 14.
3. Preface to the 1928 edition of Eliot, *SW*, London: Methuen, 1928, p. viii.
4. T.S. Eliot, *The Criterion*, October 1923, p. 153.
5. T.S. Eliot, *Selected Essays* (hereafter referred to as *SE*), London: Faber and Faber, 1951, p. 32.
6. Remy de Gourmont, *La Culture des idées*, Paris: Mercure de France, 1900, p. 255.
7. Ibid., p. 257.
8. Review of *The Sacred Wood* by J.M. Murry in *New Republic*, 13 April 1921, pp. 194–5.
9. Remy de Gourmont, *Le Problème du style*, Paris: Mercure de France, 1902, p. 162.
10. T.S. Eliot, *To Criticize the Critic*, London: Faber and Faber, 1978, p. 14.
11. Gourmont, *La Culture des idées*, pp. 14–15.
12. Ezra Pound, *Selected Poems*, London: Faber and Faber, 1928, p. x.
13. Gourmont, *Le Problème du style*, p. 109.
14. Ibid., p. 142.

15. Ibid., p. 306.

16. See F.W. Bateson, 'Poetry of Pseudo-learning', *Essays in Critical Dissent*, London: Longman, 1972, p. 133.

17. Gourmont, *La Culture des idées*, p. 43.

18. Gourmont, *Le Problème du style*, p. 162.

19. Eliot, *SE*, p. 289.

20. Gourmont, *Le Problème du style*, p. 190.

21. Ibid., p. 53.

22. Eliot, *SE*, p. 290.

23. Gourmont, *Le Problème du style*, p. 107.

24. Remy de Gourmont, 'La Sensibilité de Jules Laforgué', *Promenades littéraires*, vol. I, Paris: Mercure de France, 1904, p. 106.

25. Richard Aldington, *Remy de Gourmont: A Modern Man of Letters*, Seattle: University of Washington Bookstore, 1928, p. 11.

26. Edward Lobb, *T.S. Eliot and the Romantic Critical Tradition*, London: Routledge and Kegan Paul, 1981, p. 45.

27. Gourmont, *Promenades littéraires*, vol. I, p. 350.

28. *Le Problème du style*, quoted in T.S. Eliot, 'Phillip Massinger', *SW*, London: Methuen, 1982, p. 139.

29. Remy de Gourmont, *Promenades philosophiques*, Paris: Mercure de France, 1905; quoted in Ezra Pound, *Literary Essays*, London: Faber and Faber, 1954, p. 353.

30. Remy de Gourmont, *Le Chemin de velours*, Paris: G. Crès, 1923, p. 222.

31. Eliot, *SW*, p. 117.

32. Gourmont, *La Culture des idées*, p. 51.

33. Gourmont, *Le Chemin de velours*, p. 240.

34. Remy de Gourmont, *Esthétique de la langue française*, Paris: Mercure de France, 1899, p. 13.

35. Gourmont, *Promenades littéraires*, vol. I, p. 184.

36. Gourmont, *La Culture des idées*, p. 140.

37. Gourmont, *Le Chemin de velours*, p. 319.

38. Eliot, *SW*, p. 44.

39. Ibid.

40. Aldington, *Remy de Gourmont*, p. 21.

Appendix B
Julien Benda

F EW CRITICS SEEM TO HAVE taken seriously Eliot's admission in 1923[1]
that the French philosopher Julien Benda[2] (1867–1956) had exerted
a decisive influence on his intellectual development. The names are,
of course, sometimes linked in passing,[3] but there has never been any
worthwhile attempt to examine closely the nature of Eliot's debt.

As he was struggling to construct a quiet, ironic, and penetrating poetic
idiom, primarily the product of an enthusiastic cross-fertilization with
Symbolism, T.S. Eliot also desperately needed his own *art poétique*, so that
he could 'explain, rationalize, defend or prepare the way for his own poetic
practice'.[4] His theorizing was, therefore, a 'by-product of [his] private
poetry-workshop' and 'a prolongation of the thinking that went into the
formation of [his] own verse'.[5] Guided by Irving Babbitt, he quickly found
his raison d'être in current French criticism. He was stimulated by Remy
de Gourmont's provocative synthesis of artistic sensitivity and scientific
intelligence, which was useful enough to support his critical and poetic
predilections. To Eliot, he had easily become 'the critical consciousness
of a generation'.[6]

Yet, in his first book of criticism, written while he was still very much in
the orbit of Gourmont, we find that Benda is referred to as many times as
him and with as much awe. It is not evident as to when Eliot encountered
Benda. It is possible, as Herbert Howarth puts it,[7] that he read him in
Cahiers de la quinzaine as early as in 1910–12, but probably was not much
impressed. In his introduction to Ezra Pound's *Selected Poems*,[8] Eliot gives
him the entire credit for introducing Benda to the Anglo-Saxon world.
Although he did seem acquainted with Benda,[9] it was Pound who sent
him a copy of *Belphégor*. '*Belphégor* received and much pleased with it',
Eliot wrote to him,[10] 'If you can procure any other of Julien Benda's works
I will purchase them from you'. 'Benda's book is ripping', he would write
to Scofield Thayer[11] in a month, and to Robert McAlmon,[12] 'I am sure
Julien Benda is worth knowing'. He published with great haste an article

by Benda in one of the early issues of *The Criterion*, appending a personal note which hailed *Belphégor* as 'one of the most remarkable essays in criticism of our time'.[13] A few years later Eliot would recall how 'some of us recognised [*Belphégor*] as an almost final statement of the attitude of contemporary society to art and the artist'.[14]

In Benda, Eliot had apparently found the same 'keen sense of actuality' and 'conscientious sense of fact'[15] which he had discovered in Gourmont. He was struck by his 'formal beauty',[16] and 'the exceptional cogency and clarity' with which he manipulated his ideas.[17] Though he agreed that Benda could not supply, like Gourmont, 'the conscious formulas of sensibility in process of formation', Eliot liked his ruthless diagnosis of the decadent French society, which was gradually taken over by the middle class.

A rationalist with sound knowledge of history and mathematics, an 'agitateur d'idées' ('agitator of ideas')[18] who has been likened to Sartre, Benda had initially worked with Charles Péguy for some time and contributed to *Cahiers de la quinzaine*, before he called himself a 'free man' and started campaigning for an intellectuality which was not possible to realize in a world submerged in lyricism and romanticism. He chose Bergson as his natural foe, and his philosophy of creative evolution was ripped apart,[19] so much so that Eliot's weakness for him was cured for ever. In *Belphégor*, he censured the strange 'haine de l'intelligence' ('aversion to intelligence') in contemporary France, the 'détestation violente, consciente et organisée de l'intelligence' ('violent, conscious and organized dislike of intelligence').[20] The present society, he thought, demanded only emotions and sensations from a work of art[21] and there was no place for any kind of intellectual pleasure. Eliot who knew how much Gourmont appreciated the intelligence of Laforgue, also expresses an identical attitude when he says that there is no method 'except to be very intelligent', that 'intelligence should operate the analysis of sensation to the point of principle and definition'.[22]

Lack of intelligence, these two reformers knew full well, was the bane of much of contemporary literature. In fact, Benda's book begins with a typically tongue-in-cheek quotation from Bossuet's *Henriette d'Angleterre*: 'Le charme de sentir est-il done si fort?' ('Is the charm of feeling then so irresistible?') Criticizing the general infatuation for emotive and sensational art, Benda rejects the theory that there should be a mystic fusion of the artist with the essence of things.[23] Such a fusion, he believes, is 'aphasique' ('aphasic') and leads to confusion, imprecision, and formlessness in art. Of course, Eliot too attacked 'confusion of thought, emotion and vision'[24] with equal venom.

As a possible way out of this quagmire, Benda advocated impersonality in art, the detachment of a work from the author's psyche. Most people, says he, would like to love with Grieux, hate with Iago, tremble with Desdemona, sigh with Phèdre, and die with Werther. 'Est-ce besoin d'ajouter que l'émotion de sympathie n'a rien à voir avec l'émotion esthétique?' ('Does one need to add that real life emotion has nothing to do with aesthetic emotions?')[25] To be sure, *Belphégor* is a series of onslaughts on the *culte du moi*[26] and when Eliot was painstakingly trying to isolate the 'art emotion' from the 'particular emotions' of a writer à la Gourmont ('The difference between art and the event is always absolute'[27]), he was also paraphrasing one of Benda's major premises. At this point, it may be worthwhile to cite Eliot's quotation of Othenin d'Haussonville from *Belphégor*[28]:

Il y a une beauté littéraire, impersonnelle en quelque sorte, parfaitement distincte de l'auteur lui-même et son organisation, beauté qui a sa raison d'être et ses lois . . .

(There is a beauty which is literary and impersonal in some ways, perfectly distinct from the author himself and his organisation, beauty which has its raison d'être and laws . . .)[29]

Eliot's distrust of the psychological or biographical school of criticism and his contempt for the 'mixing of genres' are also clearly the heritage of Benda.[30]

Like Babbitt before him, Benda taught Eliot to despise originality in art. For him, it was merely a 'religion romantique' ('romantic religion');[31] consequently, he also ridiculed the 'soif de la nouveauté' ('thirst for novelty')[32] and the current fad for surprise. Eliot, we may recall, would come down heavily on the 'search for novelty'[33] ('one error of eccentricity is to seek for new human emotions') in order to justify his theory or tradition.

For both the critics, the greatness of art lies in its 'ordered presentation'[34] and its 'arrangement'. 'One needs less talent to invent things than to arrange them', says Benda[35] and cites the example of, among others, Boileau, Pascal, La Bruyère, and Corneille. He quotes conclusively from Pascal ('Inventiveness lies in the selection of thoughts') and La Bruyère ('The subject is not new, the composition is'). Surely enough, Eliot would make use of Benda's cogent and clear formulations in his own theorizing. 'If you compare several representative passages of the greatest poetry, you see how great is that variety of types of combination'.[36] He firmly believed that the genuine poet only discovers 'new variations of sensibility, which can be appropriated by others'.[37] His own poetry would testify to that.

Eliot calls him 'the ideal scavenger of the rubbish of our time'.[38] One recalls Benda's virulent assault on the uninformed writers.[39] Though he believed, like Eliot, that true art is not meant for the populace, he was optimistic that with the increase in communication between people and the greater diffusion of books, more and more professors, intellectuals, and curious amateurs would be attracted towards the new classicism he wished to promulgate.[40]

In his illuminating book on Eliot, Howarth suggests (wrongly, I think) that he differed with Benda on two precise points: his crude misogyny, and his distaste for the musicalization of literature. Benda, it is true, branded the contemporary thoughtlessness as 'feminine'[41] and castigated it. Of course, Eliot was far too sensible to think much of it, but then he, too, had personal reasons to have a deep-seated mistrust of the female sex. As for music, Benda disapproved of the 'sensibilité musicale' ('musical sensibility'), which is 'une sensation sans contour, diffuse et épandue' ('a sensation without contours, diffuse and scattered')[42] and 'son essence est absence de forme' ('it is essentially formless').[43] But he also admits that it is not so in the hands of masters. A Wagner or a Debussy, he goes on to say, were indeed able to restrain their musical impulse and add a plastic quality (which, for Benda, means formal order, clarity and firmness).[44] The name of Wagner is important. Also to be noted is the possibility of new heights that music can reach. At one point, Benda even refers to Baudelaire, whose poetry, in spite of its defects, 'semble devoir se rattacher à la musique *en tant que celle-ci serait plasticienne*'.[45] He wanted a plastic quality in all music and works of art, and T.S. Eliot would be the last person to quarrel with him on this issue.

In Charles Maurras's *L'Avenir de l'Intelligence* (1905)—another book to influence Eliot—Benda finds the subtle interplay of 'l'esprit classique' ('classical spirit') and 'l'exaltation romantique' ('romantic exaltation'). 'Voilà une anti-thèse bien romantique' ('What a romantic antithesis'), he quips sarcastically.[46] In Eliot's case, it was a romantic soul with a classical temperament. Benda had highlighted the paradox which would eventually lead to their parting of ways. 'L'Apostolat', he concluded, 'ne saurait être classique' ('Apostles cannot be classicits').[47] Benda would go on to denounce in *La Trahison des clercs* (1927) the abject surrender of the intellectuals and lambast the modern 'clergy' (like Maurras, Péguy, and Claudel) for their treachery. The value of the artist, he proclaimed, is that he *plays* human passions instead of living them. He came down heavily on Maurras for corrupting his works with political ideologies: an 'idealism' which, however, no longer satisfied the changing Eliot, who was rearranging and expanding his intellectual life by the late twenties, and mixing religion, politics, culture, and literature in a more and more Maurrassian manner. This, I think, explains Eliot's sudden reversal of opinion in 'The Idealism of Julien Benda' (1928) where he snubbed Benda for being 'infected with romance'.[48] 'You cannot lay down any hard and fast rule of what interest the clerc, the intellectual, should or should not have', he wrote. 'Where there is no vital connection, the man may be a brilliant virtuoso, but is probably nothing more'.[49] But what is learnt is never unlearnt, and by that time, Benda had left an ineffaceable mark on Eliot. (A very good example of the latter's recognition of his old debt to Benda is his decision to publish an English translation of *Belphégor* in 1929, with a foreword by Irving Babbitt).[50]

It should be apparent from this brief survey that both Benda and Eliot wished to play the role of classicist reformers, and both dreamt of an identical intellectual aesthetic. In short, both detested the so-called notion of identification in art, blasted what they thought was the myth of originality and censured vagueness and imprecision. More importantly, both stressed (like Gourmont before them) the vital role of critical intelligence in art. In spite of the intricacies imbibed from Gourmont, it is the Bendaesque spirit which seems to pervade many of Eliot's early critical writings, for some time from *The Sacred Wood* onwards. I would even go to the extent of saying that these sometimes read like an English version of Benda's discourse. There is the same persuasive, often coercive, gift of argument—the arrow that goes unerringly to the centre of the target—and the same propensity not to mince matters. If Eliot is still so highly thought of as a critic, it is primarily because of these qualities of persuasiveness and elegance.

NOTES

1. T.S. Eliot, 'Lettre d'Angleterre', *La Nouvelle Revue Française*, November 1923, p. 620.
2. *Julien Benda* (1867–1956): French thinker and novelist, who began his career with articles in the celebrated *La Revue blanche*. He collaborated with Péguy's *Cahiers de la quinzaine* for some time before proclaiming himself a 'free man'. He was highly critical of Bergsonism and sentimental criticism, and adhered to a strict, if somewhat narrow, classicism. His best-known works include *Belphégor* (1918), *La Trahison des clercs* (1927), and an autobiographical trilogy: *La Jeunesse d'un clerc*, *Un régulier dans le siècle*, and *Exercice d'un enterré vif* (1946).
3. As in René Wellek, *A History of Modern Criticism, 1750–1950*, vol. V, London: Jonathon Cape, 1986, p. 203. Wellek cursorily mentions his name in connection with Eliot.
4. T.S. Eliot, *To Criticize the Critic*, London: Faber and Faber, 1978, p. 33.

5. T.S. Eliot, *On Poetry and Poets* (hereafter referred to as *OPP*), London: Faber and Faber, 1969, p. 106.

6. T.S. Eliot, *The Sacred Wood* (hereafter referred to as *SW*), London: Methuen, 1982, p. 44.

7. Herbert Howarth, *Notes on Some Figures Behind T.S. Eliot*, London: Chatto & Windus, 1965, p. 183.

8. See the introduction by T.S. Eliot to Ezra Pound, *Selected Poems*, London: Faber and Faber, 1928, p. xxiii.

9. Eliot to Ezra Pound, 3 July 1920, in T.S. Eliot, *Letters of T.S. Eliot*, ed. Valerie Eliot, vol. I, London: Faber and Faber, 1988, p. 388.

10. Eliot to Pound, 13 July 1920, in ibid., p. 392.

11. Eliot to Thayer, 10 August 1920, in ibid., p. 401.

12. Eliot to McAlmon, 2 May 1921, in ibid., p. 449.

13. T.S. Eliot, Personal note on 'A Preface' by Julien Benda, *The Criterion*, April 1923, p. 242.

14. Quoted in Howarth, *Figures Behind T.S. Eliot*, p. 183.

15. T.S. Eliot, 'Observations', *The Egoist*, May 1918, p. 70.

16. Eliot, *SW*, pp. 41, 44.

17. Ibid., p. 44.

18. See *Dictionnaire de la littérature française et francophone*, vol. I, Paris: Larousse, 1987, p. 173.

19. Benda's *Le Bergsonisme ou une philosophie de la mobilité* (1912) was sent to Eliot by Pound (see Valerie Eliot's notes in Eliot, *Letters*, ed. Valerie Eliot, vol. I, p. 392).

20. Julien Benda, *Belphégor*, 3rd edn., Paris: Emile-Paul, 1918, pp. 17, 18.

21. Ibid., p. 1.

22. Eliot, *SW*, p. 11.

23. Benda, *Belphégor*, p. 3.

24. Eliot, *SW*, p. 158.

25. Benda, *Belphégor*, pp. 54–5.

26. Ibid., p. 105.

27. T.S. Eliot, *Selected Essays*, London: Faber and Faber, 1951, p. 19.

28. Benda, *Belphégor*, p. 140.

29. Eliot, *SW*, p. 42.

30. Benda, *Belphégor*, pp. 137–40, 158.

31. Ibid., p. 76.

32. Ibid., p. 65.

33. Eliot, *SW*, p. 57.

34. Ibid., p. 168.

35. Benda, *Belphégor*, p. 73.

36. Eliot, *SW*, p. 55.

37. Eliot, *OPP*, p. 20.

38. Eliot, *SW*, p. 44.

39. Benda, *Belphégor*, p. 91.

40. Ibid., p. 176.

41. Benda, *Belphégor*, p. 213.
42. Ibid., p. 41.
43. Ibid., p. 43.
44. Ibid., p. 40.
45. Ibid., p. 45, footnote; Benda's italics.
46. Ibid., p. 206, note J.
47. Ibid.
48. See Eliot's review of Benda's *La Trahison des clercs* in T.S. Eliot, 'The Idealism of Julien Benda', *New Republic*, 1 December 1928, p. 107.
49. Ibid.
50. S.J.I. Lawson, tr., *Belphégor*, London: Faber and Faber, 1929.

Bibliography

(A) T.S. Eliot's Works

The Complete Poems and Plays of T.S. Eliot, London: Faber and Faber, 1969, 1990 ed.

The Sacred Wood (1920), London: Methuen, 1982.

For Lancelot Andrewes (1928), London: Faber and Faber, 1970.

Selected Essays (1932), London: Faber and Faber, 1951.

The Use of Poetry and the Use of Criticism (1933), London: Faber and Faber, 1980.

Essays Ancient and Modern (1936), London: Faber and Faber, 1947.

Notes Towards the Definition of Culture, London: Faber and Faber, 1948.

On Poetry and Poets (1957), London: Faber and Faber, 1969.

To Criticize the Critic (1965), London: Faber and Faber, 1978.

Selected Prose of T.S. Eliot, ed. Frank Kermode, London: Faber and Faber, 1975.

The Waste Land: A Facsimile and Manuscript, ed. Valerie Eliot, London: Faber and Faber, 1971.

The Criterion 1922–39, 18 vols., London: Faber and Faber, 1967.

The Varieties of Metaphysical Poetry, ed. Ronald Schuchard, London: Faber and Faber, 1993.

Letters of T.S. Eliot, ed. Valerie Eliot, vol. I, London: Faber and Faber, 1988.

Inventions of the March Hare, ed. Christopher Ricks, London: Faber and Faber, 1996.

(B) French Translations of Eliot's Works

Meurtre dans la cathédrale, tr. Henri Fluchère, Paris: Ed. du Seuil, 1946.

Essais Choisis, tr. Henri Fluchère, Paris: Ed. du Seuil, 1950.

Poésie (1947), tr. Pierre Leyris, Paris: Ed. du Seuil, 1969.

(C) Works by Others

Ackroyd, Peter, *T.S. Eliot*, London: Hamish Hamilton, 1984.

Alanjouantine, Théophile, *Valery Larbaud sous divers visages*, Paris: Gallimard, 1973.

Aldington, Richard, *Remy de Gourmont: A Modern Man of Letters*, Seattle: University of Washington Bookstore, 1928.

Angelet, Christian, *La Poétique de Tristan Corbière*, Bruxelles: Palais des académies, 1961.

Anglès, Auguste, *André Gide et le premier groupe de la NRF*, 3 vols., Paris: Gallimard, 1978–86.

Arkell, David, *Looking for Laforgue: An Informal Biography*, Manchester: Carcanet, 1979.

Aubry, Jean, G., *Valery Larbaud*, Monaco: Ed. du Roucher, 1949.

Bady, René, *Littérature et Spiritualité*, Lyon: Presse Universitaire de Lyon, 1978.

Barthes, Roland, *Le Plaisir du texte*, Paris: Ed. du Seuil, 1973.

Bateson, F.W., *Essays in Critical Dissent*, London: Longman, 1972.

Baudelaire, Charles, *Oeuvres Complètes*, 2 vols., Paris: Bibliothèque de la Pléiade, 1990.

————, *Correspondance*, Paris: Bibliothèque de la Pléiade, 1973.

Benda, Julien, *Belphégor*, Paris: Emile-Paul, 1918.

————, *Le Bergonisme ou une philosophie de la mobilité*, Paris: Emile-Paul, 1912.

————, *La Trahison des clercs*, Paris: Emile-Paul, 1927.

————, *Les Sentiments de Critias*, Paris: Emile-Paul, 1925.

Benjamin, Walter, *Ecrits Français*, Paris: Gallimard, 1991.

Bergonzi, Bernard, *T.S. Eliot*, London: Macmillan, 1972.

————, ed. *T.S. Eliot, Four Quartets: A Casebook*, London: Macmillan, 1969, 1993.

Bern, Jeanne et al., *Laforgue Aujourd'hui*, Paris: Lib. José Corti, 1988.

Bettes, Madeleine, 'L'Univers de Laforgue à travers les mots', diss., University of Illinois, 1968.

Bloom, Harold, *The Anxiety of Influence*, New York: Oxford University Press, 1973.

————, *A Map of Misreading*, New York: Oxford University Press, 1975.

Braybrooke, Neville, ed., *T.S. Eliot: A Symposium for His Seventieth Birthday*, London: Hart-Davis, 1958.

Breton, André, ed., *Anthologie de l'humour noir*, Paris: Ed. du Sagittaire, 1950.

Brunel, Pierre et Yves Chevrel, *Précis de littérature comparée*, Paris: PUF, 1989.

Burch, Francis, *L'Originalité des Amours Jaunes et leur influence sur T.S. Eliot*, Paris: Lib. Nizet, 1970.

Bush, Ronald, *T.S. Eliot: A Study in Character and Style* (1984), New York: Oxford University Press, 1985.

Cattaui, Georges, *T.S. Eliot*, London: Merlin Press, 1966.

———— and Jacques Madaule, eds., *Entretiens sur Paul Claudel*, Paris: Moutin, 1961.

Claudel, Paul, *Oeuvre Poétique* (1967), Paris: Bibliothèque de la Pléiade, 1985.

————, *Théâtre Complet*, 2 vols., Paris: Bibliothèque de la Pléiade, 1949.

————, *Positions et Propositions*, Paris: Gallimard, 1928.

————, *Réflexions sur la poésie* (1963), Paris: Gallimard, 1979.

———— et André Gide, *Correspondance*, Paris: Gallimard, 1949.

———— et Jacques Rivière, *Correspondance*, Paris: Plon, 1926.

Chiari, Joseph, *Contemporary French Poetry*, Manchester: Manchester University Press, 1952.

Chiari, Joseph, *The Poetic Drama of Paul Claudel*, London: Harvill Press, 1954.

Collie, Michael, *Jules Laforgue*, London: University of London Press, 1977.

Corbière, Tristan, *Les Amours Jaunes* (1873), ed. Jean-Louis Lalanne, Paris: Gallimard, 1988.

———, *Selections from 'Les Amours Jaunes'*, ed. C.F. MacIntyre, Berkley: University of California Press, 1954.

Crawford, Robert, *The Savage and the City in the Work of T.S. Eliot* (1987), Oxford: Clarendon Press, 1990.

Culler, Jonathon, *Structuralist Poetics* (1975), London: Routledge, 1989.

Dansel, Michel, *Langage et Modernité chez Tristan Corbière*, Paris: Lib. Nizet, 1974.

Alighieri, Dante, *The Divine Comedy*, tr. Dorothy L. Sayers and Barbara Reynolds (1962), Harmondsworth: Penguin, 1975.

Debauve, Jean-Louis, *Laforgue en son temps: Langages et documents*, Neuchâtel: A la Baconnière, 1972.

Décaudin, Michel, *La Crise des valeurs symbolistes*, Geneva: Slatkine Rpts., 1981.

Dictionnaire de la littérature française et francophone, 3 vols., Paris: Larousse, 1988.

Dobrée, Bonamy, *The Lamp and the Lute*, New York: Barnes and Noble, 1964.

Drew, Elizabeth, *T.S. Eliot: The Design of his Poetry*, London: Eyre and Spottiswoode, 1950.

Durrell, Lawrence, *A Key to Modern Poetry* (1952), Norman: University of Oklahoma Press, 1972.

Ellmann, Maud, *The Poetics of Impersonality*, Sussex: The Harvester Press, 1987.

Fokkema, Douwe, *Issues in General and Comparative Literature*, Calcutta: Papyrus, 1987.

Fournier, Alain (Henri), *Le Grand Meaulnes*, Paris: Le Livre de Poche, 1983.

——— and Jacques Rivière, *Correspondance*, 2 vols., Paris: Gallimard, 1991.

——— and Charles Péguy, *Correspondance: Paysage d'une amitié*, Paris: Fayard, 1990.

Fowlie, Wallace, *Paul Claudel*, London: Bowes & Bowes, 1957.

Gardner, Helen, *The Art of T.S. Eliot* (1949), London: Faber and Faber, 1968.

———, *The Composition of Four Quartets*, London: Faber and Faber, 1978.

Gibson, Robert, *The Quest of Alain-Fournier*, London: Paul Elek, 1953.

Gordon, Lyndall, *Eliot's Early Years*, Oxford: Oxford University Press, 1977.

———, *Eliot's New Life*, Oxford: Oxford University Press, 1988.

Gourmont, Remy de, *Le Livre des Masques*, Paris: Mercure de France, 1896.

———, *Esthétique de la langue française*, Paris: Mercure de France, 1899.

———, *La Culture des idées*, Paris: Mercure de France, 1900.

———, *Le Problème du style*, Paris: Mercure de France, 1902.

———, *Promenades littéraires*, vol. I, Paris: Mercure de France, 1904.

———, *Promenades philosophiques*, Paris: Mercure de France, 1905.

———, *Le Chemin de velours*, Paris: G. Crès, 1923.

Grant, Michael, ed., *T.S. Eliot: The Critical Heritage*, 2 vols., London: Routledge and Kegan Paul, 1982.

Gray, Piers, *T.S. Eliot's Intellectual and Poetic Development 1909–1922*, Sussex: Harvester Press, 1982.

Greene, E.J.H. (Edward), *T.S. Eliot et la France*, Paris: Boivin, 1951.

Grin, Micha, *Tristan Corbière, poète maudit*, Paris: Evian, 1972.

Hiddleston, James, ed., *Laforgue Aujourd'hui*, Paris: Lib. José Corti, 1988.

Hoffman, Frederick, *The Twenties: American Writing in the Post-War Decade*, New York: Collier, 1962.

Holmes, Anne, *Jules Laforgue and Poetic Innovation*, Oxford: Oxford University Press, 1993.

Hough, Graham, *Image and Experience*, London: Gerald Duckworth, 1960.

Howarth, Herbert, *Notes on Some Figures Behind T.S. Eliot*, London: Chatto & Windus, 1965.

Hughes, Glenn, *Imagism and the Imagists*, London: Bowes & Bowes, 1960.

Humes, Joy Nachod, *Two Against Time: A Study of the Very Present Worlds of Paul Claudel and Charles Péguy*, Chapel Hill: University of North Carolina, 1978.

Huyghe, René et al., *Baudelaire* (1961), Paris: Hachette, 1966.

Kenner, Hugh, *The Invisible Poet* (1959), London: Methuen, 1985.

Kermode, Frank, *Continuities*, London: Routledge and Kegan Paul, 1968.

———, *An Appetite for Poetry*, Glasgow: Fontana, 1989.

Kunitz, Stanley J., ed., *Twentieth Century Authors: A Biographical Dictionary of Modern Literature* (1955), New York: H.W. Wilson, 1985.

La Nouvelle Revue Française, Paris: NRF, 1908–27.

Laboulle, M.J., 'T.S. Eliot and Some French Poets', *Revue de littérature comparée*, April–June 1936, pp. 389–99.

Laforgue, Jules, *Poésies Complètes*, Paris: Le Livre de Poche, 1970.

———, *Mélanges Posthumes* (1903), Geneva: Slatkine Rpts., 1979.

———, *Moralités Légendaires*, ed. Pascal Pia, Paris: Gallimard, 1977.

———, *Oeuvres Complètes*, Lausanne: L'Age d'Homme, 1986.

———, *Textes et Critique d'art*, ed. Mireille Dottin, Lille: Presse Universitaire de Lille, 1988.

Lalou, René, *Histoire de la littérature contemporaine* (1946), Paris: Presse Universitaire, 1947.

Larbaud, Valery, *Les Poésies de A.O. Barnabooth*, ed. Robert Mallet, Paris: Gallimard, 1966.

———, *Oeuvres*, Paris: Bibliothèque de la Pléiade, 1977.

———, 'A propósito de la publicación de un libro inédito de Julio Laforgue', *La Nación*, 15 April 1923.

——— and A.A.M. Stols, *Correspondance*, Paris: Ed. des Cendres, 1986.

Lasserre, Pierre, *Charles Maurras et la Renaissance Classique*, Paris: Mercure de France, 1902.

Leavis, F.R., *New Bearings in English Poetry* (1932), London: Chatto & Windus, 1971.

Lemaître, Henri, *La Poésie depuis Baudelaire* (1965), Paris: Armand Colin, 1978.

Leuwers, Daniel, *Introduction à la poésie moderne et contemporaine*, Paris: Bordas, 1990.

Litz, Walton A., ed., *Eliot in His Time*. Oxford: Oxford University Press, 1973.

Lobb, Edward, *T.S. Eliot and the Romantic Critical Tradition*, London: Routledge and Kegan Paul, 1981.

Margolis, John D., *T.S. Eliot's Intellectual Development, 1922–39*, Chicago: University of Chicago Press, 1972.

Martin, Graham, ed., *Eliot in Perspective: A Symposium*, London: Macmillan, 1970.

Martineau, René, *Tristan Corbière*, Paris: Le Divan, 1925.

Maritain, Jacques, *Réflexions sur l'Intelligence*, Paris: Nouvelle librairie nationale, 1924.

————, *Religion et Culture*, Paris: Desclée de Brouwer, 1930.

————, *Antimoderne*, Paris: Revue de Jeunes, 1922.

March, Richard and Tambimuttu, eds., *T.S. Eliot: A Symposium*, London: Frank and Cass, 1965.

Matthews, T.S. *Great Tom: Notes Towards the Definition of T.S. Eliot* (1972), London: Wiedenfeld and Nicholson, 1974.

Maurras, Charles, *L'Avenir de l'Intelligence* (1905), Paris: Nouvelle librairie nationale, 1925.

————, *Le Conseil de Dante*, Paris: Nouvelle librairie nationale, 1920.

Millet-Gérard, Dominique, *Anima et Sagesse: pour une Esthétique de l'exégèse claudélienne*, Paris: Lethieulleux, 1990.

Morice, Charles, *Tristan Corbière*, Paris: Messein, 1912.

Morize, André, *Problems and Methods of Literary History*, Boston: Ginn & Co., 1922.

Moody, A.D., *Thomas Stearns Eliot, Poet*, Cambridge: Cambridge University Press, 1979.

Partridge, A.C., *The Language of Modern Poetry*, London: André Deutsch, 1976.

Perkins, David, *A History of Modern Poetry* (1976), London: Harvard University Press, 1987.

Perse, Saint-John, *Oeuvres Complètes* (1972), Paris: Bibiothèque de la Pléiade, 1989.

Philippe, Charles-Louis, *Marie-Donadieu* (1904), Paris: Charpentier, 1951.

————, *Bubu de Montparnasse* (1901), Paris: Garnier-Flammarion, 1978.

Pinkney, Tony, *Women in the Poetry of T.S. Eliot*, London: Macmillan, 1984.

Pondrom, Cyrena, *The Road from Paris*, Cambridge: Cambridge University Press, 1974.

Pound, Ezra, *Selected Poems*, London: Faber and Faber, 1928.

————, *Literary Essays*, London: Faber and Faber, 1954.

————, *Lettres de Paris*, Paris: Cahiers Ulysse, fin de siecle, 1988.

Raboul, Pierre, *Laforgue*, Paris: Hatier, 1960.

Rousselot, Jean, *Tristan Corbière*, Paris: Ed. Seghers, 1951.

Ruchon, François. *Jules Laforgue, sa vie, son oeuvre*, Geneva: Albert Ciana, 1924.

Sencourt, Robert, *T.S. Eliot: A Memoir*, ed. Donald Adamson, London: Garnstone Press, 1971.

Seylaz, Louis, *Edgar Poe et les premiers symbolistes française* (1923), Geneva: Slatkine Rpts., 1979.

Smith, Grover, 'Tourneur and Little Gidding; Corbière and East Coker', *Modern Language Notes*, June 1950, pp. 418–21.

———, 'Charles-Louis Philippe and T.S. Eliot', *American Literature*, November 1950, pp. 254–9.

———, *T.S. Eliot's Poetry and Plays: A Study in Sources and Meaning* (1956), Chicago: University of Chicago Press, 1961.

Soldo, John, 'The Tempering of T.S. Eliot, 1888–1915', diss., University of Harvard, 1972.

Sonnenfield, Albert, *L'Oeuvre Poétique de Tristan Corbière*, Paris: PUF, 1960.

Southam, B.C., ed., *T.S. Eliot: 'Prufrock', 'Gerontion', 'Ash-Wednesday' and other Shorter Poems* (1978), London: Macmillan, 1993.

Spender, Stephen, *Eliot* (1975), Glasgow: Fontana Press, 1986.

Starkie, Enid, *From Gautier to Eliot: The Influence of France, 1851–1939*, London: Hutchinson, 1960.

Svarney, Erik, *The Men of 1914: T.S. Eliot and Early Modernism*, Philadelphia: Open University Press, Milton Keynes, 1988.

Symons, Arthur, *The Symbolist Movement in Literature* (1899), London: Archibald Constable, 1908.

Taupin, René, *L'Influence du symbolisme française sur la poésie américaine, 1910 à 1920* (1929), Geneva: Slatkine Rpts., 1979.

Tate, Allen, ed., *T.S. Eliot: The Man and His Work*, London: Chatto & Windus, 1967.

Thibaudet, Albert, *Les Idées de Charles Maurras*, Paris: Gallimard, 1919.

Turnell, G.M., 'Introduction to the Study of Tristan Corbière', *The Criterion*, April 1936, pp. 393–417.

———, 'The Poetry of Jules Laforgue', *Scrutiny*, September 1936, pp. 128–49.

Unger, Leonard, ed., *T.S. Eliot: A Selected Critique*, New York: Rinehard & Co., 1948.

———, *Eliot's Compound Ghost: Influences and Confluences*, Pennsylvania: The Pennsylvania State University Press, 1981.

Vagianos, Sylvia Caides, *Paul Claudel et la Nouvelle Revue Française* (1909–18), Geneva: Lib. Droz. S.A., 1979.

Valéry, Paul, *The Art of Poetry*, New York: Bollingen Foundation, 1958.

———, *Oeuvres*, vol. I, Paris: Bibliothèque de la Pléiade, 1957.

Van Tieghem, Paul, *Les influences étrangères sur la littérature française*, Paris: PUF, 1967.

Verlaine, Paul, ed., *Les Poètes Maudits* (1884), Cognac: Le Temps qu'il fait, 1990.

Warner, Val, ed. and tr., *The Centenary Corbière*, Cheadle, Chesire: Carcanet, 1975.

Wellek, René, *A History of Modern Criticism*, 6 vols., London: Jonathon Cape, 1955–86.

Wilson, Edmund, *Axel's Castle* (1931), London: Fontana, 1967.

Woolf, Virginia, *The Common Reader* (1925), London: Hogarth Press, 1951.

Index

www.ingramcontent.com/pod-product-compliance
Lightning Source LLC
LaVergne TN
LVHW091522170726
843492LV00004B/1018